Global Television and the
Shaping of World Politics

To Ruth,
my wife, my best friend,
who by her life
has shown me the meaning
of the word
"grace"

Global Television and the Shaping of World Politics

CNN, Telediplomacy, and Foreign Policy

ROYCE J. AMMON

McFarland & Company, Inc., Publishers
Jefferson, North Carolina, and London

Library of Congress Cataloguing-in-Publication Data

Ammon, Royce J., 1954–
    Global television and the shaping of world politics: CNN,
telediplomacy, and foreign policy / Royce J. Ammon.
        p.   cm.
    Includes bibliographic references and index.
    ISBN 0-7864-1062-0 (softcover : 50# alkaline paper) ∞
    1. Diplomacy.   2. Communication in international relations.
    3. Television in politics.   I. Title.
    JZ1305'A478   2001
    327'2 — dc21   2001030546

British Library Cataloguing data are available

Manufactured in the United States of America

Cover images ©2001 Eyewire and PhotoSpin

*McFarland & Company, Inc., Publishers
    Box 611, Jefferson, North Carolina 28640
    www.mcfarlandpub.com*

Acknowledgments

This book is possible only because of what others have entrusted unto me. Many have given of themselves; through such selfless acts, I received the necessary gifts to write this book. Where to begin in recognizing these individuals? The list is long, and, were I to attempt an exhaustive listing by name, someone to whom I am indebted would be overlooked.

Writing a book is not a *sui generis* process; it does not just spring forth of its own accord. The actual writing process itself can be long — in this case, nearly six years from the original idea to completion. But, the book that was completed during the last two years of concerted writing began long before that.

My mother, Arlene, taught me to read, to love books, and to love learning. She also encouraged my curiosity, and my dreams.

My father, John, continues to teach me to take myself less seriously. He reminds me that the people who turn out best are the people who make the best of the way things turn out.

My grade school teachers cared enough to teach me phonics and how to spell. They taught me to love words.

My high school teachers saw abilities in me that I had never seen in myself, and they actively encouraged those abilities.

Several college professors encouraged me in the direction of graduate school, despite my insistence on going another direction. When I belatedly realized that they were right, these same professors were there for me.

A close friend, Ron Boesiger, asked me a pivotal question over coffee one Friday afternoon a decade ago, a question without which this book might never have been written.

My mother-in-law, Winnie, showed by her support that she continued to believe in me during a time when it was hard for me to believe in myself.

Although incomplete, this listing suggests something of the beginnings without which this book could not have been written.

Several individuals made significant and direct contributions to the manuscript itself. The idea for this project began as a research paper in a special topics seminar during my Ph.D. program in the University of Nebraska–Lincoln Department of Political Science. From there the idea was revised and refined. Ultimately, the ideas from that research paper grew into my doctoral dissertation. The dissertation formed the core research from which the book was written. Given this, the members of my Ph.D. supervisory committee deserve special recognition for their contribution: Professors Bill Avery, David Forsythe, Phil Dyer, Ray Zariski, and Mike Stricklin.

Professor Bill Avery introduced me to the fascinating world of political science during a 1990 summer school course in American foreign policy. As chair of my Ph.D. committee, he proved to be an insightful and tenacious editor for the dissertation. He has become a close personal friend and confidant.

Professor Phil Dyer introduced me to the concept of working in the world of ideas. I have worked in other worlds (professional aviation and business); however, I consider it a distinct honor and a privilege to work in the world of ideas. Professor Dyer also provided much-needed encouragement and insight at several critical junctures during both my undergraduate and graduate education. He is typical of so many of the unsung heroes in the professoriate: He never saw his name in lights, but he was always there for his students.

Professor Mike Stricklin challenged me to new ideas. The ideas he contributed to this book were invaluable. Professor David Forsythe challenged me to sharpen the dissertation's arguments. Professor Zariski was an encourager, simply by virtue of who he is.

Eric Ryberg, one of my former students at the University of St. Thomas in St. Paul, Minnesota, deserves special mention. Of his own initiative he offered to assist me with the tedious job of converting my in-text citations to the many pages of notes that follow the text. When I explained to him that this project was not funded, that it was a labor of love, he was undaunted. I am exceedingly grateful for Eric's uncommon display of initiative, and for the willing and cheerful way he attacked a sizable project. Thank you, Eric.

Finally, this book would not have been possible without my wife,

Ruth. While I earned my Ph.D., she earned her P.H.T. (put hubby through). Ruth was willing to go back into the workforce so I could go back into the classroom. She was my primary encourager during the many years of completing my undergraduate and graduate degrees. Ruth is one of those unique individuals who offers encouragement not only by what she says, but by what she does. During my ten years of education and book writing, she was unflagging in her commitment to see both through to completion. In addition, her numerous editorial suggestions significantly enhanced the book's readability. I am one of those individuals who has been blessed to marry above himself.

The paragraphs above attest that I have received much. Although many have contributed to this work, I alone am responsible for its shortcomings. Time will determine whether this book is worthy of the gifts with which I have been entrusted. But, whatever that determination may be, it could neither repay nor dim the debt of gratitude that I owe for all that I have received.

Contents

Acknowledgments	vii
Preface	1

One. Communication and Diplomacy:
An Historic Relationship

1. The Communication-Diplomacy Link	5
2. Paradigms, Communication, and Diplomacy	12
3. Diplomacy and Communication: The Results of Linkage	48

Two. Communications and Diplomacy:
Present Realities

4. The Persian Gulf War and Telediplomacy: The Next Diplomatic Paradigm	65
5. Global Television's Ability to Drive Policy	88
6. Global Television and Diplomatic Outcomes	96
7. Global Television's Mechanisms for Driving Policy	130

Three. Communications and Diplomacy:
Future Potential

8. Today's Communications, Tomorrow's Diplomacy	151

Notes	155
Bibliography	156
Index	189

Preface

Scholars and diplomats alike have long recognized that a relationship exists between communication and diplomacy, although the effects of this relationship have not been thoroughly explored. This book contends that changes in how we communicate — the whole field now known as "communications" — have historically determined the methods of diplomatic practice. Furthermore, the recent development of global television has, for the first time, allowed communications to determine diplomatic outcomes as well. Communications can now drive world politics.

The first clear example of communications' ability to drive world politics occurred in the aftermath of the 1991 Persian Gulf War. The post–Gulf War Kurdish and Shiite Muslim refugees experienced significantly different outcomes— outcomes which demonstrated global television's ability to determine foreign policy. However, the 1994 Rwandan genocide demonstrates that there are limits to global television's ability to influence foreign policy.

Methods of communication will continue to define diplomacy's methods of practice. Furthermore, today's increasing reliance upon global television suggests that tomorrow will bring an increasing role for communications in determining diplomatic outcomes. In the final analysis, by studying today's communications we can better understand tomorrow's diplomacy.

One

COMMUNICATION AND DIPLOMACY: AN HISTORIC RELATIONSHIP

Chapter 1

The Communication-Diplomacy Link

> "[I]nternational relations have become truly global for the first time. Communications are instantaneous."
> — *Former Secretary of State Henry Kissinger, 1994*

> "[T]oday's explosive growth of telecommunications is transforming international relations.... [T]he dynamics of communication ... are central to processes of change."
> — *Richard H. Solomon, 1997; President of the United States Institute of Peace, and a former U.S. Assistant Secretary of State*

Diplomatic scholars and practitioners have long recognized that a relationship exists between communication and diplomacy. However, the extent, and especially the effects, of this relationship have yet to be thoroughly explored. This book contends that major changes in diplomatic practice occur in the aftermath of major changes in the prevailing method of communication: The historical link between diplomacy and communication suggests that prevailing methods of communication define future methods of diplomatic practice. Furthermore, by the 1990s communications could also determine diplomatic outcomes, under certain conditions.

Western diplomacy has been marked by two prevailing methods of practice, or paradigms. The first of these paradigms, "old diplomacy," was distinguished by a method of practice that relied upon privacy and secrecy. Old diplomacy's methods defined Western diplomatic practice from the time of the Renaissance until the World War I era. The succeeding diplomatic paradigm, referred to as "new diplomacy," was distinguished by methods of practice that relied upon openness. New diplomacy's methods defined diplomatic practice from the World War I era until the 1980s.

The move from old to new diplomacy resulted from a previous shift in the prevailing method, or paradigm, of communication. Specifically, the prevailing method of communication shifted from hand-written documents to the mass printing of newspapers. The accompanying shift in the communication paradigm redefined diplomacy's methods of practice from those characterized by secrecy to those characterized by openness.

The prevailing method of communication has recently undergone yet another shift. The mass printing of newspapers has given way to a new paradigm of communication, exemplified by global television. Time and space have virtually been collapsed by this recent paradigmatic shift in communication. We all can now witness events that occur half a world away. And, since the rise of global television in the 1980s, we can witness these events in real time — at the instant that they are happening. As a result of this shift in the communication paradigm, Western diplomacy's third paradigm — telediplomacy — began to emerge in the late 1980s.

Telediplomacy is distinguished by its reliance upon real-time global television. In addition, whereas communication historically has defined the *methods* of diplomatic practice, under telediplomacy communications can also determine the *foreign policies* that result from diplomatic decision-making. In other words, communications can now, for the first time, determine diplomatic outcomes.

Both diplomatic scholars and professional diplomats have recognized this linkage between diplomacy and communications. Hans Morgenthau was one of the twentieth century's most respected diplomatic scholars. By 1949, he was already arguing that the communications revolution had significantly affected diplomacy. Morgenthau contended that:

> Today diplomacy no longer performs the role, often spectacular and brilliant and always important, that it performed from the end of the Thirty Years' War to the beginning of the First World War.... [D]iplomacy has lost its vitality, and its functions have withered away to such an extent as is without precedent in the history of the modern state system. Five factors account for that decline.... *The most obvious of these factors is the development of modern communications.*[1]

Former U.S. Secretary of State Henry Kissinger echoed Morgenthau's argument half a century later, stating that diplomacy has been "radically changed" by the advent of instantaneous communications.[2] And in 1995 the world's chief diplomat, UN Secretary-General Boutros Boutros-Ghali, charged that "CNN [the Cable News Network] is the [unofficial] sixteenth member of the [fifteen member United Nations] Security Council."[3]

Communications scholars and practitioners have also recognized the relationship between communications and diplomacy. John Hohenberg has argued that in some situations "journalism has replaced diplomacy."[4] Patricia Karl contends that, in an "age of media diplomacy, statecraft may have become the hostage — if not the victim — of stagecraft.... International politics is a theater in which traditional diplomacy is increasingly an ignored understudy."[5] Former White House correspondent Timothy J. McNulty contends that "television imagery transmitted by satellite ... makes traditional diplomacy all but obsolete in times of crisis."[6] The impact of communications on diplomacy prompted scholars Keith Hamilton and Richard Langhorne to conclude that, by 1995, the media had come to represent an "alternative to diplomacy" in many situations.[7]

Something is occurring at the point where communication and diplomacy intersect. Successive advances in communications technology have affected the very methods whereby diplomacy is conducted in three specific ways: first, by displacing diplomacy's traditional methods; second, by increasing the diplomatic influence of non-traditional actors; and third, by accelerating diplomacy's pace. Furthermore, communication has historically defined diplomacy's methods of practice to such an extent that successive paradigms of diplomatic practice have emerged over the last century.

Under certain conditions communications can now exert an effect on diplomatic outcomes as well. This newfound potential, where communications can determine the policy adopted, is telediplomacy's distinguishing characteristic. Former U.S. Secretary of State James A. Baker, III, stated in 1989 that he experienced "a classic demonstration of a powerful new phenomenon: the ability of the global communications revolution to drive policy."[8]

Communications' ability to determine policy was demonstrated in the aftermath of the 1991 Persian Gulf War. The Gulf War itself stands as the first example to date of communications having shifted diplomatic practice to the emerging paradigm of telediplomacy. But communications also affected a diplomatic outcome as well: During the immediate post-Gulf War period, real-time global television coverage influenced U.S. foreign policy toward the Kurdish refugees. Global television's ability to affect diplomatic outcomes results from its role as an agenda-setter, derived from the fact that it is a unique information source that can influence public opinion, thereby becoming a diplomatic broker. However, the 1994

Rwandan genocide demonstrates that there are definite limits to communications' ability to affect policy outcomes.

This book's primary focus is real-time global television and its effect on diplomacy. Other recent advances in communication technology also have had an effect on foreign policy, but real-time global television represents the cutting edge in today's technology. Furthermore, global television exerts a unique and defining effect upon diplomacy by virtue of its immediacy and its sensory impact. Real-time global television refers to the broadcasting of events at the instant that they are occurring anywhere on earth, via the latest generation of ultra-lightweight satellite up-link technology. The terms "real-time television" and "global television" are used interchangeably throughout this book.[9]

Communication and Diplomacy: The Case for Linkage

Communication is the "act of transmitting, giving, or exchanging information," according to Webster's Dictionary.[10] For example, global television can provide instantaneous communication between a few people or it can provide communication to virtually the whole globe in real time. But global television itself is an example of communications, a "system for sending and receiving messages."[11] Where *communication* refers to the transmitting or exchanging of information, *communications* refers to the system or method by which that transmission is accomplished.

Traditionally, diplomacy has been understood to mean the "putting of foreign policies into practice" via "political contact between governments of different nations."[12] However, Sir Harold Nicolson, the noted British diplomat and diplomatic historian, observed that diplomacy is a broad concept.[13] This broader sense suggests that diplomacy encompasses the "total process" by which states carry on their political relations with other states in the world.[14] In other words, diplomacy deals with the political process on a global level, or world politics. Therefore, at the risk of oversimplification, this book will treat the terms "diplomacy," "foreign policy," and "world politics" as nearly synonymous.

Although diplomacy is a broad concept, the broad understanding of diplomacy covers seven specific functions. These include:

1) the activities associated with supporting a country's citizens as they travel abroad and conduct business in foreign countries, a function known as performing routine consular affairs[15];

2) the gathering and interpretation of information[16];

3) the signaling and receiving of governments' positions on various issues[17];

4) the official representation of a diplomat's home (or sending) government before her host (or receiving) government[18];

5) the conduct of international public relations[19];

6) negotiation[20]; and

7) crisis management.[21]

In short, diplomacy consists of these seven functions.

Communications is the field upon which the game of diplomacy is played, according to diplomatic experts. John T. Rourke argues that "[i]t is best to think expansively of diplomacy as communications."[22] Likewise, Bruce Russett and Harvey Starr contend that the "central feature of diplomacy is communication."[23] Vietnamese diplomat Tran Van Dinh argues that diplomacy is "especially influenced by the means of communication with which it is carried out."[24]

Communications scholars also agree that diplomacy is influenced by the means of communication. Communication theory has long contended that it is impossible to separate what we communicate about from the way in which we communicate. The effect of a message depends upon factors that relate directly to the way the message is actually communicated.[25] In other words, it is impossible to separate communication from the "medium through which it is transmitted."[26] The way in which we communicate helps determine *what* we communicate.

Scholars have long understood that there is a link between communications and diplomacy. But how does this link operate? Stephen Kern recognized the linkage between communications and diplomacy when he observed that diplomacy's different historical manifestations have occurred because of "changing experiences of time and space."[27] Morgenthau would agree. Forty years before Kern, Morgenthau deduced how the communications-diplomacy linkage functions when he observed that diplomacy's decline resulted from the "*conquest of time and space by modern technology,*"[28] This then is how the link between communications and diplomatic practice has operated: Advances in communication technology have progressively collapsed time and space on diplomacy.

Diplomacy and the Collapse of Time and Space: The Vehicle for Linkage

The constructs of time and space have long been recognized for their importance in defining human experience. Media scholar Harold Adams

Innis argues that civilizations traditionally have been bounded by their concept of time and space.[29] According to Innis, the media of a particular civilization may be the most significant reflection of that civilization's concept of time and space.[30]

Successive advances in the primary medium through which civilizations communicate have consistently contracted time and space. Western civilization evolved from media that emphasized time and were durable in character (such as stone, clay, and parchment) to media that emphasize space (such as papyrus and paper, which are easily distributed over large areas). Each successive advance in communication technology has served to improve communications efficiency by lessening both time and space, thereby altering a particular civilization's concept of its boundaries with regard to time and space. In other words, a civilization's concept of space and time, as represented in its primary medium of communications, has served to define that civilization's boundaries.[31]

In addition to collapsing time and space, the evolution of communications technology has consistently eroded monopolies over knowledge. For example, civilizations dominated by a medium of communication that was durable in character, but not amenable to wide distribution (such as parchment), historically have developed monopolies of knowledge in specific geographic locations around this medium. Subsequently, new media (such as paper, with its inherent ability to be widely distributed) "responded to the monopoly of knowledge" based on parchment, with its emphasis on time.[32] The ability of paper to disseminate knowledge over greater spaces challenged and consequently eroded the previous monopoly over knowledge based on parchment. Likewise, Innis argues that the move from the written production of texts to the printing of texts produced a corresponding loss of control over knowledge.[33]

Each successive advance in communications technology has served to further erode the monopoly over knowledge. Innis contends that "sudden extensions of communication are reflected in cultural disturbances."[34] Among the primary cultural disturbances accompanying inventions in communication are "realignments in the monopoly of knowledge."[35] Advances in communication likewise have altered the limits imposed by space and time upon the dissemination of knowledge,[36] rendering accessible that which was once available only to a privileged few. Collapsing time and space has persistently eroded the monopoly over knowledge.

Therefore, two phenomena have historically influenced diplomacy at its link with communication: the collapse of time and space, and the erosion of the monopoly over knowledge. History suggests that the combined effect of these phenomena has defined different methods of diplomatic practice by altering the very practices through which diplomacy is conducted. In modern times, these changes have effectively displaced traditional diplomacy's methods of practice, accelerated diplomacy's pace, and increased the diplomatic influence of non-traditional actors. In other words, successive paradigms of diplomatic practice have been defined by paradigmatic changes in communication.

The following chapter explores the paradigm concept and the history of both communication and diplomacy, histories which take on unique defining patterns when analyzed according to paradigm theory.[37] The succeeding chapters establish the historic link between communications and diplomacy and the results of this relationship. Communications' most recent effects on diplomatic practice are detailed in a case study of the 1991 Persian Gulf War. A comparative study drawn from the Gulf War's immediate aftermath, that of the Kurdish refugees vs. the Shiite Muslim refugees, highlights communications' newfound ability to influence diplomatic outcomes. A succeeding study explores the limits to communications' influence on foreign policy by examining the 1994 Rwandan genocide. Finally, the specific mechanisms by which communications can influence foreign policy decision-making are examined.

Chapter 2

Paradigms, Communication, and Diplomacy

"Gutenberg broke the monopoly of the monks who copied manuscripts by hand and guarded them jealously. They understood that knowledge was power and sometimes chained books to the shelves…. Contrast that mindset with the ability of a researcher anywhere in the world with a computer and a modem to tap into the entire database of the Library of Congress…. In today's parlance, this change constitutes a paradigm shift."

— *Walter B. Wriston, 1997; former presidential advisor and CEO of Citicorp*

"The transition from a paradigm … to a new one … is a reconstruction of the field from new fundamentals…. When the transition is complete, the profession will have changed its view of the field, its methods, and its goals."

— *Thomas S. Kuhn, 1970*

Thomas S. Kuhn theorized about the process whereby a particular discipline undergoes major changes.[1] According to Kuhn, a paradigm is the "prevailing world view" that defines a particular discipline's "methods of practice."[2] A fundamental change occurs in a discipline when there is a "tradition-shattering" change in the primary elements which define its world view.[3] Such a fundamental change constitutes a paradigm shift.

Kuhn's original discussion of paradigms was geared toward the natural

12

sciences; however, his insights about how these prevailing world views evolve are equally applicable to the histories of communication and diplomacy. The disciplines of Western communication and diplomacy have both been marked by world views that changed over time; as discussed below, each discipline has known three different world views, or paradigms. Consistent with Kuhn's paradigm theory, each of these world views served for several generations to define the very essence of communication and diplomacy.[4]

However, over time, different communication and diplomatic paradigms emerged as the essential character of each discipline changed. Paradigm changes occur gradually and only after a certain critical mass has been achieved during a transitional period. A move from one world view to its successor begins when anomalies emerge that do not fit within the existing world view.[5] These anomalies emerge incrementally.[6] Over time, there is a sense that the discipline is being reconstructed from new fundamentals that change its very defining elements.[7] This period during which anomalies appear and begin to redefine the discipline is known as the "pre-paradigm" era.[8]

Communication and diplomatic history are both marked by these transitional periods, or pre-paradigm eras, prior to major changes in world views. A paradigm shift ultimately occurs when new and unique practices emerge that are inexplicable given the existing world view, and when the occurrence of such practices is sufficient to require that a particular discipline must effectively redefine its world view. For example, although electronic communication first appeared with the railway telegraph in 1837, it was not until the 1970s that the average American consumed more words electronically than via print. The prevailing method of communications was gradually redefined from one dominated by the mass printing of newspapers, the mass-communication paradigm, to one dominated by electronics, but only following a pre-paradigm era of nearly a century and a half. In other words, between 1837 and the early 1970s, anomalous communication practices emerged that did not fit with a world view which saw the mass-circulation newspaper as the prevailing method of communication. During this period, new and unique communication methods were developed, inventions such as the telegraph, telephone, wireless telegraphy, radio, and television. By the 1970s, these anomalies had reached "critical mass" and had collectively become the dominant medium of communication — electronics. Communication had been redefined and a shift had occurred to the electronic communication paradigm.

One final point should be noted about paradigm shifts. New paradigms rarely emerge from the mainstream adherents to a particular discipline's prevailing world view. Newspaper men did not develop electronic methods of communication. Practitioners in a particular discipline have been educated in that profession's prevailing world view. This process of being socialized into a discipline's existing world view may restrict professionals' vision concerning foundational changes that originate outside the mainstream of their discipline. Consequently this process may make professionals resistant toward such changes.[9] Scientist Max Planck concedes in his autobiography that a new paradigm does not triumph by "convincing its opponents and making them see the light, but rather because its opponents eventually die, and a new generation grows up that is familiar with it."[10] Kuhn has argued that the movement from one paradigm to its successor is quite "often accompanied by resistance."[11] This resistance to change, and an unwillingness to accept its reality, is particularly apparent in tradition-bound disciplines such as diplomacy.

The histories of communication and diplomacy both take on unique defining patterns when analyzed according to Kuhn's paradigm theory. Each discipline's history has been marked by a progression through succeeding distinct world views, or paradigms. Each paradigm has ultimately been displaced by a successor, following pre-paradigm stages of differing lengths. We turn first to a consideration of communication paradigms.

Paradigms and Communication

The history of communication can be divided into rather distinct eras based on differences in the methods of communication. Scholar Ithiel de Sola Pool argues that human history has known four distinct eras on the basis of four prevailing communication methods—the oral, the written, the printed, and the electronic.[12]

Pool's four communication eras arguably define corresponding communication paradigms. According to Kuhn, a paradigm is a "prevailing world view" that forms the basis of practice within a certain discipline.[13] Each of Pool's eras of communication defines a prevailing world view, a world view that formed the basis of practice within the discipline of communication for a particular historical period. Therefore, human history has known four communication paradigms. Each succeeding paradigm has been defined by a unique prevailing method or basis of practice: speech, writing, printing, and electronics.

Paradigms can be assigned only rough historical boundaries at best. The particular era defined by a paradigm requires one to take account of an often protracted period preceding the ultimate shift from one prevailing basis of practice to its successor — Kuhn's "pre-paradigm stage."[14] Allowing for these pre-paradigm stages, Western civilization has known only three of Pool's four eras of communication.[15] These three eras correspond to the three communication paradigms in the history of Western civilization: the writing era, which this book refers to as the elite communication paradigm; the printing era, which is referred to as the mass communication paradigm; and the electronics era, which is referred to as the instantaneous communication paradigm.

The origin of Western civilization is commonly traced to the rise of ancient Greek civilization, circa 500 B.C.[16] Given this, the West has never known an exclusively oral tradition as the prevailing method of communication. Innis has argued that the ancient Greek philosopher Socrates (470?–399 B.C.) was the "last great product and exponent of the oral tradition."[17] History records that Socrates wrote nothing. However, his student, Plato (427?–347 B.C.), was a prolific writer, as was Plato's student, Aristotle (384–322 B.C.). After Aristotle, the Greek world "passed from oral instruction to the habit of reading."[18] In the *Phaedrus*, Plato has Socrates report a conversation between the Egyptian god Thoth, the inventor of letters, and the god Amon. Amon charges that Thoth's discovery of letters "will create forgetfulness in the learners' souls."[19] Communications scholar Walter J. Ong argues that Plato's philosophical foundation was "unwittingly a programmed rejection of the old ... oral culture."[20] In short, Socrates and Plato mark the great divide between the oral and written traditions in the West. Given that the origins of Western civilization are traced to the rise of classical Greek civilization, Western history originates at the end of the oral communication era and the advent of the writing era.

Innis contended in 1950 that Western civilization had experienced two historically identifiable eras of communication, the writing era and the printing era.[21] However, events subsequent to Innis's time indicate that the West has now entered a third era in communication history: electronic communication.

Pool argues that the electronic revolution is "of at least as much historical significance as the mass production of print and other media."[22] Likewise, communications scholar Carolyn Marvin contends that "the invention of the telegraph, the first of the electrical communications machines, [was] as significant a break with the past as printing [was] before."[23] With the advent of rudimentary instantaneous communication devices, such as the telegraph in the mid-1800s, scholars began to conjecture openly that electronic communication had "annihilated space and time."[24] This one-hundred-and-fifty-year-old conjecture has proved prophetic, given the truly instantaneous electronic communication that has become commonplace today.

Kuhn has argued that the evolution of paradigms is a process of creeping incrementalism.[25] The move between prevailing methods of communication has been marked by this same process of incrementalism, and includes that period of time described by Kuhn as the "pre-paradigm stage."[26] In the case of communication, the pre-paradigm era would include that period between a specific technological innovation, such as telegraphy, and its ultimate acceptance as the prevailing method of communication. Therefore, communication paradigms are roughly defined by those eras during which specific communication methods prevailed, eras that include the next paradigm's pre-paradigm stage. On this basis, Western history has been marked by three succeeding communication paradigms: the elite communication paradigm, defined by writing; the mass communication paradigm, defined by printing; and the instantaneous communication paradigm, defined by electronics.

The Writing Era and the Elite Communication Paradigm

Ronald Berkman has argued that writing before the advent of a true mass printing capability was "directed toward an educated elite."[27] Only the elite — whether in monasteries or palaces—could read the early writings, whether the printed characters were produced by a scribe or the earliest of printing presses. Consequently, that era dominated by written communication up to the development of mass printing can be referred to as the elite communication paradigm.

The elite communication paradigm is roughly defined by that period between Plato and the development of a true mass printing capability in the 1830s. The government of Athens, the ancient Greek city-state, ultimately sentenced Socrates to death for his lack of respect for tradition and for corrupting the youth. Socrates was required to down a cup of hemlock in 399 B.C., thereby committing suicide in keeping with his death sentence. Socrates and his student, Plato, are on opposite sides of the great divide between the oral and written traditions—between orality and literacy — in Western culture. Therefore, the advent of writing as a prevailing communication method can be traced to the time of Plato's first writings, circa 388/7 B.C.[28] Socrates only spoke, but Plato wrote.[29]

Printing first emerged around 868 A.D. in China, according to most scholars[30]; the development of printing in the West would have to wait almost six hundred years. Most scholars attribute the development of movable type in the West to Johann Gutenberg of Mainz, Germany, around 1440.[31] Therefore, one might argue that the writing era in Western civilization encompassed 1,828 years—that period strictly defined by Plato (388/7 B.C.) on one end and Gutenberg (1440 A.D.) on the other.

However, even though the writing era may be said to have begun with Plato, affixing this era's end date requires taking account of Kuhn's "pre-paradigm stage."[32] The writing era did not end in 1440 A.D., nor did its successor, the mass communication paradigm dominated by printing, begin in A.D. 1440 A pre-paradigm stage of nearly four centuries would elapse between Gutenberg's invention of movable type and the development of the true mass printing capability that would usher in the mass communication paradigm.

Gutenberg's new device did not catch on immediately. It was not until the end of the fifteenth century that the major European states could each boast that they had at least one important publishing center.[33] Indeed, the hand-copying of texts continued to be economically viable throughout the remainder of the fifteenth and on into the sixteenth century; this fact is attested to by the employment of nearly 10,000 scribes in just the Paris and Orleans regions of France as the fifteenth century drew to a close.[34] The high cost of producing both scribal and printed texts contributed to the continuance of the elite communication paradigm.

Printing was a handcraft in the true sense of the word during the 390 years from Gutenberg's invention until the advent of mass printing. Prior to the development of a mass printing capability, it took sixteen hours to set the type for two pages of a newspaper. Once the type was set, two skilled artisans who worked well together might be able to turn out as many as 240 sheets per hour. Each sheet then needed to dry thoroughly before the process could start all over again to print the other side.[35]

The earliest ancestor of what would, more than a century later, become known as a newspaper was not printed until 1505. In that year an Augsburg printer in the German states put out what was then called a broadside, announcing the discovery of Brazil.[36] Broadsides were usually printed on only one side, hence the origin of their name. These forerunners of the newspaper were printed on an occasional basis and lacked exact dates and serial numbering.[37] The first publication recognizable as a newspaper was printed in the German states, but not until 1609. England got its first newspaper in 1622. France got her first newspaper in 1631 at the behest of Cardinal Richelieu, who from 1624 until his death in 1642 ruled France in King Louis XIII's interest.[38] One hundred and ninety-one years had transpired between the time of Gutenberg's invention and the printing of the first newspaper in Paris, the then-recognized diplomatic capital of the world. The newspaper had been developed, and with this development, the world received its first printed method of communication capable of wide distribution.

The problem with printing, of course, had been one of control. Governments across Europe reacted to stem the "menace" of the printed word, for printing had become "a challenge to authority throughout Europe."[39] Early printing was heavily censored and tightly controlled. Broadsides, the earliest newspapers, were viewed with a wary eye by governments because of their relative ease of production and amenability to wide distribution. The first newspaper printed in Richelieu's France was an official publication of the French government, as was commonly the case across Europe. Richelieu's newspaper, Gazette de France, existed to print news for the king. Consequently, the king felt quite free to contribute his version of the news to the paper.[40]

In addition to government censorship, there were other impediments to the distribution of printed material that limited readership. Printed material was still largely for consumption by an elite audience more than two and a half centuries after Gutenberg's invention. By the end of the 1600s, the literacy rate in England, the most educated populace in the world, was only 30 percent for men. Women in the world's most educated country experienced significantly lower literacy rates than did men.[41]

The move from an elite written medium of communication toward a mass printed medium would ultimately require the acceptance of two crucial concepts: the free marketplace of ideas and the public's right to know. Although the free marketplace of ideas had historical predecessors, it was first enunciated in the modern era by Montaigne of France and Peter Wentworth of England during the 1500s.[42] The concept held that when truth was allowed to compete it would naturally and inevitably overcome falsehood.[43] The acceptance of this concept was an incremental process that required more than two centuries.

The move toward the free marketplace of ideas got a significant boost in early eighteenth-century England. This boost came in the articulation of the concept of the public's right to know. These closely related concepts—the free marketplace of ideas and the public's right to know—became two of the cornerstones for the expansion of printing as the prevailing method of communication.

Around 1720 two London newspapermen, John Trenchard and William Gordon, began to call for freedom of the press based on the public's right to know. Trenchard and Gordon wrote under the pen name of "Cato." It was Cato who first argued that truth should be allowed as admissible evidence in defense of those charged with criminal or seditious libel, both of which were crimes against the state and were punishable by immediate imprisonment. The rule had been that nothing irreverent or disrespectful could be spoken in an English court against the government or one of its officers, whether the charge was true or not. However, Cato argued that "the public had a right to know the truth about its government."[44] The public's right to know was so radical that it even shocked Britain's John Locke, a leading advocate of personal liberty. Locke's ideas would ultimately be used in crafting the American Declaration of Independence. Yet, the revolutionary nature of this right to know prompted Locke to argue against its adoption. In early eighteenth century England, the public's right to know was far from being a right as we understand it today. However, the concept of such a right had entered the marketplace of ideas. Cato's direct bequest was a right that would ultimately be realized via the printing press, the public's right to know.[45]

Although the free marketplace of ideas concept got its initial boost in the Old World, it would take its next move forward in the New World. On August 4, 1735, Peter Zenger, a little known publisher from the British Colony of New York, was put on trial for seditious libel. The charge was that in his newspaper, the New York *Weekly Journal*, Zenger had printed seditious words about the Governor of New York. It was not that Zenger had made grossly false statements about the Governor and his minions. Zenger had simply spoken ill of them in his paper — an indiscretion sufficient to incur the charge of seditious libel. And, under early eighteenth century English law, merely speaking ill of government officials, whether true or not, was punishable by immediate imprisonment and trial.[46]

The jury in the Zenger case ruled contrary to tradition, providing the free marketplace of ideas with a significant boost. Zenger was found not guilty. The legal technicality established that day in court was the admission of truth as a defense in cases of criminal or seditious libel against the state. But there were much larger issues settled that day for the freedom of the press. In time, and by a process of fits and starts, the Zenger case became a "landmark in the history of the free press in both the New World and the Old."[47]

It would be some years of course, before the main principle in the Zenger case was enshrined in law. At times, governments would attempt to bypass or suspend the legal guarantees of a free press. But, whatever else may be said about the Zenger case, truth could now appear in print, whether or not that truth was complimentary of the state or its officials. Therefore, by 1735, the free marketplace of ideas had gained a legal toehold.[48]

The Bill of Rights of the U.S. Constitution was the first official government document to protect the free marketplace of ideas and the public's right to know. These concepts became legal rights for the first time with the ratification of the Bill of Rights in 1791, thanks to the freedom-of-the-press clause in the First Amendment. James Madison, the Bill of Rights' principal advocate, argued in 1791 that "public opinion was the 'real sovereign' in every free country" and that the press—as protected in the First Amendment—"would keep the public informed."[49] Public opinion thus became the sovereign to be kept informed by the nation's free press.[50]

The Bill of Rights effectively bequeathed the continuing and predominating influence of the American experience on communication: the public's right to know and the free marketplace of ideas. However, it would be two centuries before the rest of the world would have to grapple with the reality of this bequest, a reality that would not be fully realized until communications technology had collapsed time and space and completely eroded the monopoly over knowledge. The free marketplace of ideas would only become a universal reality with the development of instantaneous global communications. With this development, communications would become the conduit for transmitting the influence of the American experience to world politics. Today, the free marketplace of ideas has become a "virtual" worldwide reality: global communications can cross governments' borders with impunity. In addition, the public's right to know is accepted in most of the world's capitals today, even if only via lip service in some.

Long before the technological millennium, however, progress was being made toward the mass communication paradigm. Government censorship had been dealt an initial blow in the 1735 Zenger case. And the mass communication paradigm had received a sizable boost with the legal protections afforded by the U.S. Bill of Rights. In fact, according to Innis, it was only with "the adoption of the Bill of Rights in the United States" that the full impact of printing even became a possibility—three hundred and forty years after Gutenberg's invention.[51] Another scholar has summarized the incremental movement towards a free press as follows:

> In the three centuries from Johann Gutenberg to John Peter Zenger, the press found only small, isolated islands of freedom in a vast sea of authoritarian control. If these islands existed mainly in England and the American colonies, it was almost entirely due to the preoccupation of the English-speaking peoples with the long struggle for individual freedom and their support of the valiant printer-publishers who challenged their governments.[52]

As a result of these challenges, governmental impediments to press free-dom were slowly falling.

However, the logistics of being able to circulate printed ideas in this free marketplace were still daunting. As had been the case in the Old World, the broadside was the precursor to the newspaper in the New World. Broadsides in America would often resemble the front page of a contem-porary English newspaper, such as the official London *Gazette*, which had the widest circulation of any newspaper in the New World. One of the ear-liest broadsides printed in America was *The Present State of the New-English Affairs*, printed in 1689 by Samuel Green.[53]

However, the first actual newspaper in America was not published until 1690. On September 25 of that year, Benjamin Harris published the first and only edition of *Publick Occurrences Both Forreign and Domestick*. Harris's publication placed a primary emphasis on foreign news in both its title and content. *Publick Occurrences* was quickly shut down by the sus-picious English Governor and Council of Massachusetts. Harris never attempted to resurrect his newspaper. His experience, however, illustrated all too well why no newspaper had been printed in the Colonies until 1690, even though printing presses had existed there since 1638.[54]

The second attempt at publishing a newspaper in the Colonies occurred in 1704. That year, John Campbell started what would become the first continuously published American newspaper, *The Boston News-Letter*. As with Harris's *Publick Occurrences*, Campbell's paper was focused upon foreign news. Approximately two-thirds of *The Boston News-Letter* contained information from London journals dealing primarily with English politics and European wars.[55]

However, this devotion to English politics would ultimately lead to the *News-Letter's* demise. The *News-Letter* had long been loyal to England's Home Government in the Colonies. The last known issue of the *News-Let-ter* was published on February 22, 1776, after a near-continuous existence of seventy-two years. Revolutionary patriots refused to tolerate the pub-lication of a pro-British paper in Boston while it was under siege by Gen-eral Washington. Ultimately, the *News-Letter's* attacks upon Washington and other Revolutionary generals resulted in its forced cessation.[56]

Censorship had contributed to the newspaper's slow development in colonial America, as did the average person's inability to afford newspa-per subscriptions. Early newspapers were very costly, given average wages. As a result, only five percent of white families in the American colonies received a weekly newspaper by 1765.[57] By this time there were only thir-teen small weeklies in the American colonies, most with a circulation that never exceeded 600 copies.[58] A subscription to the average U.S. daily paper cost about $8 per year in 1800, while prices ran about $3 per year for a weekly — this at a time when skilled labor was commanding only about $8 per week.[59] In other words, a daily newspaper subscription cost the equivalent of one week's wages. Few were able to afford this price in late 1700s America, and few would be willing to afford it today.

All of these factors combined to keep circulation figures low for those few newspapers that did survive. The largest selling newspapers in the U.S. could only boast a circulation of 4,000 by the time George Washington left office.[60] And Williamsburg, the Virginia Colony's capital until 1779, had no newspaper from 1780 to 1824.[61] In fact, had all the newspapers in America been evenly distributed in 1790, each person would have received only one paper during the entire year.[62]

Printing's potential influence was first realized in America, despite these impediments. The U.S. Bill of Rights had been the first government document to guarantee legal protections for printing, some three and a half centuries after print's development in the West.[63] And, with these protections, the transition from one communication paradigm to the next would accelerate: the transition from a culture dominated by the elite medium of writing to a culture dominated by that of printing was well under way. Within fifty years, mass printing would usher in the mass communication paradigm.

However, a move to the mass communication paradigm would ultimately require the push of technology. Although different reference points might be debated, printing was not the primary method of communication prior to mass printing's development. Prior to this development, communication via the written word was an elite medium of communication, regardless of whether the characters on the page were produced by a scribe or early printing presses. The first true mass printing capability was developed during the 1830s in the U.S.[64] Therefore, printing as a prevailing method of communication first became a technological possibility in the 1830s. And with the coming of this possibility, the communication paradigm was able to shift beyond the elite paradigm that originated with Plato's embrace of writing. By the 1830s, the elite paradigm had passed; the mass communication paradigm had emerged.

The Printing Era and the Mass Communication Paradigm

By the early 1800s, a communication paradigm based on mass printing was beginning to emerge. In 1814, the first power press was adopted at the *London Times*. Although the technology to print quickly and cheaply was invented in the Old World, it was in the New World that this technology would first revolutionize printing.[65]

The mass communication revolution truly began with the first issue of the *New York Sun* on September 3, 1833.[66] The *Sun* immediately became an innovative newspaper, adopting the latest in production technology. It was the first newspaper to be sold for one penny per copy, resulting in the term "penny press" as a generic label for the new mass-printed newspapers. The *Sun's* first machine press could turn out 200 impressions per hour; its new press the following year could turn out 1,000.[67] Within two years, the *Sun* had reached a circulation of 27,000.[68] By 1835, the *Sun's* steam press was capable of printing 22,000 copies on both sides in less than eight hours.[69] The *Sun's* immediate successor, *The Herald*, had reached a circulation of 40,000 by 1836.[70] By 1840, *The Herald* had reached a circulation of 51,000.[71] Within just four years of the *Sun* having inaugurated the penny press, total newspaper circulation figures had more than tripled in New York City.[72] And by the mid-1840s, the *Sun's* owners boasted that theirs was the largest selling newspaper in the world, a claim undisputed by scholars.[73] The development of a true mass printing capability had ushered in the mass communication paradigm. For the first time in history, printed material was available to the general population.

Pool contends that the printing press was the "foundation of modern democracy."[74] Implicit in Pool's contention is the mass communication paradigm's ability to erode the historic monopoly over knowledge that had characterized the elite paradigm. James Madison declared that it was the press that would keep the public informed, a public whose opinion Madison believed to be the "real sovereign" in a free country.[75] Pierre-Louis Roederer, a historian and contemporary of the French Revolution, argued in 1796 that Revolution newspapers had become the most influential of political media.[76] The German social philosopher Jurgen Habermas augmented Roederer's firsthand analysis by arguing that the French Revolution of 1789 was the first moment when "public opinion could dictate laws to the lawgiver"; and, thereby, public opinion "was transformed into the sovereign itself."[77] Gradually, advances in communications technology were making knowledge more widely available.

Access to knowledge was also becoming less expensive, thanks to mass printing. Newspapers cost six or more cents per copy prior to the advent of mass printing, well out of reach of the average person. However, by the 1830s, daily information about distant places was available for the price of one cent.[78] The price of purchasing a newspaper had dropped to a level that allowed ordinary people to avail themselves of these new information sources. The penny press was putting information into the hands of the masses. This fact, and the increasing rates of literacy, expanded the availability of printed material to the average person for the first time in history.

The increased reach of the penny press made it a prime method of distributing news. By becoming a daily chronicler of current events, the penny press brought these events to the lives of ordinary people. A contemporary observer of the penny press called it "the great leveler, elevator, and democratizer."[79] This observer was correct: the penny press was the first communications medium to break the monopoly of information that had been locked up in the old communication paradigm defined by writing. Mass printing was eroding the monopoly over knowledge.

Given its capacity for large circulation, the penny press set about cultivating a mass audience by appealing to readers' desire for the sensational. In the late nineteenth century, New York City papers began using the techniques of sensationalism that were subsequently referred to as "yellow journalism." Sensationalism was to become a tremendous boon to newspaper circulation.

The term "yellow press" was first used by Ervin Wardman of the *New York Press* to describe New York City's sensationalizing newspapers. The term had its origin in a comic strip character ("Yellow Kid") that was first featured in the *Sunday World*. Subsequently the *Sunday Journal* began to run the same character. However, the term "yellow press" soon became shorthand for those newspapers that boosted circulation by emphasizing visual appeal and base sensationalism. The yellow papers became infamous for trafficking in scandal, gossip, divorce, sex, etc. By early 1898, William Randolph Hearst's *Sunday Journal*, replete with the "Yellow Kid" comic character, was running between forty-eight and fifty two pages in length, sold for a mere five cents, and had acquired a circulation of more than 600,000 copies.[80] Sensationalism sold newspapers.

Although yellow journalism began in 1896 with two New York City papers, it spread quickly to other areas of the country. By the turn of the twentieth century, yellow journalism had reached its peak. A study of papers in twenty-one large metropolitan centers around the U.S. in the year 1900 revealed that fully one-third of them employed yellow journalism. By this time, the familiar sensationalism of yellow papers had been augmented by other common traits: 1) scare-tactic headlines that screamed excitement in huge print, often about relatively minor events; 2) the abundant use of pictures, some of which were "faked"; 3) the common use of impostors and frauds, who would gladly "fake" interviews and or information; 4) a huge Sunday supplement that appealed to a yearning for cheap entertainment; and 5) conspicuous sympathy for the abuses—both real and perceived — experienced by ordinary people. All were techniques designed to hold and gain circulation.[81]

Another New York City newspaper owner, Adolph Ochs, decried the yellow papers' "freak journalism."[82] Ochs had purchased the then-bankrupt *New York Times* in 1896. Ochs's purchase of the *Times* proved to be a turning point in the history of the mass communication paradigm, for he embraced a new slogan for his paper: "All the News That's Fit to Print."[83] The subsequent success of the *Times* in offering a "high-class" newspaper was largely responsible for yellow journalism's decline in prestige among newspaper publishers.[84] Indeed, with the *New York Times*, Ochs had inaugurated a new concept in newspaper publishing: "the journal of record."[85]

Readers had now received their first reliable organ of public record. Under Ochs's leadership, the *Times* made itself indispensable as a comprehensive, accurate, and impartial source of news. Within two decades of Ochs's purchase of the *Times*, it had established itself as the "first newspaper in the United States."[86] This reliable public record of each day's major events served the public's right to know and advanced the free marketplace of ideas.

The old elite medium of writing had died slowly. Although Gutenberg's invention had appeared around 1440, it was not until the 1830s that printing as the prevailing mode of communication would usher in the mass communication paradigm. In the interim, several key developments were required for the mass printing paradigm to replace the elite written paradigm: a loosening of government censorship, the rediscovery of the "free marketplace of ideas" in the modern era, the birth of the doctrine of the "public's right to know," the idea of a free press, the codification of legal protections for these novel policies, and, ultimately, the development of a mass printing capability. This long list of developments were ultimately realized by mass communication's four-century pre-paradigm era.

The Electronic Era and the Instantaneous Communication Paradigm

The move from pre-paradigm to paradigm that had required four hundred years in the case of mass communication would take less than one hundred and fifty years for electronic communication. Electronic communication had made its first appearance by the time that mass printing replaced writing as the prevailing communication method in the 1830s: The first railway telegraph was built in Britain in 1837.[87] That same year, Samuel F.B. Morse patented his code in the United States, and subsequently opened the first public telegraph line from Baltimore to Washington in 1844.[88] Therefore, the pre-paradigm stage for instantaneous electronic communication begins with the discovery of telegraphy. By 1963 more Americans received their news from television than from newspapers. The mass communication paradigm based on printing was waning. By 1977, Americans were consuming four times as many words electronically as they were via print. In less than a century-and-a-half, electronics had replaced printing as the prevailing method of communication.[89]

People began thinking differently about time and space in the early 1800s.[90] This was especially true of Morse, the man credited with being the father of commercial telegraphy in the United States. In 1832, while returning from England to the United States aboard a vessel that was attempting to make the best possible time, Morse began seriously pondering how to "eliminate time in communications between individuals across space."[91] Other would-be inventors as well were working on solving the problems posed by time and space.

Although slow and crude by today's standards, the telegraph moved humanity towards the collapse of time and space in communication. In 1790 it took at least eighteen days for an event occurring in Washington, D.C., to be known in Boston, a figure that was reduced to 2.8 days in 1841 by improved transportation.[92] However, the inauguration of telegraph service between these two cities in 1846 significantly collapsed time and space for very short, one-way messages, tapped out using Morse's code. Telegraphy's advent prompted newspaper publisher James Gordon Bennett to state that the new invention would allow the whole nation to be "impressed with the same idea at the same moment."[93] Although somewhat overstated, Bennett's claim would have seemed incredible before telegraphy.

When viewed in retrospect, the invention of telegraphy has proven to be more than just another technological advancement. Telegraphy inaugurated a "cultural revolution of the broadest scope."[94] Even though slow by today's standards, this relatively instantaneous communication device altered people's concepts of time and space; it also affected the way people thought about themselves and the present.[95] The very dimensions of thought and of life itself were being profoundly transformed, and in a way that they had never been shaped before.[96] Telegraphy was an innovation of historical significance at least equal to printing's discovery and its subsequent mass production.[97] Beginning with telegraphy, electronic communication has proven to be the technological key that unlocked profound conceptual and social changes.[98]

The rate of electronic communication's acceptance and growth outstripped that of printing. Electronic communication effectively brought about the "annihilation of time and space," as early nineteenth-century philosophers put it. Within twenty years of its invention the telegraph covered both North America and Europe, reaching even into the smallest towns, and time and space had been annihilated across an ocean. The threshold of global communication was about to be crossed.[99]

Talk about a transatlantic telegraph cable was virtually born with the idea of telegraphy. In the early-to-mid-nineteenth century, the Atlantic loomed as the ultimate prospective space for annihilation. According to communications scholar Daniel R. Headrick, "[n]o telecommunications project in history aroused more excitement, nor has any been more talked about, than the Atlantic cable."[100] By 1845, serious ventures were underway to lay a cable across the Atlantic that would carry the new invention's signals. But it was not until 1854 that the ultimate moving force behind the project appeared, the American Cyrus Field. In 1856, Field succeeded in founding the Atlantic Telegraph Company and, by 1858, he succeeded in running a cable from Newfoundland to Ireland on his third attempt.[101]

On August 17, 1858, U.S. President James Buchanan received a message that he and his Cabinet initially believed to be a hoax. The message read, "The Queen desires to congratulate the President upon the successful completion of the great international work, in which the Queen has taken the greatest interest." The message was alleged to have come from Queen Victoria herself, via a cable stretched across the floor of the Atlantic Ocean.[102] However, the suspected hoax proved to be fact: the message had crossed the Atlantic via cable.

The U.S. broke into a spirit of euphoric celebration. City after city made plans to participate in a nationwide celebration on September 1, 1858, to commemorate the technological achievement represented by the transatlantic cable. In the minds of the celebrants, the space between the U.S. and Britain had been annihilated.[103]

The technological "firsts" continued to pile up. On August 27, 1858, the first European news crossed the Atlantic Ocean via cable. It was addressed to the Associated Press. The following day, August 28, the U.S. reciprocated with the first transatlantic news transmission of its own. Yet, even as the U.S. news was being sent, the cable signals were beginning to fade. Transmissions became noticeably slower, more difficult, and at times impossible. And just as the celebrations over technology's annihilation of space began, the cable went dead on September 1.[104]

However, the idea of global communication was soon rescued by technology. In July 1865, a new and more advanced cable was being laid across the Atlantic when it broke, east of Ireland. An 1866 attempt at laying a cable met with success on July 27. And, with the successful repair of the 1865 cable, two cables spanned the Atlantic by September, 1866. The age of global communication was dawning.[105]

Technology was now beginning to triumph over the distance which had separated the Old World from the New. By early-nineteenth-century standards, time and space were collapsing at a phenomenal rate. By today's standards, however, transmissions were slow over the transatlantic cables of the mid-nineteenth century. At best they could average only seven to thirteen words per minute.[106] Yet, at the beginning of the nineteenth century, messages from the Old World to the New took, on average, two months in transit.[107] In 1865, just one year prior to the completion of a successful transatlantic cable, it took twelve days for the news of Abraham Lincoln's assassination to cross the Atlantic.[108] By these standards, the 1866 transatlantic cable represented a communications revolution.

The push of communications technology persisted in altering the constructs of time and space. Improvements in telegraph and cable technology continued to increase the speed and volume of communication that was possible. Messages that used to take a matter of hours to communicate could now be sent in a matter of minutes. And, by the 1880s, cables had reached every populated continent of the earth. Praise was heaped upon the new technology from newspapers, pulpits, and lecturers. By mid-nineteenth-century standards, the telegraph had, indeed, annihilated time and space.[109]

News from formerly distant places was now instantly available. The electronic delivery of news within the U.S. became a reality shortly after the invention of telegraphy. On May 1, 1844, the first news message was transmitted by telegraph: Henry Clay had been nominated for president by the Whig Party, with Theodore Frelinghuysen as his running mate.[110] Telegraphic news reached the nineteenth century general public largely through newspapers. Telegraphic bulletins were also posted outside newspaper and telegraph offices. In addition, a few innovative electronic bulletin boards were erected.[111] By 1866, the transatlantic cable began to provide the routine delivery of news between Europe and America. However, apart from large organizations and wealthy individuals, the personal receipt of information from distant places via electronics would have to await the next major development in communications technology — the telephone.

The telephone was invented in 1876. It was soon adapted so that individuals could personally consume public broadcasts. By 1879, sermons were being broadcast over telephone lines in the U.S. Musical performances were being sent over telephone lines in Europe by 1880. And, in an 1888 science-fiction story, the futurist Jules Verne envisioned "telephonic journalism." Like many of Verne's stories, this one proved to be prophetic.[112]

However, Verne's fantasy only preceded reality by four years. In 1892, telephonic journalism was first employed to report the U.S. presidential election returns, albeit to a limited degree. The telephone companies of New York and Chicago forwarded those election returns which they received to local hotels and clubs. Telephone bulletins were received as much as ninety minutes in advance of bulletins from local telegraph offices. Thus, telephones were beginning to collapse time and space to a degree beyond that achieved by telegraph.[113]

However, individual access to news via telephone was not widespread until the presidential election of 1896. By this time a national network could be organized for receiving and distributing election returns via the telephone. And, by the election of 1900, the Chicago Telephone Company was able to relay returns within one minute to some twenty-five-hundred subscribers in clubs and private homes where telephone parties were being hosted. With the election of 1912, technology had become refined sufficiently to allow telephone subscribers to place a call to "Election News" and hear a two-minute bulletin update on the latest returns. Subscribers could then call back in ten minutes for the next updated bulletin.[114]

The space between an individual person and distant events was being collapsed. Likewise, the monopoly over knowledge was being further eroded. Telephonic journalism brought individuals access to knowledge about events happening at previously incomprehensible distances. Yet, according to one electronic communications scholar, telephonic journalism in its early stages was little more than "telephone occasions." Single events were broadcast via telephone to scattered audiences on an episodic basis, albeit with "unprecedented immediacy."[115]

However, a telephone news feature was soon developed that foreshadowed today's instantaneous electronic media programming. In the 1890s, dedicated, independent programming was introduced for consumption by individual telephone subscribers. This new and "distinctive social feature" represented a radical change in how people acquired information.[116] Nearly ninety years later, the way in which individuals acquired information would be radically changed yet again with the introduction of all-news television programming.

The first, and perhaps only, example of sustained, independent programming for telephone subscribers in the nineteenth century occurred in Hungary. Telefon Hirmondó began regular service to about one thousand Budapest telephone subscribers in 1893. Telefon Hirmondó developed its own independent programming, used a standardized schedule and format, and emphasized news— national, international, economic, political, financial, and legal news. Subscribers could simply call Hirmondó's telephone number and listen to its programs, which were provided according to a regular programming schedule. Given its standardized schedule and news-dominated format, Hirmondó foreshadowed the all-news media of nearly a century later, especially CNN.[117]

However, telephone journalism's success soon fell victim to both financial limitations and those imposed by governments. The U.S. Telephone Herald, a short-lived imitator of Hirmondó, was developed in 1911, but quickly succumbed to financial problems. Telefon Hirmondó fared somewhat better, with nearly six thousand subscribers at one time. Yet this figure represented only one percent of Budapest's population.[118]

The limits of the Herald's and Hirmondó's success resulted from factors other than subscription cost: A subscription to the Herald's programming could be had for a nickel a day; Hirmondó's for a penny a day. Access to telephones was the limiting factor. In New York City in 1896, basic telephone service cost $20 a month, at a time when the average worker's income was about $38.50 per month.[119] In addition, the Herald had insufficient capital to finance the necessary equipment to meet its own demand. Hirmondó's demise probably resulted from official government limitations imposed on subscribers and upon those who could receive telephones.[120]

Telephonic journalism's lack of commercial success does not diminish its importance. The primary significance of Hirmondó and the Herald was that they demonstrated that a market already existed in the nineteenth century for receiving regular news and entertainment programming via personal electronic communication devices. Given that Hirmondó began in 1893, this proved to be a "radically forward-looking" medium of communication.[121] Thus, "the telephone distribution of breaking news [became] part of the transition from a passing world."[122] Telephonic journalism was, indeed, a bridge between two communications worlds: a bridge between an old world with vast expanses of time and space, and a new world where time and space would be fully collapsed for information; and a bridge between an old world where knowledge was monopolized, and a new world where knowledge would be both widespread and readily available. The instantaneous communication paradigm was on the horizon.[123]

One could argue that the age of instantaneity made its debut with the birth of wireless telegraphy in the late 1890s. True, the invention of telegraphy itself in the 1830s had marked the advent of the pre-paradigm era for the instantaneous communication paradigm. The development of the telephone had provided virtually instantaneous communication between specific points at the ends of telephone wires. Although the telegraph and telephone were rudimentary by today's standards, the vast majority of people believed that they had "annihilated space and time."[124] In light of these newfangled electronic marvels, a contemporary historian boldly proclaimed that "succession gave way to simultaneity."[125] However, it was not until wireless telegraphy that instantaneity became a reality between any two points.

Guglielmo Marconi demonstrated what he claimed to be the first truly wireless system of telegraphy in 1896. His first customer for the device was the British War Office, which, in 1900, ordered a significant number of the new machines. By 1903, Marconi had been made the sole supplier of wireless equipment for the British War Office, a concession which he held for the next eleven years.[126]

Marconi was never short on promises. Within five years of wireless telegraphy's first demonstration, Marconi claimed that he could communicate across the Atlantic by wireless. Although unverified by witnesses, Marconi claimed to have received the first transatlantic wireless transmission in December 1901: three dots in Morse Code, denoting the letter "S." Marconi had used a transmitter at Poldhu in Cornwall, England, and had received on a set manned solely by himself at St. John's, Newfoundland. By October 1907, Marconi began commercial operations that provided for poor but usable wireless service to ships all the way across the Atlantic Ocean. The vastness of the Atlantic was being further collapsed.[127]

Wireless telegraphy came into its own as a news source through tragedy. When the *Titanic* sank on the night of April 14, 1912, David Sarnoff, a wireless operator located atop Wanamaker's Department store in New York City (and later of RCA fame), was the first to receive a distress signal from sea. The signal had been relayed from the *Olympia* nearly 1,500 miles at sea. U.S. President William Howard Taft ordered all other stations to shut down so that Sarnoff could receive uninterrupted. Over the next three days, wireless technology provided Sarnoff with the names of the 700 persons that survived the sinking of the *Titanic*. She had taken another 1,500 passengers with her to the bottom of the Atlantic.[128]

Wireless's role in the 1912 *Titanic* tragedy demonstrated its ability to link land stations and ships at sea in an "instantaneous, worldwide network."[129] This was the first such network in history.[130] However, the earliest true global communications capability came with the advent of shortwave technology. Marconi, the man who moved the world into wireless telegraphy, would change the world yet again with the development of shortwave.

Marconi had long been at work on shortwave technology. However, it was not until 1923 that he discovered certain elements critical to shortwave's practical application. Then, in 1924, Marconi announced the success of his experiments and sent voice messages from England to Australia, messages that were also heard in North and South America, South Africa, and India. By the end of 1924 Marconi's voice could be received in Australia twenty-three and one-half hours per day. Instantaneous global communication was at last becoming a reality.[131]

Technology was also beginning to mount an assault on political space. According to Innis, the telegraph — wireless's predecessor — had "destroyed the monopoly of political centres."[132] However, wireless and shortwave technology introduced a radically new and unique phenomenon, the ability to literally "spray messages in all directions."[133] This ability allowed the wireless to mount an additional assault on political space, for the wireless could cross "national boundaries with impunity."[134] In other words, the wireless was the first communication device to collapse political space, as defined by state boundaries. Innis argues that the "[p]olitical boundaries related to the demands of the printing industry disappeared with the new [wireless] instrument of communication."[135] With the coming of the wireless's successor — radio — communication would be set free from political boundaries. Headrick contends that "[b]efore radio the channels of communication were physical — letters, wires— and could be guarded. Radio released information from its physical bonds and sent it out into the ether in all directions."[136] Political space was now collapsing.

Wireless technologies were also providing increased access to information. Early telephone service had inherent limits to its use as an information source: Its cost was prohibitive for the average person and it was limited to two-way transmissions. However, by contrast, the wireless had the ability to reach numerous individuals at the same time and for a cost of transmission that was largely independent of the number of people who received those transmissions. Therefore, wireless technology provided diffuse, readily available access points for information. However, wireless's successor, radio, provided the potential for near-universal access to information.

On Christmas Eve 1906, radio demonstrated its ability to carry the human voice to ships at sea.[137] By 1915, radio had demonstrated its ability to carry the human voice across the oceans.[138] These demonstrations of what was then called "radio telephony" illustrated its commercial potential. And, on election night 1920, station KDKA in Pittsburgh, Pennsylvania, inaugurated service by broadcasting election returns in what is generally regarded as the first commercial broadcast of radio.[139]

New developments in electronic communications have routinely found their initial commercial application in the delivery of political news.

The first telegraph news carried was that of Clay and Frelinghuysen's selection as the Whig ticket for president in 1844. The first telephonic journalism carried news of the returns from the 1892 U.S. presidential election. Radio's first commercial application was to deliver political news. In each case, the new technology was quickly harnessed to increase access to information on rapidly breaking political events. Knowledge was no longer monopolized and expensive; it was becoming more available and affordable.

Electronic communication was also challenging the press as a primary news source.[140] In 1923, 39 percent of U.S. cities had two or more newspapers.[141] By 1933, this number had dropped to only 17 percent of U.S. cities and continued to drop to 10 percent in 1943, and to 6 percent by 1953.[142] Consolidation accounted for some of this decrease in the number of newspapers servicing a particular city. However, with the invention of radio, the newspaper had acquired a rival in the distribution of news.[143] Thus, by the 1930s, newspapers had been displaced by radio as the primary news source, especially for bulletins.[144] Information was now available instantly and for the price of a radio.

Television, the next major advance in electronic communications, would combine radio's power of hearing with the greater power of seeing. The word "television" literally means seeing at a distance.[145] According to communications scholar Hohenberg, the invention of television was a "revolution without parallel" in the five hundred years since Gutenberg developed the printing press.[146]

Innis reminds us that "[t]he voice of a second-rate person is more impressive than the published opinion of superior ability."[147] And, Innis contends further that writing to someone records an impression that is once removed from the impression that one would convey by speaking directly to that person; likewise, reading what someone has written provides an impression that is twice removed from actually speaking directly to that person.[148]

Innis's thoughts beg an obvious question: Given his argument about the power of spoken communication as compared to writing or reading, what is the power of speaking when combined with seeing? Unparalleled impact. This answer suggests television's inherent power. Television harnessed the instantaneity of its electronic-communications forbears to the unparalleled impact of "seeing is believing."

The principles behind television had been successfully worked out by a German inventor in the late nineteenth century. By 1912, the prospect of television's existence was such a foregone conclusion that futurists were primarily concerned with whether television would be delivered to homes by radio or by telephone wires.[149] Limited television broadcasts were available in New York on an infrequent basis by 1928. By 1931, the Columbia Broadcasting System (CBS) had begun a regular schedule of broadcasting in New York City. By 1939, the National Broadcasting Company (NBC) began to offer television as a regular service.[150]

Network television was born in the immediate post–World War II era and with it a major change occurred in news delivery. In 1948, television brought national political conventions into people's homes for the first time. The subsequent inauguration of Harry Truman in 1949 allowed people to see via television an event that had previously only been described to them in newspapers. The advent of television made a tremendous difference in the way people got their news, so great a difference that "some of the largest and most powerful newspapers ... would be obliged to fight for their lives against the inroads of television."[151] By the early 1960s, more Americans received their political information from television than from newspapers. By the early 1990s, the U.S. had been dubbed "the world's first media state," thanks to television's pervasiveness. In fact, more homes in the U.S. now have a television than have a toilet.[152]

The latest development in television — global, satellite up-link transmission — has brought us to the virtual collapse of time and space. Early television could cover only "places where the camera and lights could be set up."[153] Given these physical limitations, early television could provide instantaneous communication. However, it could do so only between people in a large, fixed television studio and those few people who owned television sets, and who also happened to live in a major metropolitan area serviced by television. With the development of smaller cameras, detachable recorders, wireless microphones, and the videotape recorder, television could be "almost anywhere it wanted to go."[154] However, it remained for the development of the satellite dish and on-the-spot, satellite up-link transmission capability in the 1980s to provide truly instantaneous communication that was both audio and visual. Now, with the development of portable satellite transmission equipment, television can be broadcast from anywhere to anywhere. For the first time in history, the unparalleled impact of seeing while hearing is global.

Person-to-person global video communication is now possible. However, this personalization of global television is but the latest and most novel example of personalized electronic media. The personal electronic media source made its debut with the first telephone exchange that opened in New Haven, Connecticut, in 1878.[155] The next personal electronic media source, the radio, did not appear until more than forty years later in the early 1920s. However, the development of personal electronic media sources has accelerated significantly since 1920: the television, photocopier, personal computer, video cassette recorder (VCR), modem, facsimile (fax) machine, cellular telephone, satellite pager, camcorder, inexpensive direct broadcast satellite (DBS) dish — the list could continue. This string of inventions suggests something about the ultra-personalized media future that we can expect.

The trend toward personalized media also affects our concept of political space and the control of information within it. Media scholar Gladys Ganley argues that there is a significant connection between personal media and politics:

> The prompt global adaptation of these new [personal electronic] media to political acts, the variety of political acts being conducted with them, the ingenuity involved in carrying out these acts, the growing variety of available technologies and their interactive capabilities, and the actual political change which has already followed their uses, all sound a warning that something of very basic importance is happening.[156]

Some of the personal media sources that have had an effect on politics include photocopiers, direct-dial phones, personal computers, modems, satellite dishes, notebook computers, cellular phones, and satellite paging technology. In fact, Ganley documents twenty-seven specific innovations in personal electronic media since the end of World War II that have had an impact on politics.[157]

Several high-profile events have demonstrated the political impact of personal media. The Ayatollah Khomeini made significant use of cassette tapes to spread his brand of Islamic revolution to Iran from his exile in Paris prior to the 1979 uprising against the Shah's government.[158] The VCR and video tapes played a pivotal role during the 1986 people's revolution in the Philippines, which led to the ouster of President Ferdinand Marcos and the installation of President Corazon Aquino.[159] American-made audio tapes were key in sustaining the courage of striking shipyard workers in Gdansk, Poland, in August 1980, which led to the founding of the trade union Solidarity, led by Lech Walesa.[160] Walesa would later become the democratically elected President of Poland. During this same period in Poland, American-made FM radios played an important role by picking up Polish police-band radio.[161] Personal facsimiles supplied Panamanians with news from the outside about what was going on inside their own country when General Manuel Noriega imposed a news blackout in mid-1987.[162] Personal electronic media may, in fact, pose the ultimate challenge to government control over information.

The events of 1989 in Eastern Europe demonstrate the effect on politics of increased access to information. Romania's anti–Communist revolution of December 1989 was sparked by the cross-border broadcasting of a specific video tape, according to Ganley.[163] The government of Romanian Communist Party leader Nicolae Ceausescu had failed to restrict video equipment, largely because the government believed that it had sufficient control over the lives of its citizens. This oversight by the government allowed VCRs to become available to an increasing number of ordinary Romanians.[164] The specific video credited with sparking the Romanian revolution was initially broadcast on Hungarian television in July 1989 and was subsequently duplicated and widely viewed. It featured the Reverend Laszlo Tokes, pastor of the Reformed Church in Timisoara, Romania. On the video, Tokes spoke of the physical and emotional destruction of Romania under Ceausescu. The pastor's accusations prompted an attempt on the part of Ceausescu to throw Tokes out of his church.[165]

However, public support for Tokes and his cause grew, resulting in large public protests. When Romanian security forces attempted to squelch the uprisings by firing on the protesters, word reached the rest of the Romanian people via foreign broadcasts. These cross border broadcasts, plus those detailing the revolutions unfolding across the rest of Eastern Europe, ultimately sparked the Romanian revolution, according to Ted Koppel of ABC's *Nightline* TV news show. Koppel argues that

> The Romanian revolution against Ceausescu began in Timisoara because it was closest to Yugoslavia. Yugoslavia was still carrying broadcasts from CNN and Timisoara was seeing on CNN what was happening in the rest of Eastern Europe and were encouraged to have their own revolution.[166]

Mass outpourings fueled by these broadcasts resulted in the Romanian government being unable to keep the lid on mass public protests. Ultimately, Ceausescu's government fell from the force of these protests and he and his wife were subsequently executed for crimes against the Romanian people. Thus, Romania provides an illustrative case of communications' ability to collapse political space by increasing access to information.[167]

Cross-border broadcasting first became a reality with Marconi's 1896 development of the wireless. However, a new phenomenon has emerged from television's refinement into a personal medium for cross border broadcasting. By late 1989, this new phenomenon allowed television to become the force behind the dominoes that fell all across Eastern Europe, "as the Poles inspired the Hungarians, the Hungarians inspired the East Germans and the East Germans inspired the Czechoslovaks."[168] Historians

Jeremy D. Popkin and Jack R. Censer argue that the events of 1989 in Eastern Europe provide evidence that global media are now capable of undermining the "monolithic media of totalitarian societies."[169] Likewise, noted European scholar Timothy Garton Ash concludes that "[i]n Europe at the end of the 20th century all revolutions are televolutions."[170] In 1989, the world witnessed a new power: communications' ability to alter Europe's political geography.

Political space had collapsed; knowledge had become global. Historically, governments have attempted to control information, as witnessed by the keen threat that they felt from Gutenberg's 1440 invention. However, by 2001, information is no longer in anyone's control. And, since information is not in anyone's control, it is in everyone's control.

Since its advent in the 1830s, electronic communications technology has persistently moved humanity toward an historic destination. Today, the information superhighway affords simultaneous global knowledge transfers, while satellite technology affords real-time global television transmissions from one individual to another. Time and space no longer exist as obstacles to information transfer. The monopoly over knowledge has ended. Western civilization now exists in the instantaneous communication paradigm.

Paradigms and Diplomacy

As with communication, diplomatic scholars identify distinct eras in the history of diplomacy in Western civilization. These eras are distinguished by differences in the prevailing methods of diplomatic practice. Different scholars place various lines of demarcation between diplomatic eras and they may emphasize somewhat different practices as the defining modes for respective eras. However, numerous scholars agree that there was an "old diplomacy" that was distinctly different from the "new diplomacy" that emerged during the immediate post–World War I era.[171] Therefore, the history of Western diplomacy up to the latter part of last century may be divided into two eras on the basis of different methods of practice: "old diplomacy" and its successors, "new diplomacy."

Kuhn's paradigm concept is as useful in differentiating between diplomatic eras as it is in distinguishing communication eras. Recall that Kuhn described a paradigm as a "prevailing world view" that forms the basis of practice within a certain discipline.[172] The distinctions between diplomacy's two eras, old and new, stem from a prevailing world view, unique to each era, that formed the basis of diplomatic practice for the given era.

Thus, Western civilization has known two diplomatic paradigms. The first of these paradigms, "old diplomacy," defined Western diplomatic practice from the time of the Renaissance until the World War I era. The second, "new diplomacy," defined diplomatic practice from the World War I era until the rise of global television in the 1980s.

The historical boundaries for diplomatic paradigms are as difficult to affix precise dates to as are the boundaries for communication paradigms. Diplomacy has shifted from one paradigm to its successor by the same process of creeping incrementalism suggested by Kuhn.[173] As discussed further below, old diplomacy can be roughly bounded on one end by the mid-fifteenth century, and on the other end by the World War I era.

However, a move from one diplomatic paradigm to its successor also involves a "pre-paradigm stage."[174] During the last century of its existence, old diplomacy was gradually declining as new diplomacy was emerging. Therefore, new diplomacy's pre-paradigm stage was approximately one century in duration, roughly defined by the period between the 1814–1815 Congress of Vienna, which some have suggested as old diplomacy's zenith, and the point at which old diplomacy was finally displaced by new diplomacy during the post–World War I era. Western diplomacy is just now moving into another pre-paradigm era, that of diplomacy's next paradigm, telediplomacy.

Old Diplomacy

Diplomatists often express an enigmatic wistfulness about the good old days. This longing knows as its object the diplomacy of a bygone era, a style of diplomacy perceived to be far superior to the (changed) diplomacy that contemporaries must practice. Alas, "[d]iplomacy never was quite what it used to be."[175] Such wistful nostalgia implies a grudging recognition that diplomacy has changed. In light of these changes, diplomats yearn for the practices of a fabled era, that of old diplomacy.

The term "old diplomacy" is largely a shorthand reference to specific diplomatic institutions and practices. Many of these practices were developed by the fifteenth-century Italians; nearly all were refined and codified by the French during the seventeenth century. Cardinal Richelieu of France is credited with the professionalization of modern diplomacy. Richelieu served as chief minister to Louis XIII from 1624 to 1642. As diplomatic adviser to the king, Richelieu established a Ministry of External Affairs in 1626 that both centralized and standardized the management of France's foreign relations, the first such ministry of its kind. Richelieu also developed many of the practices and much of the protocol for what would one day be referred to as old diplomacy. Thus, by the mid-1600s diplomacy as we understand it today was beginning to take shape.[176]

Both old and new diplomacy exist within the modern diplomatic era. The term "modern diplomacy" refers to those methods of diplomatic practice in the Western world that originated during the Renaissance. Although it is impossible to ascribe a precise date to the beginning of modern diplomacy, its origin is marked by the incremental, faltering process whereby European leaders developed closer and more continuous relations. However, by the middle of the fifteenth century, certain diplomatic practices and institutions were forming in the Italian city-states that are recognizable as the forerunners of today's diplomacy. Given this fact, the origins of modern diplomacy may be traced to mid-fifteenth century Italy, or about A.D. 1450.[177]

The Italian city-states developed and codified certain diplomatic institutions that are still recognizable in today's diplomacy. The driving principle behind these procedural institutions was that diplomacy was to be thought of as "preventive and permanent, and not merely as a sporadic exercise in situations of emergency."[178] For example, the Italian city-states established the first recorded permanent diplomatic missions accredited to another country. This practice of posting resident ambassadors moved diplomacy toward becoming an ongoing exercise designed to prevent tensions between states. Diplomacy was no longer an episodic exercise reserved for times of emergency.

Scholars disagree as to the first known exchange of a regularly credited resident ambassador. Sir Harold Nicolson, the eminent British diplomat and historian, contends that Francesco Sforza, Duke of Milan, was the first permanent ambassador.[179] Sforza was accredited to the Italian city-state of Genoa in 1455. However, according to diplomatic scholar M. S. Anderson, Filippo Maria Visconti, also a Duke of Milan, posted the first permanent ambassador.[180] From 1425 to 1432, Visconti posted a resident ambassador to the court of Sigismund, King of Hungary and Holy Roman Emperor–elect. During this same period, Sigismund reciprocated with his own ambassador in Milan.[181] Hamilton and Langhorne agree with Anderson about the name and date of the first permanent diplomatic mission abroad.[182] Thus Anderson, Hamilton, and Langhorne set the date of the first resident ambassadorial exchange more than a quarter century before the date noted by Nicolson.

Such differences between scholars point up the difficulty in establishing a specific start date for modern diplomacy. Suffice it to say that during the middle of the fifteenth century the direct ancestors of today's diplomatic practices began to take shape. Given this fact, modern diplomacy began circa 1450. From this beginning, diplomacy evolved various methods which, by the time of Richelieu, comprised a style of diplomatic practice that would one day be referred to as old diplomacy.

Nicolson contends that old diplomacy was defined by five strategic factors.[183] According to Nicolson, old diplomacy was first a Eurocentric diplomacy, in that it saw Europe as the most important of continents. Second, the driving assumption was that the great powers were in fact great, and that they were greater than the small powers, which were graded according to their military capabilities. Third, given this assumption about the international system, there was a sense of *noblesse oblige* that inhered unto the great powers: as a function of the great powers' privileged (or noble) position, they had a responsibility (or an obligation) to preserve the peace among the small powers. Fourth, every European country possessed a professional diplomatic service that was nearly identical to that of every other country. These respective services were modeled upon, and a direct bequest of, the French system. Fifth, harmonious international relations were assumed to flow only from continuous and confidential negotiations that were never pressed for time. Such negotiations were seen as an ongoing process and never as episodic. Nicolson's strategic factors establish the context within which old diplomacy was practiced.

Certain macro-characteristics defined diplomatic practice under old diplomacy: it was a private, autonomous, cosmopolitan, elite, and unhurried art. Although different scholars may choose to emphasize specific traits, the same macro-characteristics are largely implicit within most descriptions of old diplomacy. Therefore, these five characteristics are generally recognized as defining the practices of old diplomacy.

First and foremost, old diplomacy was private, reticent and discreet. It was never the focus of "public emotion."[184]

Second, old diplomacy was autonomous. It was conducted by resident ambassadors who had little concern about being challenged over their position on issues.[185]

Third, diplomacy was characterized by uniformity and a cosmopolitan tradition. Diplomats of this era had a distinct world view that originated from living most of their lives outside the state of their citizenship. Thus, diplomats often felt a stronger kinship with their diplomatic counterparts than with their fellow citizens back home.[186]

Old diplomacy's kindred spirit stemmed from a fourth defining characteristic: The diplomatic community was small and intimate. It was an elite community consisting of representatives from at most forty to fifty sovereign states, with no more than a dozen of these states considered important in international relations. Diplomats of this era were preoccupied with only those few items that were of supreme international concern. These concerns included questions of war, strategy, and territorial possession, and were considered to be matters of high politics, amenable to resolution only at the ambassadorial level. Nonpolitical problems, such as economic and immigration issues, were considered by the diplomatic elite to be merely issues of low diplomacy. Such less-important problems were assigned to junior officials of less than ambassadorial rank.[187]

Old diplomacy's fifth defining characteristic was its status as an art, and not a science.[188] Diplomacy was the art of protocol, precedence, ceremony, and ritual. A French scholar, Le Trosne, captured the essence of old diplomacy when he wrote in 1771 that diplomacy was "an obscure art which hides itself in the folds of deceit, which fears to let itself be seen and believes that it can exist only in the darkness of mystery."[189] This was diplomacy's golden era, the era when diplomacy was a private, autonomous, cosmopolitan, elite, and unhurried art.

Former U.S. Secretary of State Henry Kissinger provides a window into old diplomacy's practice. Kissinger's doctoral dissertation at Harvard University describes the diplomatic maneuvering that ended the Napoleonic Wars of 1803–1815 and that subsequently ushered in a century of peace among Europe's great powers. Published under the title *A World Restored*, Kissinger's work describes how the autonomous, unhurried efforts of "statesmen of repose" rescued a Europe ablaze with war in 1812.[190] Chief amongst these statesmen was the Austrian Foreign Minister, Prince von Metternich. The ever-ambitious Austrian Foreign Minister determined in advance that his country should emerge as a principal European power "despite his Emperor's hesitations."[191] Metternich had, in fact, determined to lead Austria into war. By doing so, he would demonstrate that peace was impossible; consequently, war was necessary.

Emperor Francis I of Austria was successfully drawn along by Metternich. Although initially hesitant, the Emperor was first induced to "create an army in order to protect Austria's neutrality and then [convinced] to use this army to protect the peace."[192] In a classic diplomatic maneuver, Metternich then turned this army against Austria's former ally, France. Austria was now joined in the coalition of forces arrayed against Napoleon, leading to his defeat. Metternich had successfully maneuvered Francis I into making war on Napoleon, the husband of Francis I's own daughter, Marie-Louise. By doing so, Metternich transformed Austria's status in Europe from that of a mere "French auxiliary" into the "pivotal power of Europe." As a result, Metternich personally positioned himself as the mediator of a grand European peace, rather than merely being an intermediary in the process. Thus, during four years of calculated, incremental maneuvers, the Austrian Foreign Minister became Europe's leading statesman and the chief architect of the Concert of Europe. The Concert, which is often referred to as the "Metternich" or balance-of-power system, effectively kept the peace among Europe's great powers for a century.[193]

Metternich, the quintessential diplomat, had succeeded in plying his esoteric craft in unhurried detachment and according to the dictates of his own design. Metternich had skillfully avoided any effective accountability to his sovereign. Furthermore, in Metternich's era, there was little, if any, concern about accountability to the public.[194] Metternich's practices illustrate old diplomacy's two primary distinguishing characteristics: privacy and autonomy.

American diplomacy in the early 1800s was strikingly similar to that of Metternich, even though U.S. political leaders had denounced the schemes of Old World European diplomacy. The purchase of France's Louisiana Territory in North America provides a prime example of diplomatic autonomy. In 1803, President Thomas Jefferson instructed the American minister in Paris, Robert Livingston, to negotiate the purchase of the French-owned city of New Orleans. James Monroe was dispatched to assist with the negotiations. Jefferson authorized Livingston and Monroe to spend a maximum of ten million dollars.[195] However, acting upon his own authority and apart from any instructions from his government, Livingston proposed that the French sell the entire Louisiana Territory to the U.S.[196] The French government responded by offering to sell Louisiana to the U.S. for fifteen million dollars. Livingston and Monroe promptly accepted, without the knowledge or authorization of either their president or the U.S. Congress. As president, Jefferson would ultimately be responsible for getting Livingston and Monroe's treaty through Congress, which would have to give its advice and consent to the treaty as well as appropriate the funds to pay for the purchase of Louisiana. Livingston and Monroe had acted on the basis of diplomatic autonomy.[197]

Old diplomacy's practices were largely a function of two factors: time and space. The distances that separated diplomats from their governments required a significant amount of time for communication to traverse those distances by horse or sailing ship. For example, when the Louisiana Purchase was negotiated, a dispatch from Europe could take almost two months to reach Washington.[198]

Time and space also contributed to old diplomacy's characteristics in another way: The distances between a diplomat and his government gave the diplomat on the scene a monopoly over knowledge. The American diplomats who negotiated the Louisiana Purchase were able to significantly exceed their instructions, thanks to the two months required to communicate between Washington and Paris. This monopoly over knowledge afforded by time and space allowed Livingston and Monroe to negotiate a treaty that would require the U.S. president's support and Congress's approval, without the prior knowledge or authorization of either.

Jefferson was at first embarrassed by the treaty to purchase Louisiana. It doubled the size of the U.S. and Jefferson had made political commitments to sharply limit the power of the federal government. Furthermore, the Constitution contained no provisions under which the U.S. government could acquire new territory. Given that Jefferson believed in a strict interpretation of the Constitution, he was uncertain as to whether he had the authority to accept such a treaty. Likewise, Congress was taken unawares. However, as was the case with Jefferson, Congress would ultimately support the treaty by giving its approval and appropriating the funds to pay for Livingston and Monroe's purchase.[199]

Time and space, and the resulting monopoly over knowledge, largely defined old diplomacy. However, as conceptions about time and space began to change, the very context in which diplomacy functioned was changing. And, with these contextual changes, old diplomacy itself would be forced to change, giving way to new diplomacy.

Affixing the end-date for this old style of diplomacy is a subjective process. However, most scholars agree that the breakdown of diplomatic mediation which resulted in World War I was the harbinger of a fundamental change in diplomatic practice. Nicolson, who served as a British diplomat to the Versailles Peace Conference concluding World War I, designates the final settlement negotiated by the Council of Europe, the Balkan Crisis of 1913, as both the finest example and the end of old diplomacy.[200] Anderson contends that, in retrospect, it is easy to see that old diplomacy was "slowly coming to an end" by 1914.[201] Most scholars would agree. World War I marked the end of diplomacy's golden era and the beginning of something different.

New Diplomacy

Diplomatic scholars often fix U.S. President Woodrow Wilson's participation in World War I and the Peace of Versailles as the beginning of new diplomacy. The first of Wilson's Fourteen Points, issued January 8, 1918, is often noted as the "biblical text for open diplomacy."[202] Wilson declared that henceforth diplomacy should be characterized by:

> Open covenants openly arrived at, after which there should be no private
> international understandings of any kind, but diplomacy shall proceed
> always frankly and in the public view.[203]

This push for openness, which Wilson had called for in his Fourteen Points,
has incrementally come to characterize diplomacy since World War I.
Thirty years after Wilson, Morgenthau argued that "[d]iplomatic negotiations of the traditional type have ... become virtually obsolete."[204] Therefore, the World War I era is often viewed as the great divide between old
and new diplomacy.

The watershed in practice between old and new diplomacy was
between that of privacy and openness. According to Eban, the "new public diplomacy" has come to mean that "[t]here is no way of putting the
clock back to an era in which the early and intermediate stages of negotiation were sheltered from the domestic constituencies of the negotia-
tors."[205] According to Nicolson, the transition from old to new diplomacy
was brought about by "the belief that it was possible to apply to the conduct of external affairs, the ideas and practices which, in the conduct of
internal affairs, had for generations been regarded as the essentials of lib-
eral democracy."[206] These beliefs brought about a unique style of diplomacy that was largely defined by one macro-characteristic — openness.
Whereas old diplomacy had several defining macro-characteristics — a private, autonomous, cosmopolitan, elite, unhurried art — new diplomacy
can be characterized by the single concept of openness.

This emphasis on diplomatic openness stemmed from the belief that
secret diplomacy among Europe's great powers was the principal cause of
World War I. Morgenthau, perhaps this century's most respected diplomatic scholar, contends that

> During and after the First World War, wide currency was given to the opin-
> ion that the secret machinations of diplomats shared a great deal, if not the
> major portion, of responsibility for that war, that the secrecy of diplomatic
> negotiations was an atavistic and dangerous residue from the aristocratic
> past.[207]

Morgenthau argues further that, following this assessment of diplomacy
in the wake of World War I, the operating assumption became that "international negotiations carried on and concluded under the watchful eyes
of a peace-loving public opinion could not but further the cause of
peace."[208] Former Israeli diplomat Eban argues that "[a]ny discussion of
changes in the diplomatic system must begin with the most potent and

far-reaching transformation of all: the collapse of reticence and privacy in negotiation."[209] The concept of openness is, therefore, the defining distinction between old and new diplomacy.

At the risk of inordinate brevity, one could argue that old diplomacy was what new diplomacy is *not*. Although old diplomacy was an autonomous, cosmopolitan, elite, and unhurried art, the watershed distinction between the practice of old and new diplomacy is between that of privacy and openness. Where old diplomacy was characterized as private, new diplomacy is characterized as open. Likewise, new diplomacy is what old diplomacy was *not* with regard to old diplomacy's other defining characteristics, subtle differences in degree notwithstanding.

Where old diplomacy was autonomous, new diplomacy is *not*. The practitioners of old diplomacy enjoyed virtual autonomy from both their sovereigns and their publics. Diplomats under new diplomacy have become increasingly accountable to both political masters and democratic publics at home. Today, the ambassador is likely to find herself upstaged by presidential or prime ministerial diplomacy, summit meetings, or cases where his "political masters do much of the negotiation and usurp some of [the] symbolic function in celebrating and dramatizing international friendships."[210] In addition, new diplomacy is often referred to as "democratic" diplomacy in the context of increased accountability to home publics. This accountability has contributed to an increasing uncertainty of result from the diplomatic process, according to some.[211] This increased accountability requires that diplomats deal with the challenges posed by two-level bargaining, wherein diplomats conduct business with their diplomatic counterparts and their interests as is normally the case; however, in addition, diplomats must at the same time conduct business with their own domestic public opinion and its unique interests.[212]

Where old diplomacy was cosmopolitan, new diplomacy is *not*. The practitioner of old diplomacy often developed a closer relationship with his professional colleagues than with his own fellow citizens back home because of the diplomat's long years abroad. However, such "cosmopolitan solidarities" are breaking down with the dramatically increasing number of states and diplomats, and the resulting dilution of that "common culture and form of expression" which characterized old diplomacy. Today, especially with the increasing habit of states to appoint as diplomats those individuals who are wealthy or who are personal friends of heads of state, "those in political control of international relations are less likely to have recognized qualifications in that domain than their own junior officials." Furthermore, the diplomat's increasing accountability to the public at home has also contributed to a more parochial, less cosmopolitan, perspective.[213]

Where old diplomacy was characterized as elite, new diplomacy is *not*. The proliferation of new sovereign states in the last decade alone is legend; yet, two decades ago there were already more than fifty thousand officials in the world holding diplomatic credentials.[214]

The most noticeable change between old and new diplomacy may be the loss of diplomacy's unhurried nature. Old diplomacy was driven by the commonly accepted assumption that "time alone is the conciliator." Thus, diplomacy was the "art of timing," an art exemplified in the practice of a Metternich. But vast resources of time are no longer at the diplomat's disposal.[215]

Scholars and practitioners agree that diplomacy is no longer an unhurried art. Nicolson contends that under new diplomacy "things move with great celerity. There is less time for reflection."[216] James Der Derian argues that technological advances and speedy communication have conspired to rob diplomacy of its "reflective decision-making."[217] According to Der Derian, in an era of instantaneous response times, "diplomacy becomes governed as much by the velocity of the events as by the events themselves."[218] Likewise, Adam Watson criticizes the contemporary diplomatic environment as one which expects governments to "react with increasing speed to events and the actions of other governments, so that they are less and less able to wait for the reasoned comments distilled by their diplomatic organization in the field and at home."[219] Collapsing time and space, and the resulting erosion of the knowledge monopoly, has robbed diplomacy of a valuable resource — time.

Diplomacy is also experiencing the erosion of its status as an art. A contemporary diplomat has lamented that diplomacy is not yet recognized as a "science."[220] Eban believes that increased professionalization of new diplomacy might be found were the "science" of international relations to increase its authority.[221] However, were diplomacy to become more "scientific," it would suffer further loss of another of old diplomacy's defining macro-characteristics: its status as an art. Science is not art, and diplomacy cannot be both science and art.

By reviewing what new diplomacy is *not*, we can deduce something about what new diplomacy *is*. Simply put, new diplomacy's methods of practice have displaced those of old diplomacy. New diplomacy's principal characteristic is openness, in part because of the media's intrusion into the diplomatic process. New diplomacy is largely defined by the following trends: diplomats' increasing accountability to both their governments and their home publics; greater parochialism amongst diplomats, who are increasingly dependent upon a personal relationship with heads of state for their positions; a burgeoning number of diplomatic actors, including non-traditional actors, such as the media, who have not historically been considered as players in the diplomatic arena; and a significant acceleration in diplomacy's pace. Some may quibble about what new diplomacy is; however, most would agree that these trends represent what old diplomacy was *not*.

The old has gone and new diplomacy has come. Although specific degrees of difference between old and new diplomacy may be debated, few would argue that post-World War I diplomacy is the same as that plied by Metternich during the 1814-1815 Congress of Vienna or by Livingston and Monroe during the purchase of Louisiana. These watershed changes in diplomatic practice have come from the push of communications technology. Thus, almost four decades ago one diplomatic historian was already arguing that "[n]othing has had so revolutionary an effect upon the conduct of diplomacy in the past century and a half as improvements in the art of communication."[222] Communications developments during the last four decades have revolutionized diplomacy yet again.

Chapter 3

Diplomacy and Communication: The Results of Linkage

"The elite, secretive discriminating world of the traditional diplomats has been irreversibly invaded by the rude, revealing, and random eye of the television camera."
— *William H. Sullivan, 1984; former U.S. Foreign Service Officer with ambassadorial rank*

"The Information Revolution is taking the initiative in policy-making away from governments.... How policymakers react to and cope with the fact that their hands are being forced by the mass media has created a new set of challenges for ... diplomacy."
— *Richard H. Solomon, 1997; President of the United States Institute of Peace and a former U.S. Assistant Secretary of State*

Shifts in the communication paradigm historically have defined methods of diplomatic practice. Such was the case with the shift from old to new diplomacy, which resulted from a preceding shift in communication paradigm from the elite written paradigm to that of mass printing. By the mid-to-late 1800s, advances in communication were beginning to have an effect upon diplomacy's methods. Queen Victoria argued in 1876 that the "time for Ambassadors and their pretensions [is] past," given the speed of the newfangled electronic communications.[1] Communication was diminishing old diplomacy's privacy, its autonomy, and its cosmopolitan, elite, and unhurried character, as well. And, by the time of World War I, the old style of diplomacy was passing away.

Diplomatists contemporary to these changes were not unaware of communications' effect upon their craft. Some of old diplomacy's more foresighted practitioners recognized the nature of what was happening to their craft. British diplomat Charles Lister lamented in 1914 that "diplomacy is dead."[2] French Foreign Minister Jules Cambon observed in 1905 that the effects of faster communication and the press had displaced diplomacy.[3]

The displacing of old diplomacy was not a sudden or a conscious refutation of its methods. Rather, old diplomacy's demise resulted from a kind of creeping incrementalism whereby its practices were gradually displaced by different processes, the unhurried, deliberative pace of old diplomacy was accelerated, and non-traditional actors were afforded influence in the diplomatic arena. Communication was exerting its effects upon old diplomacy, gradually shaping new diplomacy's methods of practice.

Displacing Old Diplomacy's Methods of Practice

Recall that traditional diplomacy has performed several specific functions. In addition to routine consular activities, diplomacy historically has performed the functions of gathering and interpreting information, signaling and receiving, representation, international public relations, negotiation, and crisis management. However, the shift from the elite to the mass communication paradigm produced significant changes in the way diplomacy performed these functions. This displacing of old diplomacy's methods would, by the time of World War I, result in the emergence of new diplomacy.

Modern, or "old diplomacy," emerged as an institution because of the increasing need for information about other countries. The diplomat's single most important function historically has been the "gathering and sending back to his government information about the state in which he was stationed."[4] The principal purpose for the modern diplomat has been to "know as much as could be known," "gather information," and "convey news."[5] In other words, modern diplomacy was established as a vehicle to facilitate communication in an era where the prevailing methods of communication had not changed appreciably for two millennia.

Diplomacy's original intent was to bridge the gap created by geographic distance between governments. Nicolson makes the case that, "In the days before newspapers existed and when foreign correspondents were unknown, an ambassador was regarded first and foremost as a source of news."[6] In fact, according to Nicolson the "main cause of the establishment of permanent missions" was the "overriding importance attached to the quick receipt of news."[7] Thus, old diplomacy's original purpose was to gather information.

However, as the 1800s progressed, the primacy of diplomats as a news source eroded. The persistent push of communications technology began to displace diplomacy's information-gathering function. Nicolson contends that this function gradually came to be performed by the telegraph agencies and the newspapers.[8] Likewise, Innis has argued that "The diplomatic institutions and techniques of an age of dynastic cabinet politics failed to work in a situation characterized by the press [and] electrical communications...."[9] Implicit in Innis's argument is communications' challenge to old diplomacy's reason for being — to gather news.

Advances in communication would also erode the autonomy and privacy diplomats enjoyed under old diplomacy. British Foreign Secretary Lord Castlereagh's performance at the 1814 Congress of Vienna illustrates old diplomacy's autonomous methods. Prior to attending the Congress, Castlereagh received specific instructions from the British cabinet not to involve Britain in hostilities. However, Castlereagh chose to violate his cabinet's instructions and threatened war, a war that he had specifically been instructed against. Fortunately for Castlereagh, war was averted and he was not confronted with the consequences of his disregard for instructions. Castlereagh's autonomy stemmed from the distance and time between Vienna and London in 1814, a distance that would ultimately collapse under the weight of advances in communications.[10]

The time and space between diplomats and their governments also allowed old diplomacy to move at a decidedly unhurried pace, even in crisis-management situations. Nineteenth-century statesmen, such as Castlereagh, were "statesmen of repose," operating in their own private, unhurried atmosphere.[11] The atmosphere of the early nineteenth century afforded the "time for diplomacy and conferences," even in the midst of crises.[12] For example, in 1827 Greece received the decisive military support of the three dominant members of the European Congress (Britain, France, and Russia) in the Greek war for independence from the Turkish Empire. With the military aid of the Congress members, Greece was successful in defeating the Turkish fleet at the Battle of Navarino. However, questions relating to Greece had been debated in the European Congress system for some eight years before the military action was taken at Navarino.[13] Gentlemen of state had plied their crisis-management craft in unhurried detachment for eight years.

But old diplomacy's methods of unhurried detachment and free-wheeling autonomy were born of the time and space that existed between diplomats and their governments. In 1815 it took Castlereagh twenty-eight days to travel from London to the Congress of Vienna.[14] By 1822 the record time from Vienna to London for the most urgent of dispatches was still one week — and this for a light diplomatic pouch, not the much slower entourage with which diplomats had to travel.[15]

However, by the 1870s these distances between diplomats and their governments were beginning to collapse. The telegraph now covered both North America and Europe, reaching into even the smallest towns.[16] The autonomy that diplomats had once enjoyed belonged to the era of dynastic cabinet politics: Castlereagh was able to ignore his government's instructions and threaten war; Livingston and Monroe were able to strike a deal on the Louisiana Territory that far exceeded their instructions; and Greek independence was discussed in unhurried detachment for eight years before the Great Powers supported Greece at the Battle of Navarino. This type of autonomy belonged to a communications paradigm of the past.

Yet, diplomats reared under this old communications paradigm would soon be forced to ply their craft under radically changed methods of communications. Diplomats of the old era, with their "ancient and sacred rituals, entered the age of speedy communications with reluctance."[17] The Austro-Hungarian Emperor at the outbreak of World War I in 1914, Franz Joseph, was steeped in diplomacy's ancient and sacred rituals. Franz Joseph had refused to allow any telephones or telegraphs to be put in his palace, the Hofburg in Vienna. For him, and for his diplomatic colleagues of that era, the telephone and telegraph broke down formal barriers of distance and allowed an immediacy of access that was deemed inconsistent with proper diplomatic protocol.[18] The aging Emperor was wedded to the traditions of dynastic cabinet diplomacy, and divorced from the existing reality of speedy communications.

But, Franz Joseph was of a different diplomatic era. He was eighty-four years old and had been on the throne for sixty-six years when World War I began. In fact, he had come to the throne during the last year that Metternich — the examplar of an old-style diplomat — served as Austria's foreign minister, 1848. Diplomats and political leaders reared in the era of dynastic diplomacy would struggle to comprehend and manage the new communications technology. Yet, the new speedy communications would not only transform diplomacy's ancient and sacred rituals, but would significantly accelerate its pace, as well.

Accelerating Diplomacy's Pace

Communications' effect upon the pace of crisis management was highlighted during the July Crisis preceding the outbreak of World War I. The climactic period between July 23 and August 4, 1914, demonstrates the then unprecedented pace of events afforded by the telephone and the telegraph. This pace itself is often cited as one of the causes of World War I. The sheer rush of events facilitated by the telephone and the telegraph was "itself an independent cause that catapulted Europe into War."[19] The telegraphic exchanges at the highest level "dramatized the spectacular failure of diplomacy, to which telegraphy contributed with crossed messages, delays, sudden surprises, and the unpredictable timing."[20] The increased speed of communication was, itself, one of World War I's causes.[21]

Between July 23 and August 4, five separate diplomatic ultimatums were delivered between the primary actors in the prelude to war. Each of the ultimatums was delivered via the new technology of telegraph.[22] And, because of the telegraph's immediacy, each ultimatum carried with it a formerly unthinkably short time limit in which to respond. Diplomats proceeded as if the mere availability of this new timesaving technology legitimized diplomatic interactions that pushed a highly dangerous situation to the brink of war, rather than concede.[23] When time ran out and the Austrians finally declared war on Serbia on July 28, Austria delivered her war message as no war message had ever been delivered before in history—by telegraph.[24]

Statesmen from a slower age failed to grasp the effects of instantaneous communications. The most pronounced of these was a destruction of the "ameliorating balm of delay."[25] Electronic communications lent a shocking speed to these events "for which statesmen were completely unprepared, having been raised in a slower age, before electrical communications had affected the relations between states."[26] In the final analysis, "There is abundant evidence that one cause of World War I was a failure of diplomacy, and one of the causes of that failure was that diplomats could not cope with the volume and speed of electronic communication."[27] Diplomacy was now being forced to operate within a paradigm that had shifted beyond old diplomacy.

The communications paradigm had actually begun to shift eighty years prior to World War I, with the development of a true mass-printing capability in the mid-1830s, but diplomacy had failed to recognize this shift. During the run-up to World War I, diplomacy was still attempting to operate apart from the reality of the new communication paradigm that had bypassed many of old diplomacy's practices. But the consequences of speedy communication would redefine diplomacy. By the end of World War I, old diplomacy gave way to new.

Increasing the Diplomatic Influence of Non-Traditional Actors

The watershed distinction between old and new diplomacy was that of privacy *vs.* openness. Advances in communications technology served effectively to open the diplomatic process up to different actors, actors who had not previously played a foreign policy role. Among these new diplomatic actors were political leaders, communications media, and public opinion.

Hamilton and Langhorne have argued that the net effect of communications advances upon old diplomacy was to shift power from the diplomat to foreign offices.[28] Eban agrees that under new diplomacy the shaping of high policy was "now moving away from the embassies, and few ambassadors would claim to be filling as formidable a role as in the past."[29] The development of telegraphy initiated this shift in power. The once autonomous diplomat in the field now became — in the words of a British diplomat — nothing more than a "marionette" at the end of a telegraph wire.[30] Likewise, the quaint, slow rhythm of diplomatic correspondence was of declining importance in an age of increasingly rapid communication. The diplomat's actions now were governed effectively by telegraphic instructions.[31]

By the end of the nineteenth century, control over diplomats was exerted through cables and wires.[32] This bureaucratic control replaced the "free-wheeling agents of the frontier period" and resulted in the fact that "[a]fter the turn of the century, no one any longer hears much about independent proconsuls."[33] The power of ambassadors was reduced with the "introduction of the telegraph in the late 1840s."[34] Sir Horace Rumbold, a British Ambassador to Vienna before the turn of the century, reflected upon the impact of these changes when he spoke of the "telegraphic demoralization" of diplomats in the face of communication technology's advance.[35] Communications had forced diplomacy to shift paradigms beyond the unhurried detachment of the Greek civil-war crisis, and beyond the autonomy practiced by Castlereagh, Livingston, and Monroe. By the beginning of the twentieth century, communications was bringing an end to a "diplomacy merely of statesmen and diplomats."[36]

Throughout the 1800s communications itself was also beginning to become an actor in foreign policy. As early as 1805 one European diplomat stationed in Berlin argued that "The gazettes are worth an army of

300,000 men to Napoleon."[37] A French historian argued that by the late 1800s the increased pace of communication "brought distant events to the foreground with burning actuality and necessitated rapid and often ill-considered responses."[38] By 1900 a reputable French newspaper asserted that "[e]ach day the press becomes ... more of a diplomatic force of the first order."[39] The "technology of mass communication" had itself become a factor in diplomacy.[40] By the turn of the century the two traditional pillars of national security, the military and diplomacy, were being challenged by a "third pillar of national security," telecommunications.[41]

However, communications' most important impact did not result from its direct effect upon diplomacy in the 1800s. According to defense and media scholars Peter Young and Peter Jesser:

> Until the emergence of the printing press, public opinion was governed by the teachings of the Church or the demands of the State. Public opinion was molded by these authorities, who dominated what representative machinery existed, and who could be relied upon to represent their own interests.[42]

And, in keeping with this Church/State — molded character of public opinion, Nicolson argues that under old diplomacy "it would have been regarded as an act of unthinkable vulgarity to appeal to the common people upon any issue of international policy."[43] But with the advent of the printing press and ultimately mass communication, "public opinion developed into a political force *external* to parliament or any other authority."[44] This indirect effect of communications upon foreign policy via public opinion would prove to be communications' most transforming effect upon diplomacy.

First the printing press and then mass printing had eroded the monopoly of knowledge. Both had informed and given voice to a formerly unknown diplomatic actor, public opinion. Public opinion came to be an actor in international relations through

> cheap newsprint; new technology which made it possible to attract readers by printing illustrations relatively cheaply; growing mass literacy...; mass newspaper readerships; a resulting growth of mass public feeling, often emotional and volatile, on international questions; all these were adding another element to the changing picture [of foreign relations].[45]

Even before the development of mass printing, Sir James MacIntosh argued in 1803 that "The multiplication of newspapers has produced a gradual revolution in our government by increasing the number of those who exercise some sort of judgement on public affairs."[46] Communications was giving a formerly unknown actor a voice in foreign policy.

Scholars and practitioners both agree that public opinion's introduction into the diplomatic arena had a defining impact upon diplomacy. Eban contends that public opinion's influence is one of the factors demarcating old from new diplomacy.[47] Morgenthau agrees, arguing that public opinion contributed to the decline of traditional diplomatic practice.[48] Likewise, Hamilton and Langhorne argue that the impact of public opinion in foreign affairs is one of the defining themes of new diplomacy.[49] Kern has argued that the immediacy of news distribution via the newspapers presented diplomats with a historically unprecedented phenomenon: having to do business simultaneously with their opposition and their own public opinion back home.[50] And another diplomatic scholar contends that the "annihilation of distance" and "instantaneous means of communication" caused a "widening up of diplomatic activities."[51] Communications had now widened the field of diplomatic actors to include public opinion.

Under old diplomacy, public opinion was not an actor in foreign policy. Metternich, Austria's Foreign Minister from 1809 to 1848 and the architect of European order in the post-Napoleonic era, was the quintessential practitioner of old diplomacy. According to Nicolson, Metternich regarded the very notion that the public should even have any knowledge, or opinion about, foreign policy as both "dangerous and fantastic."[52] Furthermore, Metternich considered the courtship of public opinion as "a pretension that is misplaced in a statesman."[53]

But with the coming of mass printing and electronic communications, public opinion began to exert an influence. In 1805 one European diplomat contended that "Public opinion is the most powerful of weapons."[54] Former British statesman and Prime Minister (1827) George Canning argued that public opinion was "a power more tremendous than was perhaps ever yet brought into action in the history of mankind."[55] By the century's end, the changes wrought by communications would lead the brilliant German military strategist von Moltke to argue that "[i]t is no longer the ambition of princes; it's the moods of the people ... which endanger peace."[56]

The run-up to the 1898 Spanish-American War illustrates the emerging and complex relationships among communications, public opinion, and diplomacy. The owner of the *New York Journal*, William Randolph Hearst, dispatched the famous artist Frederic Remington to Cuba in late 1896.[57] The artist's job was to investigate the plight of Cubans under Spanish rule and to send back pictures for Hearst's paper. Shortly after arriving in Cuba, Remington is alleged to have cabled Hearst that all was quiet on the island, there was no trouble, and that there would be no war. Remington then asked to return home. Hearst is alleged to have cabled back the following terse reply: "Please remain. You furnish the pictures and I'll furnish the war."[58] No copies of the telegrams exist, suggesting that this story could be apocryphal. However, the incident was first recounted by a *Journal* correspondent in 1901 and has been corroborated sufficiently that most scholars rely on its authenticity to establish Hearst's exceedingly strong desire for war, if not some personal involvement in its coming.[59]

Hearst's interests in war were certainly financial, if not personal and political as well. Foreign war news sold papers. The so-called "yellow press," which was not above exploiting the misfortunes of those close to home in the interests of increasing circulation figures, proved especially adept at exploiting war news to increase circulation. During the Spanish-American War, a competition arose between Joseph Pulitzer's *New York World* and Hearst's *New York Journal* in which each paper tried to out-sensationalize the other. At the height of the war, circulation figures for the largest New York papers surpassed the one-million mark per day.[60] The coming of peace only confirmed the boom in circulation that war could provide: after the war's conclusion, circulation figures quickly shrank back to their normal levels.[61]

The war in which Hearst had such an interest did not come overnight. The Cuban insurrection against their Spanish colonial masters broke out in early 1895, at which time U.S. newspaper editorials began to attack Spain for its allegedly barbarian treatment of Cubans. The press began calling for war during the 1896 presidential campaign and Hearst dispatched Remington to Cuba in December of that year. President William McKinley's March 1897 inaugural address struck a moderate tone on both the troubles in Cuba and the calls for war. Hearst and other publishers yearning for war were openly derisive of such moderation, calling it "vague and sapless."[62]

War would not come until April 24, 1898. On February 15, 1898, the U.S. battleship *Maine* was sunk while at anchor in Havana harbor, a fortuity for those seeking a pretext for war. The following day Hearst's *Journal* carried an offer of a $50,000 reward for information that would convict the perpetrators of the *Maine's* sinking, while in the same issue the *Journal* ran a presumptive headline that read: "Destruction of the War Ship Maine Was the Work of an Enemy."[63] When Congress voted two months after the sinking to approve President William McKinley's war message, Hearst announced to his staff that this was "Our War."[64] Shortly after the war began, Hearst's paper trumpeted a headline that asked: "How Do You Like the *Journal's* War?"[65]

Whatever Hearst's actual personal involvement in fomenting the war with Spain, he certainly desired to communicate that he had been involved directly in causing the war. No one would suggest that Hearst single-hand-edly landed the U.S. in a war with Spain, even with the assistance of his warmongering journalistic colleagues, such as Pulitzer at the *New York World*. However, several scholars[66] would agree with Hohenberg who has argued that "[i]t is possible that the national war fever might not have risen to the height required for [McKinley to request] a declaration of war if the press had not done so much to stimulate it."[67] In other words, a com-plex, new relationship was emerging between mass communications, pub-lic opinion, and important foreign-policy decisions.

Journalism professor Philip Seib argues that the Spanish-American War was "Mr. Hearst's War."[68] However, Seib does not argue that Hearst himself was directly responsible for the U.S. decision to declare war on Spain. Rather, Seib contends that the indirect influence of warmongering journalism like Hearst's stirred American public opinion to the point that President McKinley "followed — rather than led — public opinion."[69] Still, the public's desire for war had not emerged overnight. Nearly two and one-half years were required before the tide of public emotion was able to rise above McKinley's moderation. Furthermore, the journalism used to fuel these emotions was not the dispassionate reporting of facts. Rather, Hearst, Pulitzer, and their colleagues engaged in openly inflammatory warmongering.[70]

Ultimately, however, McKinley took the politically expedient posi-tion and bowed to war fever. Seib concludes by arguing that, "If the press had not been so vitriolic or if McKinley had been more assertive, public opinion might merely have simmered rather than boiled over."[71] As it was, the "press's assertiveness" fueled the public opinion that "overwhelmed" McKinley's lack of leadership on this particular issue, all of which helped produce the Spanish-American War.[72] The run-up to the Spanish-Ameri-can War foretold a pattern that would be repeated in the future: a lack of leadership on a critical foreign-policy issue had created a vacuum that sub-sequently was filled by the influence of other actors, namely the press and public opinion.

The run-up to the Spanish American War also foretold an impend-ing redefinition of diplomatic practice, as did the run-up to World War I. Where the run-up to the Spanish American War illustrated the increasing diplomatic influence of non-traditional actors — the press and public opin-ion — in the face of McKinley's lack of leadership, the rapid exchange of telegraphic ultimatums during the run-up to World War I demonstrated the effects of accelerating diplomacy's pace. Both cases indicated that a shift in the diplomatic paradigm was about to occur. In addition, both cases suggested the consequences for political leaders and diplomats who were still struggling to operate apart from the reality that the communication paradigm had shifted, bypassing many of diplomacy's traditional practices. New diplomacy was displacing the old.

Diplomats have historically operated according to diplomacy's rituals and traditions. As a result, diplomacy is at times oblivious to changes in the prevailing communication paradigm. This pattern, which was suggested by the run-up to the Spanish American War, would repeat itself again in the case of the U.S. war in Vietnam. During Vietnam, electronic communications was just becoming the dominant paradigm and, in its wake, the outlines of a different diplomatic paradigm, telediplomacy, were visible on the horizon. Television would exert its first effects on foreign policy during the Vietnam war.

The U.S. government's actions in Vietnam were carried out in a way reminiscent of a previous communications era. However, by 1963 Americans were, for the first time, receiving more of their news from television than from newspapers.[73] Under the former communications paradigm, most Americans had been spared the horrors of war. But, during the Vietnam era, war's hell would be graphically televised into people's living rooms. The new electronic communications paradigm resulted in Vietnam being dubbed the first living-room war.[74]

Television had substantially eroded the U.S. government's knowledge monopoly. Yet, the government was still attempting to operate under the former communications paradigm. Consequently, the government was also operating under outdated diplomatic practices. The government failed to establish effective control over the new electronic information sources, unlike the restrictions placed on the press in former wars. This fact suggests the government's inability to comprehend the new communications medium's inherent power. The government's failure to comprehend existing communications realities resulted in Vietnam becoming the first uncensored war in U.S. history.[75]

Foreign-policy information could effectively be crafted to suit government's purposes, so long as official government communication was the primary source of foreign-policy news. As late as the 1950s, television cameras were physically incapable of being at trouble spots around the world. Foreign news coverage was still very weak on the popular, but relatively new, television news broadcasts. This lack of international news coverage allowed government to craft the pictures it wanted held in people's minds on foreign events. John Foster Dulles, Secretary of State during the Eisenhower Administration, took to having regular press conferences and acquired his own television and radio advisor. Dulles became adept at giving press conferences, speeches, and statements when he either departed for or arrived home from foreign destinations. In effect, world events were portrayed from the government perspective — as seen through "Dulles's eyes."[76]

However, an event in 1963 provided early evidence of government's failure to comprehend that communication was moving to a different paradigm. On the morning of June 9, 1963, a Buddhist school teacher named Thich Quang Duc ignited gasoline that had been poured over him while sitting in a busy intersection in downtown Saigon. The Buddhist monk's self-immolation was captured on film by an Associated Press photographer. According to James Aronson, these pictures "jolted the United States and the world."[77] Full-page newspaper advertisements were subsequently taken out in both the *New York Times* and the *Washington Post* by anti-war groups and clergy opposing American involvement in Vietnam. In other words, an anti-war, anti-government sentiment was being fueled by communications' erosion of the knowledge monopoly. Government, and its foreign-policy apparatus, had failed to understand the new communications technology's impact.[78]

Vietnam also offered other examples of government being oblivious to a change in the prevailing method of communications. On February 27, 1968, CBS news anchor Walter Cronkite concluded his evening news broadcast with a graphically illustrated, personal report on the recent North Vietnamese Tet offensive. Cronkite closed by commenting that the war had become a "bloody stalemate" and that the time had perhaps come to get out of Vietnam.[79] At that moment U.S. President Lyndon Johnson (LBJ) turned to his aides and said, "It's all over."[80] LBJ continued by predicting, "If I've lost Cronkite, I've lost Middle America."[81] Although the Tet offensive was a military defeat for the North Vietnamese, the psychological effects of this surprise offensive eroded U.S. public support for the war. LBJ's February 27 prediction came true: he had lost middle America. And, on March 31, LBJ stunned the nation by announcing during a televised address that he would neither seek nor accept his party's nomination to become a candidate for president in 1968. A U.S. president had declined to seck re-election, in part because television had brought the ferocity of a "failed" enemy offensive home to American living rooms.[82]

Advances in communications technology were crafting a new relationship between the mass media and foreign policy. LBJ's comment in the aftermath of Cronkite's broadcast suggests television's increasing role as a diplomatic actor. Graphic portrayals of a war half a world away had become common public knowledge, information to which the public would not have had unfiltered access in a former era. The impact of seeing while hearing had burst onto the foreign policy scene in the wake of the Tet offensive. Although still in its infancy, television had exerted an effect; and its diplomatic counterpart, telediplomacy, was just over the horizon.

A new phenomenon was emerging: the connection between mass communications, public opinion, and foreign-policy decision-making. Diplomatic scholar Noel Cohen described this relationship as "affecting the perceptions of both policymakers and the interest groups and general public to whom they are responsive," thereby allowing the media to "influence the course of foreign policy itself."[83] The relationship between the press and public opinion had operated in an unprecedented way in the case of the Spanish-American War; likewise, the relationship between television and public opinion had operated in a way not envisioned by the government during Vietnam. The mass media influenced public opinion, which in turn influenced foreign policy. In other words, media had influenced foreign policy.

Subsequent advances in communications technology would enhance the diplomatic influence of non-traditional actors such as public opinion and the media. The mass media — public opinion relationship foreshadowed by the Spanish-American War would continue to mature; the increasing pace of diplomacy evidenced during the run-up to World War I would continue to accelerate; and television's impact, which had been hinted at during Vietnam, would intensify with global television's real-time immediacy. Nearly a century after the Spanish American War, the mass media — public opinion relationship would exert a decisive influence on foreign policy in the post-1991 Kurdish refugee crisis. In the Kurdish case, a diplomatic outcome would be determined by these non-traditional actors, and it would not require two and one half years and an openly inflammatory press, as had been the case during the Spanish-American War. But, by 1991 the media–public opinion relationship had been strengthened by global television's immediacy and impact.

The communication paradigm had shifted yet again by the 1990s. By the mid-1980s, public opinion had become an influential foreign policy actor. Former Israeli diplomat Eban argues that a diplomat must now transact business simultaneously with his diplomatic counterpart and his own public opinion, a reality that suggests the emergence of a different diplomatic paradigm.[84] Vietnamese diplomat Tran Van Dinh implicitly recognized this shift when he argued that instantaneous communications had "transformed the substance of diplomacy."[85] With this shift to instantaneous communications, diplomacy would experience a corresponding shift. The ability to influence foreign policy that had required two and one half years of warmongering journalism in the 1890s, and weeks to produce a delayed reaction during Vietnam, would be more immediate and deci-sive in the 1990s. All that would be required were live, real-time pictures. Diplomacy was, yet again, being forced to operate a paradigm shift beyond its traditional practice. Telediplomacy, the next paradigm of diplomatic practice, was emerging.

The following chapter details communications' effects on diplomatic practice during the 1991 Persian Gulf War. Succeeding chapters explore communications' effects on diplomatic outcomes. Communications' abil-ity to influence foreign policy had only been hinted at during the run-up to the Spanish-American War. However, this influence over policy proved to be decisive in the aftermath of the Gulf War. Specifically, real-time global television was the deciding factor in the different diplomatic outcomes experienced by two groups of post-Gulf War refugees, the Kurds in north-ern Iraq and the Shiite Muslims in southern Iraq.

Two

COMMUNICATIONS AND DIPLOMACY:
PRESENT REALITIES

Chapter 4

The Persian Gulf War and Telediplomacy: The Next Diplomatic Paradigm

CNN was "the most efficient way for one government to speak to another during the [Persian Gulf War] crisis."
— *Peter Tarnoff, 1991; President of the Council on Foreign Relations*

The 1991 Persian Gulf War represents the culmination of instantaneous communications' effect on world politics, resulting in telediplomacy. *USA Today's* foreign editor, Johanna Neuman, contends that the Gulf War experience should be taken as a reminder that communication's cycle of change is once again about to affect diplomats and policymakers, only this time the cycle of change is going to roll through "with a loud thunder."[1] Diplomatic scholars Lawrence Freedman and Efraim Karsh argue that even diplomats from "earlier in the television age" would have been astounded by "the speed with which information reached them" during the Gulf War, as well as the "influence of raw and undigested information" that reached the public and policymakers at the same instant.[2] The Gulf War truly represented a "media war," after which "it will never again be possible to discuss the conduct of war without reference to the media."[3]

The Persian Gulf War's beginning and ending time both suggest the unique relationship that now exists between world politics and the media. The Gulf War began during America's evening network newscasts. Bombers from an American-led coalition of countries conducted air raids on Bagh-dad a few moments before 7:00 p.m. Eastern Standard Time on January 16, 1991. Thus, the opening salvos of the war occurred at "an appropriate media-age time."[4]

Media-age considerations also played a role in the war's conclusion. Hostilities with Iraq ceased following television coverage of the Mutla Gap carnage, exactly one hundred hours after the ground war had begun, end-ing at 12:00 a.m. on February 28. Extensive television coverage was given to the death and destruction that coalition warplanes had inflicted on Iraqi forces that were retreating along the road through the Mutla Gap north of Kuwait City. Bush Administration officials were concerned about the per-ceptions created by the extent of this carnage. They were concerned that the coalition forces might be seen as "piling on" against an enemy that was already decisively defeated.

U.S. officials admit that the Gulf War's ending time contained media overtones, much as did its beginning. Richard Haass, a Bush Administra-tion National Security Council (N.S.C.) staffer, believes that television cov-erage of the carnage played a part in Bush's decision to halt the war.[5] General Norman Schwarzkopf, commander of coalition forces, contends that the one-hundred-hour figure was chosen by the administration because it "really knew how to package an historic event."[6] Likewise, Bush's Undersecretary of Defense, Paul D. Wolfowitz, concedes that "[t]he deci-sion to end the war when we did is one that may have been influenced by television."[7] Nick Gowing of Britain's Independent Television News (ITN) has concluded that "those [television] pictures did play a major part in Bush's decision to halt the ground war at a moment which coincided con-veniently with 100 hours of battle."[8] The Gulf War's beginning and its end suggest the impossibility of discussing this war apart from the media. Something had changed about the relationship between world politics and the media: it may never be possible to discuss future wars without also discussing the media's role in them.

However, the Gulf War's beginning and ending demonstrate one thing that had not changed about the relationship between media and world pol-itics: the influence of political leadership. This point will be developed further in succeeding chapters, but the fact is that the changes in com-munications have not "changed the fundamentals of political leadership and international governance."[9] The selection of beginning and ending times that coincide with the media clock illustrates leaders' ability to influence news coverage. This ability is often referred to as attempting to manipulate the messenger.[10] Such attempts have as their objective obstruct-ing the "flow of information to the public."[11] These manipulations are usually subtle and conducted within the "letter, if not the spirit, of the First Amendment's insistence on freedom of the press."[12] The Gulf War does demonstrate communications' affect upon diplomatic practice. However, it also illustrates that political leaders can retain control of news coverage.

The Gulf War also offers a more overt example of controlled news coverage — the media pool system. During the Gulf War, only selected journalists were given permission to accompany coalition forces to cover the war. Originally this number was limited to fifty reporters, but grew to include upwards of 200. These reporters were to provide copy to the more than 1,500 journalists that had gathered to cover the war.

Reporters who attempted to operate independent of this pool system were at times arrested and confined. But even the reporters who abided by the pool system saw it as a violation of the traditional professional competitiveness between rival news organizations. Reporters also saw the media pool as a breach of journalists' watchdog role. The pool system is often charged with having kept to a minimum the amount of coverage opposing the Gulf War effort.[13] The Gulf War's media pool demonstrated once again that political leaders do retain the ability to "make policy choices, and to lead."[14] However, in order to do so, leadership must be united and have a clear policy. The bottom line is that leaders must lead. If they fail to, or if policy becomes ambiguous, communications will quickly move to fill any policy void resulting from the absence of leadership.[15]

Advances in communications technology had, by the time of the 1991 Persian Gulf War, moved the industrialized world into the instantaneous communication paradigm. Leaders do have the ability to lead on news coverage. Nevertheless, the effects of this paradigm shift are redefining contemporary diplomatic practices. Former U.S. Assistant Secretary of State Harold Saunders contends that, despite what diplomatic theory may say, the actual practice of diplomacy has been significantly altered by instantaneous communications: "The use of satellites to broadcast to ... other nations is a fact of diplomacy today.... It is a fundamental fact that international relations theory has not caught up with yet — television is a significant part of international relations interaction."[16] Former newspaper editor and author Michael O'Neill has observed that the communications revolution is the "supreme catalyst of change" and that it holds the "codes to the future."[17] Given this, O'Neill argues that trends that the communications revolution is "generating today provide crucial insights into tomorrow's world."[18] And so it is with diplomacy: today's communication provides insight into tomorrow's diplomacy.

Telediplomacy: The Next Diplomatic Paradigm

Communication's persistent collapse of time and space is precipitating the next diplomatic paradigm: telediplomacy. U.S. Ambassador John W. Tuthill conducted a seminar ten years ago entitled "American Diplomacy in the Information Age" for senior-level diplomatic and media personnel. Tuthill concluded that a "rapid breaking down of the limitations posed by time and space" marks our age.[19] Bosah Ebo argues that the current information revolution has dramatically changed international relations.[20] Walter R. Roberts, a retired U.S. Foreign Service Officer, argues that the changes wrought by the recent communications revolution have had their most profound impact in the world of American diplomacy.[21] Etyan Gilboa contends that recent advances in communications technology are opening up a significant role for the media in diplomacy.[22] And former U.S. National Security Adviser Zbigniew Brzezinski, while reflecting upon the effects of instantaneous communications, contends that if foreign ministries and embassies "did not already exist, they surely would not have to be invented."[23] For the second time in history, communications is redefining Western diplomatic practice.

The advent of real-time global television marks a significant departure from the past. This development has enabled communications to become a major player in the arena of foreign policy.[24] Madeleine Albright, while serving as U.S. Ambassador to the United Nations (U.N.), made the case for real-time television's significance when she claimed, "There is no question that television has become the sixteenth member of the [U.N.] Security Council."[25] Two factors afford real-time global television its unique influence, factors that distinguish it from all previous advances in communications technology: its immediacy and its impact. Likewise, these same two characteristics distinguish telediplomacy from its diplomatic predecessors.

Comparisons between the Persian Gulf and Vietnam Wars illustrate real-time television's immediacy. During the Vietnam War, America's first "living room war," battlefield footage was days old by the time viewers saw it.[26] A complicated logistical process was involved: getting the film out of the battlefield, driving it to an airport, flying it to the West Coast of the U.S., editing the film, and finally transmitting the edited version over expensive, leased telephone lines to New York. The finished product would finally be shown on evening newscasts two to three days after it was shot in Vietnam.[27]

By comparison, the Gulf War twenty-five years later has been called America's first "television war."[28] In this war, people literally experienced war in real-time.[29] Viewers saw what was happening from half a world away at the same time that the events occurred. The public was treated to instantaneous switching between anchors and action in Baghdad, Dharan, Tel Aviv, London, and New York. The public was also served up visuals that had been shot by a video camera located in the nose of a smart bomb homing in on its target. The distinction between Vietnam and the Gulf War is the difference between three days' delay vs. experiencing a war in real-time. Put simply, the difference is one of immediacy.[30]

Real-time global television also enjoys a unique impact by virtue of its intimately graphic imagery. Former White House Counsel Lloyd N. Cutler has observed that "TV news has a wider reach and faster impact that must now be taken into account. If a picture is worth 1,000 words, sounds and pictures together must be worth 10,000."[31] Then-U.N. ambassador Madeleine Albright, while testifying before the Senate Foreign Relations Committee, lamented that "Television's ability to bring graphic images of pain and outrage into our living rooms has heightened the pressure both for immediate engagement in areas of international crisis and immediate disengagement when events do not go according to plan."[32] Old diplomacy was characterized by secrecy; new diplomacy, by openness. Telediplomacy is characterized by real-time television's immediacy and impact.

Former U.S. Secretary of State James Baker's experience demonstrates the significance of global television's break with the past. Baker recounts a phenomenon that he experienced a few minutes before 7:00 p.m. Eastern Standard Time on January 16, 1991, a phenomenon unique in all of human history.[33] Baker watched, in real-time, the opening salvos of a war half a world away that he personally had helped plan. And he watched it begin on CNN.

Why CNN?

The immediacy and impact that characterize telediplomacy have reached their zenith in CNN. Therefore, references to telediplomacy are often synonymous with references to CNN. Former Secretary of State Lawrence Eagleburger contends that the most important factor transforming foreign policy today is

> the whole impact of CNN. We have yet to understand how profoundly it
> has changed things. The public hears of an event now in real time, before
> the State Department has had time to think about it. Consequently, we find

ourselves reacting before we've had time to think. This is now the way we determine foreign policy — it's driven more by the daily events reported on TV than it used to be.[34]

Former State Department spokesman Nicholas Burns concurs with Eagleburger, observing that the pervasiveness of CNN's coverage sometimes makes it "an actor itself in global politics."[35] Eagleburger's and Burns's remarks imply the reasons that CNN and telediplomacy are virtually synonymous: CNN's format and the nature of its coverage.

Ted Turner, founder of CNN, inaugurated a unique type of television format in 1980 — a twenty-four hour, all-news network via satellite.[36] In the early years CNN was regularly lampooned by the big three networks as "Chicken Noodle News."[37] But by 1991, ABC, CBS, and NBC had stopped laughing at CNN.

During the 1991 Gulf War, CNN's ratings outpaced those of the big three networks, reaching ten times their normal value.[38] Polls reported CNN as the public's first or second overall choice for news.[39] CNN was the sole news organization in the world capable of keeping up with satellite-fed communications — presenting, transmitting, and distributing live coverage twenty-four hours a day.[40] During the opening hours of the Gulf War, CNN provided seventeen hours of continuous live coverage.[41] The other networks could not match this feat.[42] As a result of CNN's capabilities, it became a primary channel of communication between the antagonists in the conflict — U.S. President George Bush and Iraqi President Saddam Hussein.[43] Thus, by the end of the Gulf War, CNN had emerged as the "most dynamic" media development to date; it was now an "unavoidable player in international relations."[44]

CNN's influence in international relations stems in part from its increasing coverage of international news. The network's broadcasts were available in only 105 countries in 1991[45], but were received in 265 countries by 1994, according to CNN Executive vice-president Ed Turner.[46] The gross revenues of CNN International increased sevenfold between 1991 and 1994.[47] And, while the three major networks were eliminating foreign correspondents, CNN was opening new foreign bureaus at a rate that left it with as many reporters stationed abroad by the end of 1992 as ABC, CBS, and NBC combined. CNN's coverage now originated from almost twice as many countries as that of the three major networks combined. According to Stephen Hess, "The networks [ABC, CBS, and NBC] are now basically out of the foreign news business."[48] CNN had come into its own during the Gulf War; it was a high-visibility international crisis that was ready-made for CNN to capitalize on its unique format and coverage.

CNN persists as a significant player in international affairs for the same reasons.[49]

CNN's real-time coverage has also contributed to its status as a force in foreign policy. The fact that CNN's coverage is available in a continuous, real-time format has allowed it to become, in Lewis Friedland's characterization, a "diplomatic party line."[50] CNN could carry a live speech by Saddam Hussein and the subsequent, live State Department response. This type of instantaneous coverage made CNN a part of diplomacy itself during the Gulf War.[51]

CNN also derives its importance in world affairs from its viewership, an importance that exceeds the sheer number of viewers. CNN's viewership is numerically smaller than the viewing audiences of the three major networks, except for CNN's coverage of major international events. The key to CNN's influence in international affairs is the unique nature of the audience that is attracted by its format and coverage.[52] Leaders and foreign policymakers from around the world monitor CNN for breaking developments.[53] CNN has been described as "a common frame of reference for the world's power elite.... A kind of world-wide party line, allowing leaders to conduct a sort of conference call...."[54] In fact, so effective are CNN's format, coverage, and, consequently, the character of its audience, that one communications expert concludes that CNN "appear[s] to have transformed diplomatic practice."[55]

Once again, communications has transformed diplomacy. CNN is only the most recent manifestation of this transforming force. CNN epitomizes that force which has historically transformed diplomacy: successive advancements in communications technology. The shift from the elite to the mass communication paradigm caused the subsequent shift from old to new diplomacy. Likewise, the current shift from the mass to the instantaneous communication paradigm is once again redefining diplomatic practice. Real-time global television is causing the next diplomatic paradigm, telediplomacy, to emerge.

The Persian Gulf War and Communication's Effect on Diplomatic Practice

The 1991 Persian Gulf War demonstrates that diplomacy today is different from the style of diplomacy that emerged in the immediate post–World War I era. Recall that communication historically has affected diplomatic practice by displacing diplomacy's traditional methods, accelerating its pace, and by shifting the relative balance of diplomatic influence from traditional to non-traditional diplomatic actors. By the time of the 1991 Gulf War, communications had brought us what former Secretary Baker calls "diplomacy via television," or telediplomacy.[56]

Today, diplomacy's practice is different from those practices employed under the post-World War I new diplomacy. The way in which six of diplomacy's seven functions are performed has been changed by real-time global television. Although the seventh function, routine consular activities, has been affected by electronic information flows, the inherent nature of consular activities, combined with their lack of high visibility, has left this diplomatic function relatively unaffected by real-time television. However, the methods of performing diplomacy's other six functions have been redefined by global television. Telediplomacy is gradually displacing new diplomacy's methods in the conduct of information gathering, official representation, signaling and receiving, international public relations, negotiation, and crisis management. By 1991, telediplomacy had already become a reality under certain conditions.

Displacing New Diplomacy's Methods of Practice

The nature of real-time global television gives it a unique ability for information gathering during fast-breaking, high-visibility crises. A comparison between the 1962 Cuban Missile Crisis and the Gulf War illustrates the changed nature of information gathering between that of an earlier television era and the present real-time environment. By 1963, just one year after the Cuban Missile Crisis, more Americans were receiving their news from television than from newspapers.[57] Yet, JFK's Defense Secretary Robert McNamara recalled, "I don't think I turned on a television set during the whole two weeks of that [Cuban Missile] crisis."[58] However, on the eve of the 1991 Gulf War, Bush's Defense Secretary Dick Cheney admitted that he was getting most of his information from CNN, the same source that average Americans were using.[59] Both U.S. Joint Chiefs of Staff Chairman Colin Powell and the Air Force general responsible for the air war over Iraq used CNN as a primary information source, as did Saddam Hussein himself.[60] Likewise, during the Gulf War top members of the former Soviet Union's Foreign Ministry Policy Planning Staff relied on CNN for information, rather than Soviet intelligence.[61] Although the Cuban Missile Crisis and the Gulf War were less than thirty years apart, these two crises were, in fact, separated by a shift in diplomatic paradigms.

Foreign policy decision-makers confirm the changed methodology of information gathering during the Gulf War. Interviews conducted with thirty-five top foreign policy decision-makers during January and February of 1991 indicate that eighty-seven percent recalled cases where the media were the only information source available for decision-making.[62] Furthermore, sixty-five percent of these interviewees agreed that the media were often the fastest source of information for decision-making.[63] The Gulf War confirmed that, when it comes to information gathering, "the diplomatic importance of satellite television [makes] the slower rhythms of the [diplomatic] pouch and cable seem quaint."[64]

Individual decision-makers also attest to information gathering's changed methods. George Bush argues that, "You end up hearing statements for the first time not in diplomatic notes, but because you see a foreign minister on the screen. I really mean CNN. It has turned out to be a very important information source."[65] Judith Kipper, an advisor to past administrations on Middle East politics, has charged that in "[a]ny crisis where you need on-the-spot information, the media information is more accurate and the government relies on it."[66] Likewise, former U.S. Assistant Secretary of State Langhorn Motley contends that during international crises CNN gets information out before "official sources could get geared up to let Washington know what was happening."[67] One U.S. diplomat has summed up the nature of information gathering in the era of instantaneity: "There is a diminished value in classical diplomatic reporting. If you had a choice between reading the [diplomatic] cables in your box and tuning in to CNN three times a day, you'd tune in to CNN."[68] Diplomatic practice and individual decision-makers both suggest that new diplomacy's methods of gathering and reporting information were displaced during the Gulf War.

Likewise, real-time global television also has affected traditional methods of diplomatic representation and the signaling and receiving of governments' positions. The Persian Gulf War offers several examples of the changes to these diplomatic functions. During the run-up to hostilities, Secretary Baker's diplomatic channel of last resort to avert the impending crisis was not the traditional diplomatic cable or ambassadorial contact. Rather, both Baker and President Bush relied on CNN as their diplomatic channel of choice. Baker made his "last appeal to reason" via CNN on January 11—"a public démarche not as easily ignored as the President's [Bush's] letter had been in Geneva [during Baker's last meeting with Iraqi Foreign Minister Tariq Aziz on January 9]."[69]

Interestingly, the U.S. and Iraq still maintained formal diplomatic relations at the time of Baker's CNN appearance. The U.S. had five credentialed diplomats remaining in Baghdad on January 11, diplomats who did not depart for the U.S. until *after* the CNN démarche.[70] In fact, formal diplomatic relations between the U.S. and Iraq were not suspended until February 6, 1991, approximately three weeks after the air war against Iraq had commenced.[71] Baker later explained the rationale behind his use of this non-traditional diplomatic channel prior to war:

> The "CNN effect" has revolutionized the way policymakers have to approach their jobs, particularly in the foreign policy arena, and it started frankly only about 1987 or '88, whenever CNN began their CNN international program. We learned very early, in 1989, that the best way for us to get a message to a foreign head of state was to get on the tube, to get out there on CNN. Particularly in the Gulf War, we knew that Saddam Hussein watched CNN. You didn't send a message to the embassy or an ambassador; that delayed it a lot.[72]

U.S. Ambassador and former State Department official Newsom argues that the conventions of traditional diplomacy were "largely ignored or set aside in the Gulf crisis."[73] Clearly, Baker's practice during the run-up to hostilities in the Gulf War indicates a style of diplomacy that is a paradigm shift away from those methods employed under new diplomacy.

Real-time television's ability to perform signaling and receiving functions was illustrated by one particular Gulf War example. Immediately following Iraq's invasion of Kuwait in August 1990, Turkey's President, Turgut Ozal, was watching live on CNN a press conference by President Bush. In response to a reporter's question about Turkey's position on the crisis, Bush stated that the first thing he was going to do following the press conference was to call President Ozal. At the close of the conference, Ozal got up from his chair and walked into the adjoining room, where the telephone promptly rang. When Ozal answered he found Bush on the other end of the line, quite as he had expected. Ozal then expressed his unqualified support of Bush's hard-line position toward Iraq.[74]

Ozal, like most world leaders, was up to speed on real-time diplomatic communication and interaction. He was a regular CNN watcher and routinely consulted it for information, even during personal meetings with Secretary Baker.[75] Like many leaders and foreign ministries around the world, Ozal kept his television turned on with the "mute" button on throughout the day, monitoring CNN for new developments.[76]

These changes to representation, signaling, and receiving have been brought about by the advent of real-time television. When real-time global television was still in its infancy, traditional diplomacy was already being ignored in favor of "media diplomacy."[77] By the early 1980s one communications scholar had observed that governments were not so much talking to each other as "at each other through the media. 'Theater warfare' and 'diplomatic channels' have taken on new meanings in an age when communications satellites have replaced traditional means of communication."[78] By 1986, the U.S. government admitted that real-time television had affected diplomatic representation. In an official publication, the government acknowledged that diplomacy via public media was "part of the worldwide transformation in the conduct of international affairs.... Government-to-government communications [have] become less important...."[79]

Gulf War practice confirmed the U.S. government's report of five years earlier. Several top policymakers interviewed during the Gulf War argued that the media operated as an out-of-control "front channel" for diplomatic communication, quite apart from traditional diplomatic channels.[80] Peter Tarnoff contends that CNN was "the most efficient way for one government to speak to another during the crisis."[81] Warren Strobel, White House and former State Department correspondent for the *Washington Times*, concludes that during the Gulf War "Bush, Saddam, and other leaders used CNN as a tool to send near-instantaneous messages to one another ... fulfilling a function once reserved for embassies and foreign ministries."[82] In other words, new diplomacy's methods of signaling, receiving, and representation were being displaced by different methods of diplomatic practice.

The diplomat's methods of conducting international public relations have also been changed by the latest advances in communication. International public relations conducted via real-time television was a staple of the Gulf War. George Bush often used CNN as the vehicle for specifically targeted international public relations efforts directed at the Iraqi people. Former NBC News and PBS (Public Broadcasting System) president Lawrence Grossman recounts one such example.[83] While watching Peter Arnett's live reporting on CNN from Baghdad, Bush observed the Iraqi people cheering Saddam Hussein's first announcement that he was going to pull out of Kuwait. Strictly on the basis of what he was seeing on CNN, Bush decided to give a speech and included in it an exhortation to the Iraqi people to overthrow Hussein's government. According to Grossman, "[Bush] got that from watching television, and he made a decision to pump it back into Iraq via a speech in Washington that he knew would be seen on CNN in Baghdad."[84] Bush got his information from real-time television (via the same method and at the same time as other Americans watching CNN) and immediately responded via the same "diplomatic channel" with a public-relations message targeted to his adversary's public half a world away. The communication loop had come full circle.

Bush's use of CNN during the Gulf War illustrates a change in international public relations, a change afforded by real-time global television. By the early 1990s, the use of the media to address other national populations had become routine and expected.[85] But as Dennis Ross, former staff member of the N.S.C., has argued, recent communications developments have allowed real-time television to be used to communicate "over the heads of governments in a way that makes them feel a need to respond in some fashion."[86] The ability to address a hostile adversary's entire population is a recent phenomenon in international relations. Today, an enemy's population can be addressed immediately, and it can be addressed in such a way that compels a response.

International crisis management has also experienced real-time television's effects. Crisis management's high visibility renders it uniquely susceptible to the influence of real-time television. Negotiation, particularly when conducted in the context of international crisis management, is subject to communications' effects. Crisis negotiations are especially susceptible to communications' ability to accelerate the pace of decision-making. This acceleration results in pressure to make decisions apart from diplomacy's traditional deliberative bodies.

Diplomatic practitioners and media experts agree that real-time television has affected diplomacy's crisis management and negotiation functions. Former U.S. diplomat David Newsom argues that television has become a player in U.S. diplomacy, especially in crisis situations where foreign-policy officials "pay as much attention to CNN and the networks as to embassy dispatches."[87] President Bush went so far as to say, "I learn more from CNN than I do from the CIA."[88] According to Gowing, global television brings two significant developments to crisis management: "the instant power of real-time television and the loss of government control of information...."[89] Colonel Bill Smullen, special adviser on public affairs to General Colin Powell when Powell was chairman of the Joint Chiefs of Staff, argues that these two developments have become significant factors in diplomacy's crisis-management function.[90]

But Israeli diplomat Eban argues that "[a]ny discussion of changes in the diplomatic system must begin with the most potent and far-reaching transformation of all:" the changed nature of negotiation in the television age.[91] McNulty contends that "television imagery transmitted by satellite ... makes traditional diplomacy all but obsolete" during crisis negotiations.[92] Indeed, much of the evidence above from the Gulf War argues for the changed nature of crisis management. However, one particular example illustrates global television's effects on negotiating diplomatic outcomes during times of international crisis.

On February 15, 1991, networks in the U.S. and around the world broke the news that Saddam Hussein was offering to withdraw from Kuwait. Peace was at hand and spontaneous celebrations of the war's end erupted.[93] George Bush realized the potential damage such publicity posed to the military effort underway by the U.S. and its twenty-six allies. Bush told his advisers, "We've got to get on the air fast to answer all these people who either don't know what to do or want us to do something we don't want to."[94] Marlin Fitzwater, Bush's spokesman, recounts what happened next:

> The "quickest and most effective way [to respond] was CNN, because all countries in the world had it and were watching it on a real-time basis ... and 20 minutes after we got the proposal ... I went on national television ... to tell the 26 members [of the coalition fighting against Saddam Hussein] ... that the war was continuing."[95]

The most significant thing about this incident is what it implies about diplomatic negotiation and crisis-management decision-making. Fitzwater recounts what transpired during the twenty minutes that elapsed between Hussein's overtures and the subsequent U.S. response:

> The course of action was set. There was no talk of cables back to the embassies or phone calls back to heads of state. In most of these kinds of international crises now, we virtually cut out the State Department and the desk officers.... Their reports are still important, but they often don't get here in time for the basic decisions to be made.[96]

In other words, the traditional instruments of diplomatic analysis and negotiation — the State Department, its desk officers, consultations with other heads of state — had been displaced by the negotiating dictates of a real-time media.

However, the most instructive aspect of the peace overture's rejection is the traditional crisis-management processes that were *not* present. Fitzwater mentions nothing about an expert appraisal of Saddam's offer. In fact, quite the opposite was true: the experts were "cut out," according to Fitzwater.[97] Former chair and CEO of Citicorp and presidential advisor Walter B. Wriston contends that

> In this and many other instances, the elite foreign policy establishment and its government-to-government communications were bypassed. No highly trained foreign service officer meticulously drafted a note, no secretary of state signed it, and no American ambassadors called on foreign ministers....[98]

Rather than being driven by diplomacy's traditional deliberative organs and the merits of the proposal, this decision was driven by a real-time media clock. The final decision was taken by officials more attuned to public relations strategy than the strategies of international crisis management. And, in keeping with telediplomacy's increasing influence, the official U.S. government response to Saddam's overture was not delivered through an ambassador or a diplomat: it was televised over the public airways. Careful analysis may have shown that Saddam's peace overture was not viable on the merits; however, there is no record of any such analysis having been performed. Traditional diplomacy had yielded to media expediency.

Comparisons with an earlier age illustrate diplomacy's changed nature in the era of real-time. The unthinkable happened in July 1914 when Austria delivered her war message to Serbia by cable. Austria's action was considered so surrealistic on the afternoon of July 28, 1914, that the Serbian prime minister suspected that he had been the victim of a practical joke.[99] But Austria's decision to begin a war followed more than three weeks of intense diplomatic negotiations, the last five days of which had seen virtually non-stop negotiating.[100] However, in 1991 the U.S. government took a decision to continue war in twenty minutes, without engaging in the traditional processes of international crisis management and negotiation.[101] Having made this decision, the U.S. government subsequently "entrusted a vital diplomatic message to a private television company seen by the whole world."[102] Saddam and the citizens of the world got the message at the same time. But another, more far-reaching message was sent, as well: International crisis management, and negotiations related to it, would be managed differently in the media age.

America's decision-making and response to Iraq in 1991 mark the arrival of a different diplomatic era, just as the novelty of Austria's action in 1914 was symptomatic of old diplomacy's passing and new diplomacy's arrival. Both Austria in 1914 and the U.S. in 1991 have proven Morgenthau's clairvoyance in 1949: the conquest of time and space via modern communications has reduced the importance of traditional diplomacy.[103] Communications has, for the second time in history, redefined traditional methods of diplomatic practice. And, communications has had an equally defining effect upon the pace of diplomacy, as well.

Accelerating Diplomacy's Pace

Just prior to the dawn of real-time global television, diplomatic scholar Eric Clark contended that "[i]n an age of fast communications the diplomat, to many, is an anachronism."[104] Clark may have understated the diplomat's relevance in a real-time future. However, his contention implicitly recognizes the changes that instantaneity would bring to diplomacy's practice. Real-time global television has "accelerated the often cumbersome process of diplomacy...."[105]

A few comparisons with prior diplomatic practice illustrate telediplomacy's changed pace. When the Berlin Wall went up in 1961, fifteen hours elapsed before President Kennedy even received word that the East Germans had begun to build barricades. It took three days for film of the first barricades going up in Berlin to be broadcast to American viewers. Kennedy proceeded cautiously, well aware of the potentially explosive nature of the geopolitical situation. In fact, Kennedy made no public statements about the border closing for eight days, and no statements were allowed to be issued in his name. When JFK did finally speak on the subject he was measured in his approach and signaled the Soviets that he planned to do nothing that might turn Berlin into the opening salvos of World War III.[106]

In 1989 citizens of the world watched the Berlin Wall come down in real time. After the unprecedented events of 1989, European expert Timothy Garton Ash concluded that "In Europe at the end of the 20th century all revolutions are telerevolutions."[107] Diplomacy was now forced to function in the real-time mode of telediplomacy, even though the geopolitical climate in Eastern Europe was as potentially explosive in 1989 as it had been in 1961. However, communications' collapse of time and space forced President Bush to make a statement within hours of the Wall's destruction.

Bush's statement was measured and cautious, given the tenuous nature of the rapidly unfolding events sweeping across the former Soviet Union and Eastern Europe during the closing days of the decade. Yet, in contrast to Kennedy's caution after an eight-day period of reflective silence, Bush's caution following only a few hours of silence was roundly criticized as being tepid and unsympathetic. And the criticism came in real time, from German citizens themselves, the media, and members of the U.S. Congress.[108] Bush's minimal delay and his diplomatic caution seemed somehow antiquated and out of place, an anachronism in the real-time 1990s. Real-time television had wrenched diplomacy from its traditional, deliberative pace.

The Bush Administration's response to another event in 1989 was more in keeping with diplomacy's accelerated pace. China's 1989 suppression of pro-democracy demonstrators in Tiananmen Square was broadcast in real time to viewers around the world. The U.S. was the first government to issue a formal response to the crackdown. According to

Marlin Fitzwater, the quick U.S. response had been driven by instantaneous video communications, and not traditional deliberative diplomacy. However, the Administration still found itself falling short of the demands created by real-time television's immediacy and impact. Fitzwater admitted during an interview that

> [The U.S.] was the first government to respond, labeling it an outrage and so forth, and *it was based almost entirely on what we were seeing on television.* We were getting reporting cables from Beijing, but they did not have the sting, the demand for a government response that the television pictures had.... *You couldn't devise words to match the images.* There was no word too "hot." For example, *we were saying words like "outrage" and "brutality"— pretty tough words — and they were just being dismissed as not caring.*[109]

Global television's immediacy and its graphic imagery were outstripping telediplomacy's ability to respond. Though the Bush Administration had been the first government to respond to events in Tiananmen Square, real-time imagery demanded even a tougher response than was conveyed by the Administration's uncharacteristically strong language.

Real-time television's demands are particularly acute during times of crisis. Richard Haass, Middle East specialist on the N.S.C. at the time that Iraq invaded Kuwait, contends that "television tends to really telescope and accelerate the pace of events."[110] Haass also reflected on the significant changes that had occurred in diplomacy from earlier in the television era during the Kennedy Administration. In 1962, JFK had six days in which to formulate carefully an official response to the Soviet Union's emplacement of nuclear missiles in Cuba. However, when Iraq invaded Kuwait, Bush was expected to react almost immediately. According to Haass, "We didn't have six minutes in some ways to contemplate it, and certainly not six hours or six days, if you'll look at the night when we first found out about it and then at every breaking event since then."[111] The diplomatic paradigm had shifted radically between the time of the Cuban Missile Crisis and Iraq's invasion of Kuwait.

The Persian Gulf War was the first major international crisis conducted at telediplomacy's accelerated pace. The preceding discussion of events surrounding Saddam Hussein's peace overture highlights diplomacy's increased pace during the Persian Gulf War: The U.S. government received, decided about, and responded to a peace overture from Hussein within twenty minutes.[112] State Department spokesman Richard Boucher has noted that the pace of events surrounding the peace overture illustrated not the exception but more nearly the rule for diplomacy's pace during America's first real-time war:

During the Gulf War, Saddam Hussein could make a speech and have it carried on CNN at 11 a.m. Then I would have to react at twelve o'clock [noon]. That's damn hard. Foreign policy cycles are not the same as media cycles. You can't do foreign policy on the fly.[113]

Traditional diplomacy's deliberative pace has yielded to the dictates of telediplomacy.

Senior-level U.S. policymakers also attest to real-time television's influence on diplomacy's pace. Former Secretary Baker argues that instead of days and weeks in which to consider a response diplomats must now "react in minutes or hours."[114] One anonymous senior-level policy adviser argues:

There's really no time to digest this information, so the reaction tends to be from the gut, just like the reaction of the man on the street. It is worrisome that high-level people are being forced essentially to act or to formulate responses or policy positions on the basis of information that is of very uncertain reliability.[115]

Former U.S. Secretary of State Lawrence Eagleburger draws a stark contrast between the pace of past and present diplomatic practice:

If you're on the receiving end; if you're trying to figure out what the policy ought to be, let me tell you: I would love to have had the period of time it took to decide we were going to war with Spain. When you have something like the Sarajevo event [marketplace massacre in February 1994], and the President is in the office fifteen minutes later: come on! The time frame and the amount of time you're permitted to think through the consequences of what you're going to do is much reduced.[116]

Philip M. Taylor, an international relations and media scholar, concludes that diplomacy's accelerated pace results in policy being determined "more by CNN's ability to break stories first with pictures rather than by any sober calculation of US national interests."[117]

Global television, by virtue of its immediacy and its impact, has now become an actor in the diplomatic arena, according to such top-level officials as Fitzwater, Boucher, and Eagleburger. The shift to telediplomacy has enhanced the influence of this non-traditional actor to the degree that former Secretary Baker has charged that the "vital national interest is now determined by what is covered on television."[118] However, communications advances also have enhanced the influence of other non-traditional actors.

Increasing the Diplomatic Influence of Non-Traditional Actors

The third effect that communication historically has exerted upon diplomatic practice is to increase gradually the diplomatic influence of non-traditional actors at the expense of traditional diplomatists. The bottom line is that recent advances in communication technology have

> transformed the international system from one almost exclusively dominated by nation-states whose political intercourse centered on bargaining bilaterally and multilaterally for national advantage, to a more diverse system in which nonstate players introduce nonnational issues into the bargaining.[119]

The recent shift in communication paradigms has diminished the nation-states' former absolute domination and afforded four non-traditional players increasing influence in the diplomatic arena: real-time global television; elected political leaders; those who formerly had no diplomatic standing and/or non-state actors; and public opinion. Although various actors' relative diplomatic influence has changed incrementally over time, the advent of global television has shifted this balance more in favor of non-traditional actors.[120] This shift in influence has become so pronounced that global communications itself, under certain narrowly circumscribed conditions, can drive policy, effectively defining the outcome of foreign-policy decision-making. Suffice it to say that the advent of real-time global television has shifted the relative balance of influence away from traditional diplomatic actors and toward the non-traditional.

Real-time television understands its increasing status as an independent diplomatic actor. During the 1991 Gulf War CNN chairman Ted Turner stressed the importance of what his network was about during a phone call to the network's Baghdad producer: "We're a global network. If there's a chance for peace ... it might come through us. Hell, both sides aren't talking to each other but they're talking to CNN. We have a major responsibility."[121] Likewise, CNN Vice President Peter Vesey argues that the "process of diplomacy and the process of government are being demystified" by real-time media, with the result that CNN has changed the form of diplomacy on major issues.[122] One foreign policy scholar concludes that real-time media such as CNN have become direct and "significant players in foreign policy making."[123] Former Secretary Baker concurs: "[T]he real-time coverage of conflict by the electronic media has served to create a powerful new imperative for prompt action that was not present in a less frenetic time."[124] Global television itself has now become a force that must be considered in diplomatic calculations.

Moreover, real-time television also provides a highly effective platform for other non-traditional players in the diplomatic arena. One such "player" is elected political leaders. Elected politicians have played an increasingly important diplomatic role in the foreign policies of democratic societies for some time. However, global television has accorded these politicians increased influence. Harold Nicolson argued in 1939 that allowing politicians to take part in diplomacy was a "dangerous innovation."[125] He was concerned that the limited amount of time at politicians' disposal might unduly rush the diplomatic process during personal visits to other capitals on matters of state.

Concerns about rushed personal visits seem dated and quaint in the real-time 1990s. Diplomats today do not share Nicolson's concern about the amount of time available during something so leisurely as a personal visit. Rather, today's diplomat must deal with the time compression of instantaneous electronic diplomacy. Former U.S. State Department Official Newsom contends that "I've always trembled when a president picks up the phone to talk to his counterparts."[126] By the time of the Gulf War, Kathleen Hall Jamieson suggested the degree to which diplomacy had been accelerated and compressed when she argued that "Ordinarily to get to the president, you've got to go through layers of bureaucracy. Once you know he watches CNN, if you're a world leader, you go on CNN."[127] Personal diplomacy via real-time television represents a paradigm shift well beyond the concerns registered by Nicolson relative to new diplomacy.

Personal-leader diplomacy via real-time television can, at times, replace traditional diplomatic experts. Although schooled in the traditions of dynastic diplomacy, King Hussein of Jordan demonstrated his understanding of the shift in diplomatic methods by the time of the Gulf War. On one occasion when Hussein was being criticized by the U.S. government for his support of Iraq in the Gulf crisis, he responded in the quickest and most effective way possible. Rather than calling an ambassador or enlisting the services of his foreign minister to lodge a formal protest with the Bush Administration, King Hussein called CNN in Atlanta, Georgia, and delivered his personal rejoinder via a live interview.[128] Newsom argues that during the Gulf War President Bush and Saddam Hussein literally "hurled messages back and forth via television."[129] The net result is that, "To the horror of the professional, diplomacy has become the politician's sport, with heads of government making policy by television...."[130] Real-time television has shifted the relative balance of diplomatic influence away from traditional diplomats and toward political leaders who often lack diplomatic credentials or expertise.

Global television also grants influence to those who formerly had no diplomatic standing at all. Former *Los Angeles Times* correspondent Tom Rosenstiel argues that the CNN linkage has "changed the nature of diplomatic communication and provided a voice for tinpot dictators" and actors "who otherwise lacked political standing."[131] The real-time media now have the ability to introduce non-state actors into the foreign policymaking process. As a result of this ability, the real-time media have upset the "historical incremental change characteristic of foreign policy and opened it up to 'shocks' in the form of issues and players which appear on the foreign policy agenda with little historical background, requiring new policies as well as changes in existing positions."[132] Those who traditionally have had no diplomatic standing can now influence the foreign-policy process.

The ability of non-diplomatic players to influence diplomacy may increase as technology further reduces the remaining impediments to true point-to-point global broadcasting. Ted Koppel of ABC News suggested a future where satellite broadcasting by individuals would become a reality. In testimony before the U.S. House of Representatives Committee on International Relations, Koppel argued that

> In the future you will have thousands of individuals who have the ability to broadcast from any point in the world to any point in the U.S. You will no longer have us—the networks, editors, etc.—as filters. There is a democratization of technology going on right now. So you are going to have on a global level the end result that any government, any rebellious group, any political group that wants to send its message directly to American viewers can do so without going through a network and without going through a station.
>
> The technology has already outstripped that [the ability of Congress or the networks to control what is covered and what is not]. There are other people reporting and by-passing us altogether.[133]

These technological capabilities will grant increasingly unfiltered access to the foreign-policy arena. And this access will enhance the influence of those who previously had no diplomatic standing.

Public opinion's influence has been enhanced to a greater degree than that of any other non-traditional diplomatic actor, thanks to real-time television. Dom Bonafede argues that, "In essence, public opinion, shaped to a large extent by the media, has become the common arbiter among competing policies, politicians, and statesmen."[134] By 1986 an official U.S. government report had already acknowledged that "International events are increasingly played out, and their outcome shaped, in the arena of world public opinion.... [W]orld leaders compete directly for the support of citizens in other countries.... Public opinion is increasingly influential in shaping foreign policy."[135] David Gergen, a senior communications official and adviser to several U.S. presidents, describes public opinion's increasing influence in foreign policy decision-making:

> ...[This practice] marks a serious departure in American diplomacy. For most of U.S. history, diplomats have been guided by their own judgments and only later have worried about public reaction.

> Increasingly during the 1980s, government officials have shaped their policies with an eye toward generating positive and timely television coverage and securing public approval. What too often counts is how well the policy will "play," how the pictures will look, whether the right signals are being sent, and whether the public will be impressed by the swiftness of the government's response — not whether the policy promotes America's long-term interests.[136]

Public opinion's influence in foreign policy is on the rise.[137]

Most early research into the public-opinion-foreign-policy connection tended to suggest that the public was largely powerless to affect foreign policy.[138] Not surprisingly, interviews conducted with officials in the State Department's Bureau of Public Affairs during the 1960s and '70s found that they had only a moderate interest in public opinion. And, to the extent public opinion was considered at all, it was only public opinion's need to be educated. Little concern was given to any potential impact of public opinion on foreign policy.[139]

A different attitude toward pubic opinion emerges from former Secretary Baker's experience at the State Department twenty years later. During a recent discussion, Baker reminded his audience that what is a vital national interest is often driven by what is on CNN.[140] Baker was subsequently asked whether it might not be better if he, as a policymaker, would just ignore CNN. He responded emphatically:

> No. No. The reason you can't do that is the reason I mentioned at the beginning of our discussion here [on why policymakers must pay attention to the media]. For any policy ... to be successful, you have to have a consensus of the public behind you, supporting you. No foreign policy can be successful for very long that doesn't enjoy a strong domestic political consensus.[141]

One of the first researchers to explore the relationship between public opinion and foreign policy characterized the prevailing attitude of State

Department officials toward public opinion in the 1960s as "to hell with public opinion."[142] By way of comparison, Baker's response suggests public opinion's increased influence in foreign policy by the 1990s.

Public opinion's increased foreign-policy influence is largely attributable to advances in communication technology. But the increase also results from a shift in diplomatic influence away from traditional diplomatic actors, such as the State Department and its diplomats, and toward public opinion. Recent statistical research bears out the increasing importance of public opinion in foreign policy decision-making. The factors most often cited for this increase are the loss of consensus between the public and the U.S. government following Vietnam; the end of the Cold War and the demise of the Soviet Union, the nation's long-standing external enemy, suggesting that foreign policy decisions must now rely for their support upon public opinion rather than appeals to imminent external threat; and the advent of new communications technologies.[143] In fact, recent research suggests that public opinion is even more influential in foreign policy than was previously believed.[144] Much of this increasing influence is due to advances in communications technology.[145]

Recent surveys of State Department officials also indicate a change in attitude toward public opinion's influence. State Department officials now feel an imperative to move foreign policy into line with the public's wishes.[146] Data indicate that U.S. foreign policies correspond with majority public opinion 90 percent of the time.[147] Furthermore, when large and sustained changes occur in public opinion, U.S. foreign policy will change to follow opinion more than two thirds of the time.[148] State Department officials have changed their beliefs from two decades ago when public opinion was seen as something to be ignored, or, at best, educated.

Earlier State Department attitudes toward public opinion merely reflected the then prevailing paradigm of diplomatic practice. Prior to the media becoming a factor in foreign policy, "diplomacy was the sport of kings and, as such, it had little or nothing to do with public opinion."[149] This was largely the case under telediplomacy's immediate predecessor, new diplomacy.

Recall that most scholars date the beginning of new diplomacy to Woodrow Wilson's Fourteen Points and the immediate post–World War I era. Wilson pledged to lay all international agreements before the court of world public opinion in an attempt to preempt further cataclysms such as World War I, which Wilson called "the War to End All Wars." Yet, Wilson's personal practice differed markedly from his pronouncements. Less than a year after Wilson announced his Fourteen Points, he began work on the Peace of Versailles to conclude World War I. Wilson, who had called for "open covenants openly arrived at," conducted highly secretive negotiations to conclude World War I, negotiations that excluded the following: other diplomatists, including the members of his own diplomatic delegation; all of the minor parties to the conflict; Germany and her allies, the adversary who was militarily undefeated but had negotiated for a cease-fire on the basis of Wilson's own Fourteen Points; and Russia, one of the original allies with Britain and France against Germany. (Although Russia had become the Soviet Union following the Bolshevik revolution of November 1917, and subsequently withdrew from the war, she had absorbed a significant amount of Germany's lethal force and had experienced staggering losses as a result.) Wilson closeted himself with the leaders of Britain and France alone during the negotiations. Furthermore, Wilson only allowed personally approved, meager press bulletins to be released.[150] By the 1990s, former U.S. Secretary of State Baker's experiences — and presidential adviser Gergen's observations — suggest the degree to which public opinion's influence has increased during the shift to telediplomacy. Diplomatic practice today stands in sharp contrast to that of Wilson.

However, to appreciate fully the potential influence of non-traditional actors such as public opinion, we need to move just beyond the conclusion of the ground war in the 1991 Gulf conflict. Communications has not only shifted the relative balance of diplomatic influence from traditional to non-traditional actors; under certain conditions this shift in influence can be so pronounced as to actually determine policy. One particular event shortly after President Bush called a halt to the fighting at 12:00 a.m. on February 28, 1991, demonstrates the ability of both public opinion and the media to influence policy in the real-time era. Indeed, in the case of Kurdish refugees fleeing Saddam Hussein's repression immediately following the Gulf War, non-traditional actors determined U.S. policy. Or, to borrow former Secretary Baker's words, global communications drove policy toward the Kurdish refugees, a case that will be examined further in Chapter 6.[151] Communications had affected a diplomatic outcome, one of the unique distinctions of telediplomacy. It is to this subject that we turn in the next chapter: the ability of real-time television to produce different diplomatic outcomes.

Chapter 5

Global Television's Ability to Drive Policy

"[T]elevision is our lifeline to the politicians who want nothing to do with us or hope that the problem will go away from public consciousness…. Without you [television coverage], we have no weapon at all."
— *Sylvana Foa, 1994; UN High Commissioner for Refugees*

"We need the pictures, always the pictures."
— *Official of the UN High Commissioner for Refugees*

"You have to have the pictures."
— *Roy Gutman, 1997 Pulitzer Prize-winning reporter for Newsday*

Today, the nexus between communications and diplomacy can determine diplomatic outcomes, under certain conditions. Although paradigmatic shifts in communication historically have worked to move diplomatic practice from one paradigm to its successor, the recent development of live satellite coverage also affords communications the potential to determine foreign policy. Specifically, real-time global television alone gives communications this potential to affect diplomatic outcomes.

Real-time television's immediacy and impact are the operative forces that allow communications to influence foreign policy. Former White House Counsel Lloyd N. Cutler argued that, already by 1984, television news had a "much greater effect on national policy decisions—especially foreign-policy decisions—than print journalism has ever been able to and more than most experienced observers realize."[1] Likewise, former Secretary Kissinger has argued that, "The print media have almost no impact at all.... But the big power is TV reporting."[2] And, while discussing the unique impact of satellite television, Kissinger contends that where diplomats seeking his counsel used to ask what they should do, "Now they ask me what they should say."[3] The high visibility that global television brings to bear on a particular situation is one of the specific conditions required for communications to affect a diplomatic outcome. The official U.S. government response to China's June 1989 crackdown on pro-democracy demonstrators in Tiananmen Square demonstrates both real-time television's immediacy and its impact.

Had there been no real-time video images of Tiananmen Square, would the U.S. response have been the same? The probable answer to this question suggests something of the break with the past that Tiananmen represented. James F. Hoge, Jr., editor of *Foreign Affairs* magazine, has argued that satellite coverage of events in Tiananmen Square marked the beginning of what has become a dramatic increase in live television reporting of international crises.[4] This new type of crisis coverage lent a unique immediacy and impact to the events unfolding in China. The graphic imagery coming from Tiananmen demanded a rapid response, which the U.S. delivered in uniquely undiplomatic language.

Principals close to the decision-making process agree that the U.S. response was driven by real-time global television. Recall that the U.S. was the first government to issue a formal response to China's crackdown. According to Bush spokesman Marlin Fitzwater, this response was driven almost entirely by live satellite coverage, not traditional diplomatic processes.[5] Former Secretary Baker concurs with Fitzwater on this point. While reflecting upon the Tiananmen Square incident some years later, Baker recognized that "The terrible tragedy of Tiananmen [Square] was a classic demonstration of a *powerful new phenomenon: the ability of the global communications revolution to drive policy.*"[6] This is telediplomacy's unique distinction: global communications' ability to "drive policy," in Baker's words.[7]

Recall the discussion in Chapter IV about the U.S. response to Saddam's televised peace overture during the Gulf War. This response also suggests global communications' ability to affect policy outcomes. In short, an important foreign policy decision, the decision to continue war, was driven by the processes of communication, not diplomacy.

Three Caveats

However, three caveats about communications' ability to affect policy decisions are in order. First, one basic fact must be recognized about potential cause-and-effect relationships in human experience: The ultimate motivations of the individual human heart are impossible to determine from external observation. Therefore, discussions about global communications driving policy must have this basic fact as their point of departure. And, although the external evidence indicates that the U.S. responses to both Tiananmen Square and Saddam's peace overture were driven by real-time television rather than traditional foreign policy decision-making processes, only George Bush knows for certain what motivated him in making these decisions. This caveat notwithstanding, the evidence does suggest that communications was a primary causative factor in both policy decisions.

A second caveat flows logically from the first. Definite cause-and-effect relationships are difficult, if not impossible, to determine in foreign policy. Given that the ultimate motivation of the human heart is impossible to determine from external observation, attempts at determining cause-and-effect relationships must rely largely upon comparing highly similar cases.

For example, the cases of the 1991 Kurdish and Shiitic uprisings discussed in this chapter both happened at the same time and under similar conditions; resulted from similar provocations; and occurred in the same country. These uprisings resulted in very different outcomes, however. Although other differences do exist, one key variable distinguished these two cases: a marked difference in real-time global television coverage. This difference in coverage arguably determined the different outcomes. Thus, real-time television's ability to drive policy can be established by comparing these two similar cases.

The final caveat regarding communications' ability to affect policy outcomes is implied by the first two: real-time television rarely, if ever, is the sole cause for a particular outcome. Real-world events seldom provide us with distinct cases that are identical in every detail, except for the real-time television coverage accorded each case. Factors in addition to global television are almost always at work, as is discussed in the Kurdish and Shiitic cases below. Moreover, when the evidence suggests that communications has affected policy, global television is merely the primary cause; other cause-and-effect relationships must almost certainly be factored into any diplomatic outcome. In other words, when global television affects policy, its presence is a *necessary* condition for that particular outcome to occur; rarely is global television alone a *sufficient* condition. The opposite also holds true when communications drives policy: the absence of global television coverage is likely to lead to a different outcome than otherwise would have occurred, had global television been present. Therefore, global communications can be said to have affected diplomatic outcomes when its presence is necessary for a particular outcome, even though other factors are also at work.[8]

Five Conditions for Global Television's Ability to Drive Policy

Communications can affect diplomatic outcomes only under certain conditions. Global television's ability to affect diplomatic outcomes depends on five specific criteria. First, the opportunity for real-time television to affect policy depends on the issue: global crises or complex humanitarian emergencies are the most likely candidates. In other words, communications' ability to affect policy is issue specific. The second and third conditions are closely related: The events must be rapidly unfolding, and/or there must be an absence of clear policy direction from the political leaders involved. In other words, in addition to fast-breaking events, there must be a leadership vacuum. Fourth, global television must have access to the unfolding events and be able to operate without restrictions. And, finally, the situation must become highly visible to a wide viewing audience.

Issue Specific

Certain events lend themselves more readily to global television's ability to affect policy than others. Some degree of crisis must exist, such as a global political crisis or a complex humanitarian emergency (CHE). A complex humanitarian emergency exists when man-made factors, such as civil wars, create significant humanitarian consequences, such as mass refugee movements.[9] A global political crisis has traditionally been defined as a situation in which "(1) two or more countries have important national interests involved, (2) there is a possibility of war, and (3) there is a limited time to reach a solution."[10] However, the post–Cold War movement towards recognizing human rights as international law requires some revisions to this traditional definition.

Today, global political crises can also be created by violations of universally recognized standards for human rights. But one condition is essential before human rights violations can rise to the level of a global political crisis: There must be a "world-wide *perception*" of indiscriminate human rights violations.[11] Situations involving human rights can become global political crises when these perceived violations result in significant international pressure for outside intervention to solve the situation. Therefore, a CHE becomes a global political crisis when there is significant pressure for outside intervention to resolve the humanitarian emergency.[12]

Real-time television coverage determines whether a particular complex humanitarian emergency will ultimately become a global political crisis. A CHE can only rise to the level of a global political crisis when real-time television coverage generates the necessary pressure for outside intervention. Calls for this intervention are usually justified on the basis of the human rights standards that are perceived as having been violated. Today, such violations often result in global crises, given the changed nature of world politics in the post-Cold War era. Global political crises are, by definition, high-visibility situations. And, given this, global political crises are uniquely susceptible to communications' ability to drive policy.[13]

The mass refugee flows that can occur during civil wars are prime candidates for becoming global political crises. The human consequences of such emergencies must be dealt with by political, military, and relief institutions.[14] CHEs are normally characterized by civil conflict and a national government's greatly diminished ability to exert political control. Inevitably, these conditions result in humanitarian consequences, including mass population movements stemming from the need to find food or avoid conflict, significant economic dislocation, and a marked decline in the ability to secure food. In the case of CHE's, these consequences result from man-made emergencies.[15]

Real-time television's immediacy and impact are most likely to affect policy in global crises and/or CHEs. Negotiations about economic assistance to a tiny or strategically unimportant state, such as the East African state of Burundi, will attract neither the media visibility nor the international attention necessary for communications to drive policy. The events that pose the greatest opportunity for global television to influence policy are issue specific. In addition to CHEs and global political crises, transnational issues such as drugs and the environment are potential candidates for global television's influence.[16]

Fast-Breaking Events and/or a Leadership Vacuum

In order for communications to affect policy, events must be either fast-breaking and/or involve a situation where there is a leadership vacuum that can be easily filled by global television. Global crises and complex human-itarian emergencies both tend to be rapidly unfolding events with limited time to react. Conditions that afford limited time for decision-making are more susceptible to communications' influence, in part because the sheer pace of events can outstrip political leaders' ability to craft clear and well thought-out policy responses.[17] A leadership vacuum can result from this type of policy confusion.

The absence of clear leadership is essential for communications to affect diplomatic outcomes. A vacuum is created when there is an absence of a carefully defined leadership position that corresponds with reality and long-term public preferences, and/or when political leaders are well behind the pace of events on the ground.[18] The resulting leadership vacuum is likely to be filled by a non-traditional diplomatic actor. Such a vacuum lends itself particularly well to being exploited by the media. Ted Koppel describes the conditions under which television's influence increases at leadership's expense: " a.) the administration has failed to enunciate a clear policy, and b.) [the administration] has done little or nothing to inform the American public on the dangers of intervention or failing to inter-vene."[19] Given a leadership vacuum, instantaneous media can trump polit-ical leaders' influence in the policymaking process.[20] But, before telediplomacy can affect policy, there must be an absence of leadership.

The Cold War's demise compounds the problems of foreign-policy leadership. Whatever else may be said about the Cold War, it provided a continuous frame of reference within which most foreign policy decisions could be cast. In the post-Cold War era, U.S. foreign policy has been char-acterized by a lack of overarching philosophy. This inability to provide a consistent foreign-policy framework has been captured by Robert J. Lieber in the title of his edited volume *Eagle Adrift: American Foreign Policy at the End of the Century*.[21] In addition, Seib has argued that "When politi-cal leaders fail to provide clearly defined policies as a foundation for con-sidering the events reported by the news media, a vacuum results."[22] And the news media themselves can move to fill the resulting vacuum.[23]

The bottom line on political leadership *vs.* news media influence on policy is simple: leadership *can* always trump journalism. But the reality of this simple truth is that political leaders *must* lead *if* they desire to main-tain control over policy. Strobel has observed that "When there is a vac-uum created by weak leadership ... the media's impact on policy increases."[24] *USA Today* foreign editor Neuman argues that "pictures drive diplomacy ... only when there is a vacuum of political leadership."[25] and Neuman concludes that "It is not inevitable, or even desirable, that lead-ers cede this power to television. It is also not the fault of television."[26]

The process whereby journalism can move to fill a leadership void is described by Strobel:

> If officials let others dominate the policy debate, if they do not closely monitor the progress and results of their own policies, if they fail to build and maintain popular and congressional support for a course of action, if they step beyond the bounds of their public mandate or fail to anticipate problems, they may suddenly seem driven by the news media and its agenda. They may discover what has been called the "dark side" of the CNN effect, a force — as sudden, immediate, and powerful as an avenging angel — that can sweep them along in its path. This [is a] seemingly random, but in fact predictable, exercise of media influence ....[27]

In other words, journalism can trump normal foreign policy decision-making processes in the absence of political leadership.

Moreover, under certain conditions, global television's power can actually overcome political leadership's ability to control policy. When leadership finds itself out of step with reality on the ground or long-term public preferences, political leaders may find the center of influence over policy shifting toward the media. The U.S. response to the 1991 Kurdish refugee crisis, discussed below, demonstrates just such a shift. Bush had made a definite decision to stay out of internal Iraqi problems between Saddam Hussein and the Kurds.[28] However, television images of fleeing Kurdish refugees pushed President Bush toward a different policy, according to Strobel, even though these images "did not appear in a policy vacuum."[29] By early April 1991, there was a disparity between official U.S. policy and reality on the ground in northern Iraq. In addition, the Bush Administration found itself significantly out of step with U.S. public opinion. Ultimately, the center of influence over policy shifted toward global television. The Kurds were granted a reprieve.

Media Autonomy

In order for global television to influence policy, the environment must be such that policymakers cannot control the media. Specifically, real-time television must have both access and virtual autonomy of action. The media are much more likely to magnify any gaps that exist between government's position and the facts on the ground when media are free to operate on their own, rather than having to depend upon governments for information and access.

For example, a lack of control during the war in Vietnam ultimately allowed the media to magnify gaps between official U.S. government statements and reality on the battlefield. On the other hand, the high degree of control exerted over the media during the 1991 Persian Gulf War resulted in few media stories contradicting official U.S. government statements and policy. In other words, absence of control over the media is essential before global television can affect policy. This absence of control, or media autonomy, can stem from government indifference, political anarchy on the ground, or other contextual factors that render control of the media a virtual impossibility. Media autonomy is essential if communications is actually to affect policy outcomes.[30]

High Visibility

High visibility is the final condition needed for communications to influence policy. All four factors above — a global political crisis, with fast-breaking events, that is characterized by a leadership vacuum and media autonomy — must produce a situation that evidences a high degree of visibility before communications can affect diplomatic outcomes. And, as established above, a need for high visibility is synonymous with attracting the attention of real-time global television.

Two events in world politics demonstrate communications' recent ability to influence policy; a third illustrates the limits to this ability. The cases of the 1991 Kurdish refugees in northern Iraq and the Shiite Muslim refugees in southern Iraq both illustrate communications' ability to influence policy. However, there are limits to this ability, as was demonstrated in the case of the 1994 genocide inside Rwanda. It is to this ability of communications to influence diplomatic outcomes, and its limits, that we turn in the following chapter.

Chapter 6

Global Television and Diplomatic Outcomes

"Public pressure for our humanitarian engagement increasingly may be driven by televised images, which can depend in turn on such considerations as where CNN sends its camera crews."
— *Anthony Lake, 1994; Former National Security Advisor*

The Bush Administration launched a massive humanitarian intervention on behalf of the Kurdish refugees fleeing northern Iraq immediately after the 1991 Persian Gulf War. Global television played a decisive role in this foreign policy decision. A similar, and virtually simultaneous, humanitarian crisis in southern Iraq received no global television coverage; consequently, no international assistance was forthcoming in the crisis in southern Iraq, which involved the Shiite, or Shiah, Muslims. The Kurdish and Shiite crises demonstrate communications' ability to drive policy, given the similarity between the two crises, the different television coverage accorded each, and, consequently, the markedly different outcomes of each crisis. British international relations scholar Martin Shaw argues bluntly that television was the "essential difference" between the Shiite and Kurdish rebellions and their suppressions.[1] Television had affected a diplomatic outcome.

Rwanda demonstrates the limits to global television's power. The 1994 humanitarian tragedy that engulfed Rwanda can be divided into two phases, a genocidal phase which occurred inside Rwanda itself and a refugee phase that spread Rwanda's misery into neighboring Tanzania and

96

Zaire. Both phases received wide coverage in the global media. Yet, as Peter Shiras, director of government relations and public outreach for InterAction, a coalition of more than 150 U.S.-based relief organizations, has argued, "[M]edia coverage of Rwanda during the period of genocide was extensive but provoked no large-scale international response until refugee flows began."[2] As the lack of any meaningful international response to the Rwandan genocide demonstrates, there are limits to communications' ability to affect diplomatic outcome.

The Kurdish Refugees: A Case of Global Television's Ability to Drive Policy

On April 5, 1991, shortly after Kuwait had been liberated during the Persian Gulf War, George Bush declared that "American lives are too precious for us to get sucked into a civil war" between Saddam Hussein's forces and Kurdish refugees fleeing for their lives.[3] Several days later Bush again stated categorically, "I do not want one soldier or airman shoved into a civil war in Iraq.... I'm not going to have that."[4] Yet, only three days after this statement, Bush announced that the U.S. was preparing to launch what ultimately would become the largest American humanitarian relief operation ever mounted. Subsequently, the U.S. dispatched 5,000 troops (half of the total number involved) and sufficient air cover to ensure that no Iraqi aircraft could operate in a major portion of their own country north of the 36th parallel.[5] In less than two weeks, the Bush Administration had moved from a firm policy of non-intervention to providing for a *de facto* Kurdish state within Iraq's borders.[6] Daniel Schorr, senior news analyst for National Public Radio, concluded that "the president had been forced, under the impact of what Americans and Europeans were seeing on television, to reconsider."[7] Shaw contends that "This was TV news' finest hour."[8] Global television had affected the outcome of foreign-policy decision-making.

A Complex Humanitarian Emergency and a Global Political Crisis

At 12:00 a.m. February 28, 1991, President Bush declared a cessation of hostilities in allied coalition efforts to liberate Kuwait from its Iraqi occupiers. By March 1 civil unrest began to erupt in Iraq, threatening Saddam Hussein's continuance in power.[9] The Kurds that were located in northern Iraq were part of this uprising. They had long been in search of their own state and had a history of being brutalized by Saddam, most recently in 1988 when his forces had used fire and chemical weapons to eradicate entire Kurdish villages, including the village of Halabja near Iran, where 5,000 Kurds were gassed.[10] Once the coalition defeated Saddam's forces, the Kurdish resistance moved quickly.

By March 21 almost the entire Kurdistan region of northern Iraq was under Kurdish control. Kurds had even regained control of Kirkuk, the richest city in northern Iraq. By March 25 the Kurds enjoyed virtually free rein in the north.[11]

The collapse of a concurrent anti-Saddam Shiitic rebellion in the south, however, freed up Iraqi troops that were then quickly transferred to help put down the Kurdish rebellion in the north. Fixed-wing aircraft, helicopter gunships, and Iraqi Republican Guard troops went on the attack. By March 29 the city of Kirkuk had been re-taken and Saddam's forces were rapidly advancing northeastward toward the Turkish border. The Kurdish rebellion was being ruthlessly crushed. As a result, between one and two million Kurdish refugees fled toward the borders of Turkey and Iran ahead of Saddam's advancing troops. Conditions were ripe for this complex humanitarian emergency to become a global political crisis.[12]

Between 500,000 and one million Kurdish refugees wound up in the snow-covered mountains on the border between Iraq and Turkey. The vast majority had fled before Saddam's rapidly advancing troops with literally nothing but the clothes on their backs. Most were ill-clad for the freezing winter weather into which they had fled: the young, the old, and the sick had fled without any prospect of shelter, food, or medicine.[13] The scale of this human catastrophe reached epic proportions. According to Save the Children, an international humanitarian relief organization which targets its efforts at children, the daily death rate exceeded that of the worst Ethiopian famine.[14] Starvation and exposure to the elements resulted in daily death counts of somewhere between 1,000 and 2,000.[15] Upwards of 100,000 Iraqis died as a result of Saddam's crushing the domestic rebellions that threatened his regime, more than the number that died during the entire 1991 Gulf War.[16] This was not a natural disaster but a man-made catastrophe. The Kurdish refugee situation began as a complex humanitarian emergency. Thanks to global television, it would soon become a global political crisis as well.

Fast-Breaking Events and the
Opening of a Leadership Vacuum

Within a two-week period, the Kurdish rebels had been able to liberate 95 percent of Iraqi Kurdistan. The Kurdish leadership subsequently invited other Iraqi opposition factions to join them in setting up a provisional coalition government in Kurdistan.[17] But by March 25 events were turning swiftly against the Kurds, and within three days the Kurdish uprising had been quashed by Saddam's forces.[18] The speed of the uprising's spontaneous beginning was surpassed by the swiftness of its demise.

Western political leaders had a hand in creating the Kurdish uprising. On February 15 Bush issued a call for the Iraqi people to rise up against Saddam:

> There's another way for the bloodshed to stop. That is for the Iraqi military and the Iraqi people to take matters into their own hands, to force Saddam Hussein, the dictator, to step aside, and to comply with the UN, and then rejoin the family of peace-loving nations.[19]

This message was broadcast into Iraq by the "Voice of America."[20] According to one source, Bush instructed the CIA in January of 1991 to provoke a Kurdish insurrection.[21] And, at the end of March, a CIA-supported radio station called the "Voice of Free Iraq" was still calling for a Kurdish uprising to depose Saddam.[22] Significant evidence, including first-hand statements from Iraqi Kurds, points to major Western responsibility for the Kurdish uprising.[23]

The Kurdish leadership accused Bush of having "personally called upon the Iraqi people to rise up against Saddam Hussein's brutal dictatorship"[24]; yet, when resistance forces inside Iraq heeded that call and then were suppressed, the West offered no diplomatic recognition, no support, and no assistance of any kind. In response to the first reports of uprisings against Saddam, White House spokesman Marlin Fitzwater stated, "We don't intend to get involved in Iraq's internal affairs," a somewhat dubious disclaimer given the Western coalition's degree of existing and former activities inside Iraq.[25] Although it had a hand in encouraging the uprising, the Bush Administration was clearly not prepared for the events that transpired in the wake of this encouragement. By March 26 the Administration had made a firm policy decision not to intervene in support of the rebels.[26]

The Administration's decision was allegedly driven by concerns about dismembering Iraq. However, such concerns were somewhat belated and misplaced. The Bush Administration had encouraged the Kurdish uprising, well aware of the Kurds' long-standing history of seeking a separate state. The Administration simply had no carefully developed plan on how it intended to deal with the consequences of the very events that it had encouraged. By the end of March, events on the ground were well ahead of Western political leaders' contingency plans.[27]

There was an apparent contradiction between U.S. pronouncements and U.S. policy. According to one anonymous diplomat, "A climate was created which seemed to say: 'If some of you people get together and rise up against Saddam, we won't dump you...' Well, we did."[28] No explicit promises had been made to the Kurds, in part because of concerns about the effects that an independent Kurdish state in northern Iraq might have on neighboring Turkey's Kurdish minority. The U.S. notion of post-Saddam rule in Iraq obviously did not include the Kurds, and probably leaned more toward a "compliant military regime" in Baghdad.[29] U.S. Vice-President Dan Quayle is the only Administration member to have raised questions about whether the U.S. had any moral obligation to the Kurdish insurgents that it had encouraged.[30]

Not surprisingly, the first public questions about the West's responsibility to the Kurds surfaced at the same time that Saddam Hussein began ruthlessly suppressing their rebellion. On March 26 a British Broadcasting Corporation (BBC) report contained the first public call for the West to redress its lack of responsibility. BBC correspondent Jim Muir reported that "[the Kurds] are disappointed at the failure of the West to come to their aid, after they encouraged them to revolt against Saddam's rule."[31] The Kurds were not seeking military aid, but political and humanitarian support.

However, Western leaders quickly made clear that they were under no obligation to provide assistance of any kind. *The New York Times* reported that the Bush Administration had "decided to let President Saddam Hussein put down rebellions in his country without American intervention."[32] On April 2 Bush, while golfing in Florida, brushed aside reporters' inquiries about U.S. responsibility: "I feel no reason to answer to anybody. We're relaxing here."[33] Two days later British Prime Minister John Major bristled when queried about potential Western responsibility for having encouraged the Kurds to rebel: "I don't recall asking the Kurds to mount this particular insurrection.... We hope very much that the military in Iraq will remove Saddam Hussein."[34] Even after the Bush Administration changed course and announced a major U.S.-led relief effort for the Kurds on April 16, Bush himself still angrily denied suggestions that the U.S. had any responsibility for events in Kurdistan:

> Do I think that the United States should bear guilt because of suggesting that the Iraqi people take matters into their own hands, with the implication being given that the United States would be there to support them militarily? That was not true. We never implied that.[35]

Yet, Bush's National Security Advisor Brent Scowcroft did admit that the administration had not expected the severity of reprisals against the

Kurds.[36] In the rush of events that had overtaken them on the ground, Western leaders had been caught without a coherent policy toward the very events that, in part, had been unleashed in response to Western encouragement.

By early April 1991 a leadership vacuum existed between official policy and reality. Western leaders were also about to learn that official government policy was out of step with public opinion. In fact, the citizens of Western democracies "forced their generally reluctant governments to support international intervention."[37] An April 11 *Newsweek* poll showed Bush's public approval rating dropping from the historic high of 92 percent down to 80 percent because of his position on the Kurdish issue.[38] Shaw noted that "what the media did was to make explicit a nexus of responsibility already established by the actions of the Western-led coalition in the Gulf War and their appeals for the overthrow of the Iraqi regime."[39] As a result, "Televised pictures of Kurdish refugees massed along the Turkish border built on a Western consensus that an obligation to them existed, growing out of the stand already taken against Iraq."[40] The bottom line is that "[t]here was no time for traditional diplomacy. Statesmen were too busy trying to catch up to their publics."[41] The gap between official policy and reality was about to be filled by real-time global television and public opinion.

Media Autonomy and Its Consequence: High Visibility

Global television had significant access to the unfolding Kurdish crisis. Gowing explains the process whereby the Kurds garnered world attention and the results of this unprecedented visibility:

> Through the new, highly-mobile satellite technology, television overcame the power of politicians and legislators to control it. No longer did enormous distances or political and logistical obstructions prevent transmission of sensitive pictures. In the final hours of the Gulf War, and the subsequent weeks of 'peace,' news management broke down. Politicians no longer set the agenda. Television images dictated the agenda for them.[42]

The Gulf War had attracted more than 1,500 journalists to the region.[43] The media management and pool systems that had been in place during the war effectively came to an end with the February 28 cease-fire.[44] The winding down of the Gulf conflict had set these journalists free to cover other related stories.[45] Furthermore, in a unique departure from its normal restrictions, Turkey allowed journalists, with their television cameras and portable satellite dishes, access to the unfolding crisis.[46] The "open television coverage" afforded by the coalescing of these elements proved to be a "major factor in motivating coalition governments to intervene in establishment of 'safe havens' inside Iraq."[47] In the case of the Kurdish refugees in 1991, global television's access and autonomy ultimately would shift the power of agenda-setting away from political leaders and toward the real-time media and public opinion.[48]

Within a matter of days, the plight of the Kurdish refugees became a high visibility crisis. By the end of March 1991, the BBC had a camera crew on the ground in northern Iraq, the first news organization to do so. Although reports had appeared earlier in the print media, it was left to the power of television images to transform the Kurds from being merely rebels opposed to the Iraqi government into victims of Saddam's merciless repression. By April 3 the Kurdish crisis dominated television news.[49]

The Kurds' heightened visibility via television directly linked Western leaders to the hapless plight of the victims on the screen. The imagery was powerful: pictures of horrific suffering in northern Iraq's freezing mountains and of crowds outside the White House protesting Bush's refusal to help the Kurds, juxtaposed with pictures of Bush golfing in Florida while denying any obligation to help. Even though television reporters and anchors made no overt calls for Western action, the moral construction afforded by the television imagery created a compelling case that the West ought to help. Walter Wriston summed up the impact of television:

> [The Kurd's] plight never attracted the attention of the world until vivid images of starving children appeared on television screens around the world. While the principle of noninterference in the internal affairs of a sovereign power has long been a tenet of international law, the television images of these pathetic children swept it aside, and allied forces eventually were forced by public pressure to go into Iraq to protect the Kurds and feed the hungry.[50]

The final condition necessary for communications to affect policy — high visibility — was coming into play.[51]

The first Western leader to suggest that the West had some moral responsibility to the Kurds was President François Mitterand of France. Mitterand's personal concern was, at least in part, influenced by his wife, Madame Danielle Mitterand, who had a long-standing interest in helping the Kurds.[52] However, British Prime Minister John Major soon experienced a change of heart on the Kurdish crisis, thanks to global television's exposé.[53] Major's change of policy towards the Kurds is traceable to one

Sunday morning, when he was moved by the television pictures he saw while putting on his socks at the Prime Minister's official residence, No. 10 Downing Street.[54] Major was so moved by the human tragedy that he saw unfolding on the television screen that he defied the advice of British diplomats. Subsequently, Major sketched out his own policy on the back of an envelope en route to a European Community (EC) meeting in Luxembourg, where he worked to persuade both his EC partners and President Bush to create "humanitarian enclaves" within Iraq itself.[55] Although the French had been the first to argue that something should be done to protect the Kurds, Major's presentation to the heads of the EC on April 8 was the first concrete proposal for Western assistance.[56] Thus, global television brought a change in Major's policy, which subsequently changed Western policy towards the Kurds.

Real-time television pictures were also critical to Bush's change in official policy.[57] Bush himself referred to the power of the images pouring out of Kurdistan. During his April 16 news conference, Bush announced what was called a "greatly expanded and more ambitious relief effort."[58] He continued by admitting, "No one can see the pictures or hear the accounts of this human suffering — men, women, and, most painfully of all, innocent children — and not be deeply moved."[59] Bush's Under-Secretary of Defense, Paul Wolfowitz, admitted that the "vividness of television images probably heightened the sense of urgency."[60] Haass, director of Near East and South Asian affairs on Bush's N.S.C. staff, concedes that "[t]elevision and press accounts created public and congressional as well as international calls for a response" to events unfolding in Kurdistan.[61] Haass elaborated on the way in which communications affected the policy that ultimately was adopted by the Bush Administration towards the Kurds:

> [T]elevision probably had the greatest impact at this time in pushing us through the various phases of policy than at any time during the [Gulf] crisis: the need — not just a cynical, political, need, but also just the human need.... The political and the human desire to respond to what was unfolding on the screen had a sizable impact.[62]

Bush's April 16 deployment of U.S. troops and aircraft to protect the Kurds marked a "clear change of policy."[63] However, this change only occurred after the Administration had issued more than half-a-dozen refusals to get involved over a two-week period. In the final analysis, "TV reporting about Iraqi atrocities against the Kurds after the Gulf War placed the Kurdish issue on the international agenda, against all the *realpolitik* wishes of

Western governments."[64] The power of real-time television and public opinion had overcome Bush's—and others'—concerns about the possible dismembering of Iraq, sovereignty, and the lack of a U.N. mandate to intervene.

Global television had been the necessary condition for a change in Western policy toward the Kurds. Lionel Rosenblatt, a former U.S. foreign service officer and the current president of Refugees International, argues that it was not until global television first got access to the Kurdish refugees and then broadcast their plight that a "public constituency" developed in favor of assisting the Kurds.[65] Likewise, Save the Children consultant David Keen contends that "the strong international response in 1991 [to the plight of the Iraqi Kurds] sprang from exceptional circumstances, in particular from the visibility of the Iraqi Kurds (on television)."[66] Former U.S. diplomat and journalist David Pearce concludes that "in the Spring of 1991 televised pictures of Kurdish refugees streaming into Turkey from Iraq ... caused the Bush Administration to reverse a decision not to provide aid."[67] This degree of visibility would not have been possible had real-time television not enjoyed both access to northern Kurdistan and the autonomy to operate there.

The Kurdish rebellion of 1988, however, did not have the visibility that global television afforded the events of 1991. In 1988, upwards of a thousand Kurdish villages were destroyed and thousands of Kurds were gassed, all beyond the visibility of real-time television. According to some scholars, more Kurds died in the 1988 uprisings than in those of 1991, yet no assistance was forthcoming in 1988.[68] Although Saddam's March 1988 use of nerve gas against the Kurds was the largest use ever against civilians, only eleven stories on this subject made it onto the network evening newscasts. Even fewer stories appeared on the networks following Saddam's use of poison gas five months later.[69]

One of the differences between the events of 1988 and 1991 and their respective outcomes was the difference in media access and visibility. In 1988, the fledgling real-time media had virtually no access to the affected regions inside Iraq and had to rely primarily on the accounts of Kurdish refugees who escaped into Turkey. Although other distinctions could be drawn between the events of 1988 and 1991, there was a significant difference in media attention. The magnitude and nature of the 1988 carnage, and its inability to garner significant international attention, provides an instructive comparison with the events of 1991 and the degree of international attention that they attracted. The international community's differing treatment of these two events, when combined with the differing media coverage received by each, argues for the likelihood of media visibility as a primary cause of the international community's response.[70] Global television alone may not have been a sufficient condition to cause this response; it was, however, a necessary condition.

Global Television and Diplomatic Outcomes

The Kurdish refugee crisis demonstrates the potential for communications to affect diplomatic outcomes. According to Gowing, the Kurdish crisis was the first identifiable incidence of television exerting this type of impact upon foreign policy decision-making.[71] Bernard Kouchner was the French Secretary for Health and Humanitarian Action during the Kurdish crisis and is currently serving as the U.N. Mission Chief for Humanitarian Affairs to the war-torn Kosovo region of Yugoslavia. According to Kouchner, the Kurdish crisis was "probably the first time that information saved a people and forced the international community into a humanitarian intervention."[72] Media and politics scholar David L. Paletz argues that "Television coverage of the flight of Iraqi Kurds compelled the administration and its allies to intervene with humanitarian aid."[73] Shaw concludes that the Kurdish intervention "is the only clear-cut case, of all the conflicts in the early 1990s, in which media coverage compelled intervention by the Western powers."[74] Furthermore, Shaw argues that the Kurdish intervention represented a major diversion from planned policy that was "forced overwhelmingly by television."[75] All five necessary conditions for communications to affect policy existed in the 1991 Kurdish case. For perhaps the very first time, communications, in the form of real-time global television, had arguably driven policy.

The Marsh Arab Uprising: The Absence of Global Television's Influence

While the Kurds were saved by global television, the Shiite Muslims who attempted to resist the power of Saddam Hussein became the "Marsh Arabs." The Shiites were forced to flee into the vast marshlands of southern Iraq for protection from Saddam Hussein's repression, without the benefit of global television coverage and its ability to force a humanitarian intervention on their behalf. In 1993, fully two years after the humanitarian intervention on behalf of the Kurds, Amnesty International issued a bitter complaint in a full-page newspaper campaign: "You've probably

never heard of the Marsh Arabs before. You probably never will again."[76]
While serving as the U.S. Ambassador to the U.N., Madeleine Albright
drove to the heart of Amnesty International's complaint by raising a trou-
bling question: "What I'm concerned about is what happens in the non-
CNN wars—those [that] are not on CNN. The question is how the
international community deals with that."[77] The complex humanitarian
emergency involving the Marsh Arabs never made it onto CNN, and the
international community did not deal with it. The lack of visibility meant
that this humanitarian emergency never became a global political crisis.

The Shiite Muslim uprising in Iraq came to a very different end than
did the simultaneous Kurdish rebellion. The Marsh Arabs were ruthlessly
crushed by Saddam's elite Republican Guard forces. And, unlike the Kurds,
the Shiites would receive no assistance or protection from the West, even
though Saddam's crushing of the Shiah was far more savage than was his
repression of the Kurds.[78] Although accurate numbers are impossible to
come by, some sources claim that upwards of 500,000 Shiites may have
been slaughtered, with as many as 800,000 more displaced and hiding in
the marshes of southern Iraq, and more than 100,000 refugees fleeing to
Iran.[79] The "essential difference" between the Shiite and Kurdish rebellions
and their outcomes was the difference in real-time media attention.[80] Gowing concludes that "[T]he power of TV images during the Kurdish crisis
is confirmed by the west's simultaneous reluctance to take action to protect the Shiah in southern Iraq."[81]

The difference in real-time media coverage is the primary distinction
between these two cases. Other factors may well have been involved, and
some of these are addressed below. However, as was implied by Amnesty
International's advertisement, the West *did* hear a lot about the Kurds
between late March and the end of April 1991, but the West did *not* hear
much about the Shiah between the end of February and the end of April
1991. Furthermore, the West has heard virtually nothing about the Shiites
since. When compared with simultaneous events in Kurdistan, the Shiitic
crisis exemplifies a complex humanitarian emergency that occurred beyond
the reach of real-time television's ability to affect diplomatic outcomes.

A Complex Humanitarian Emergency,
but Not a Global Political Crisis

The internal uprisings against Saddam Hussein following the Gulf War
first began in the southern portion of Iraq. Southern Iraq is home to the bulk
of the Shiah Muslims living in Iraq, second in number only to the Sunni

Muslims as the most common sect of Islam. Although the Shiites constitute a majority of the population in southern Iraq, and a plurality of the Iraqi population at large, they have been largely excluded from Saddam Hussein's secular Baathist Party dictatorship. Hussein's regime depends largely on the Sunni Muslims, who are politically much more powerful in Iraq.[82]

Anti-Saddam rebellions erupted among Shiites in southern Iraq even before the allied coalition began its ground war. On February 10 a crowd in the predominantly Shiite town of Diwaniyya staged the first domestic anti-Saddam uprising of the Gulf War period. Diwaniyya's Shiitic rebels protested Saddam's refusal to relinquish Kuwait, shouted anti-Saddam slogans, and killed ten officials of Saddam's ruling Ba'th party. On February 15 George Bush made his explicit call for either the Iraqi people or military to rise up and take matters into their owns hands and topple Saddam. On February 24, two weeks after the first Shiitic revolt, the U.S.-led Gulf War coalition launched its ground offensive inside Iraq itself. Within a matter of days, coalition troops liberated Kuwait and occupied the southeastern one-fifth of Iraq.[83]

By March 1 civil unrest was spreading across Iraq, and was of sufficient gravity to threaten Saddam's regime. In the closing days of the ground campaign, unrest had erupted in Basra, Iraq's second largest city and one that had a predominantly Shiah population. Soldiers returning from the war were also staging anti-Saddam demonstrations in Baghdad. Several signs pointed to the fact that Saddam was losing control, especially in the Shiite south and the Kurdish north, but in Baghdad as well. The Shiite uprising had pre-dated that of the Kurds and spread very quickly to other southern cities such as Nasiriyah and the Shiah holy cities of Najaf and Karbala. By March 3 the uprising had gained considerable momentum among the Shiites of the south, who had endured not only Saddam's continued repression but the brunt of Iraq's eight year war with Iran. On March 7 the Iraqi government made its first public admission that it was facing a serious internal revolt.[84]

Events soon began to conspire against the Shiah. On March 3 Iraqi senior military commanders met to discuss armistice arrangements with the commander of coalition forces, General Norman Schwarzkopf. During these negotiations, Schwarzkopf made what, at the time, appeared to be a very limited and reasonable concession to the Iraqi commanders. Given the devastation wreaked by the coalition on Iraq's internal communication and transport system, Schwarzkopf agreed to allow the Iraqis to fly helicopters, even those that were armed, inside of Iraq. Although this appeared to be a simple gesture at the time, Schwarzkopf's concession virtually sealed the fate of the Shiitic uprising.[85]

The Iraqis began airlifting elite Republican Guard forces into Basra on the same day that Schwarzkopf made his seemingly innocuous concession. In addition, they immediately deployed Soviet-made helicopter gunships against the Shiah as had been so effectively employed by the Soviet Union in Afghanistan. The Republican Guard plunged into its job of putting down the Shiites with particular ferocity and brutality, eager to redeem itself from its poor showing during the Gulf War. Cities were reduced to rubble by shelling from artillery and tanks. Women and children were indiscriminately shot. Tens of thousands were randomly killed. The total casualties will never be known, but, whatever the total, most scholars are agreed on one fact: Saddam's crushing of the combined Kurdish and Shiitic uprisings exacted more Iraqi deaths than did the entire Persian Gulf War.[86]

By late March the Shiite uprising had been effectively put down, although sporadic fighting continued in pockets of resistance. Many of the remaining rebels and their families fled into the relative safety of the surrounding marshes. According to the official U.S. Army history of the Gulf War, a good deal of the fighting and slaughter occurred within full view of U.S. forces, who watched the Republican Guard kill thousands of their fellow Iraqis just across the military demarcation line established by the armistice.[87] No one seriously proposed that protection be extended to the Shiites.

The repression of the Shiah constituted a complex humanitarian emergency, but failed to achieve global crisis status. The Shiites had had the misfortune of staging a non-CNN war. Therefore, the international community had come under no public pressure to deal with it, as Ambassador Albright implied in her rhetorical question cited above. British Foreign Secretary Douglas Hurd admitted during the early days of the Gulf crisis that, "like it or not, television images are what forces foreign policy makers to give one of the current 25 crises in the world greater priority."[88] Another British official echoed what had been dubbed as "Hurd's Law:" "We are under no pressure to do something about crises that are not on TV."[89] The Shiite uprising had occurred just over the horizon from real-time television and its high visibility. Therefore, the uprising lacked an essential requirement for becoming a global crisis.[90] Rather than becoming a global political crisis, the anti-Saddam Shiah Iraqis became merely the Marsh Arabs.

Fast-Breaking Events and a Lack of Leadership

The Shiite uprising was effectively over by the end of March. It had spread quickly, but lasted only one month. The speed and extent of its reach had caught not only the leadership in Baghdad by surprise, but the leadership in Washington, as well.

True, on February 15 Bush had encouraged the Iraqi people to rise up and topple Saddam. And, whether as a direct result of Bush's call or not, the Shiites had engaged in an anti-Saddam revolt. However, some scholars have suggested that Bush did not really intend to encourage either a Shiitic or a Kurdish revolt. Rather, they speculate that Bush, and especially his Turkish and Saudi allies, were hoping that a Sunni general would finally get fed up with Saddam and oust him in a palace coup.[91] History does lend some credence to such a hypothesis, given long-standing U.S. support for militarily imposed stability in other countries.[92]

Still, the Shiitic rebels' objectives are worth noting. The Shiah were involved in a spontaneous uprising directed against Saddam personally. They had no desire to separate from the state of Iraq, unlike the Kurds who had long been seeking their own separate state. In the early stages of the Shiitic revolt, there was no evidence that the civil unrest was coordinated by any one local leader. Neither was there any evidence that the Shiites had been incited by external governments or were stimulated by the weak and divided Iraqi Shiite opposition in exile. Rather, the Shiah were simply demanding political power and representation in the Iraqi government proportionate with their plurality in the population at large.[93]

Furthermore, the Iraqi Shiites had never expressed a desire to establish a fundamentalist Islamic state on the Iranian model. However, by the middle of March, the Shiite government of Iran was beginning to show a clear interest in the unrest inside Iraq. Iran had begun calling upon Saddam to resign and, according to Kuwaiti and other allied officials, Iran began to provide humanitarian and military aid to the Shiitic rebels at this point. But the basic Shiite goal often had been expressed by their leaders: Their revolt was directed against Saddam personally, and not against the Iraqi state. The Shiah were engaged in the very type of anti-Saddam revolt for which George Bush had called on February 15.[94]

The Bush Administration persistently advanced concerns about the potential dismembering of Iraq as a justification for not intervening on behalf of either the Kurds or Shiites. Yet, in the case of the Shiah, this was a hollow justification. The Shiites had never sought to separate from Iraq. Rather, they had adopted their primary identity as that of being Iraqis. The Kurds, however, have long-standing aspirations for self-rule and have engaged in several revolts aimed at achieving that specific end. Given the respective political objectives of the Kurds and the Shiah, and the Bush Administration's oft-expressed concerns about dismembering Iraq, one would have expected the administration to aid the Shiites rather than the

Kurds. However, the administration rescued the Kurds and abandoned the Shiah to Saddam.[95]

The Bush Administration declined to engage in any talks with the Shiitic opposition. On March 12 a senior U.S. diplomat sketched the U.S. official position: "Better the Saddam Hussein we know than an unwieldy coalition, or a new strong man who is an unknown quantity."[96] Laurie Millroy, an analyst with the Washington Institute on Near East Policy, argued that the U.S. government was "paying the price for an inexplicable failure to talk to the Iraqi opposition... With tens of thousands of people dying within Iraq, we should be giving close air support to the rebels."[97] Shiite frustration with U.S. inaction was correspondingly expressed by one rebel: "Bush said that we should rebel against Saddam. We rebelled against Saddam, but where is Bush? Where is he?"[98] By the end of March many of the large coalition combat units had left southern Iraq. By May 8 all coalition armed forces had departed without ever having extended any assistance to the Shiah.[99]

The events that transpired in southern Iraq during late February and early March caught the Bush Administration without a clearly defined policy for such contingencies. Most evidence suggests that the administration made a political decision to remove any hint of support for the uprisings, effectively signaling Saddam that he had a green light from the coalition to move against the rebels however he saw fit.[100] The U.S. openly publicized both its "hands-off" policy with regard to the rebels and its plans for the withdrawal of troops from southern Iraq.[101] An extensive analysis of the Shiite uprising and the lack of any U.S. response to it, has led one observer to conclude that

> Coalition leaders, especially Bush, must however take a great share of responsibility for the disaster. They had deliberately stoked the fires of revolt, hoping that popular dissatisfaction would lead to a *coup d'état* in which new Iraqi leaders would sue for peace on Western terms. They had deliberately allowed ambiguity to exist about their war aims, so that while their manifest goal was liberating Kuwait, they appeared to have the covert aim of toppling Saddam. They could not express surprise when many of the long-suffering Iraqi people took the opportunity of the coalition victory to press their own cause. They were faced with a direct choice at the end of February, when it was clear that US-led forces could make the difference between success or failure of the revolt. Bush chose to halt the West's war and leave the people of Basra to their fate.[102]

Whatever else may be said, Bush's call for the Iraqi people to force Saddam aside had not anticipated any protection or assistance for an anti-Saddam

Shiitic revolt. The nature, and speed, of the events that unfolded in the immediate aftermath of the Gulf War exposed a gap between official U.S. policy and events on the ground inside Iraq.

The memoirs of two principals within the Bush Administration suggest the absence of any clear policy toward internal uprisings in Iraq. Bush's Secretary of State, James Baker, provides essentially a parallel comparison of both the Kurdish and Shiite uprisings.[103] Baker admits that the administration was being criticized for not doing enough to protect both revolts, for allegedly having incited the revolts, and then for having abandoned both to Saddam's repression.[104] Baker contends that the U.S. was fearful of dismembering Iraq and he recognizes that the Kurds clearly had separatist political ambitions. He subsequently assesses the potential pitfalls associated with further U.S. military involvement in Iraq and argues that the operative concern was that the war was over and that it should not be restarted. However, Baker then moves to a description of how the U.S. launched, on behalf of the Kurds inside of Iraq, the "largest military relief operation ever undertaken."[105] Aside from oblique suggestions that the Shiah were perceived as aligned with Iran and that by helping them the U.S. might be helping the ayatollahs in Tehran, Baker provides no further indication as to why a commensurate relief operation was not mounted on behalf of the Shiites.

According to N.S.C. adviser Haass, the U.S. had neither the political nor the legal mandate to get involved.[106] Getting involved might have led to an open-ended commitment or the breakup of Iraq. Yet, in the same analysis, he states that the U.S. overcame its reluctance and intervened on the part of the Kurds—with no mention being made of the open-ended commitment that this represented to protecting a de facto Kurdish state within Iraq.[107] No further mention is made of the fate of the Shiah following their February-March 1991 uprising. Neither is there any mention of why the U.S. failed to intervene on their behalf.

Haass concludes by discussing the overall efficacy of humanitarian intervention. He judges the international community as having been "wrong" in not doing more to stop Hitler in Germany and Pol Pot's bloody communist rule in Cambodia, and as having been "right" in intervening to protect the Kurds in 1991.[108] Given Haass's analysis, one wonders whether it would have been wrong or right to intervene on behalf of the Shiah. Haass fails to address this subject.

However, Haass and Baker both provide evidence for one of the distinguishing factors of U.S. policy toward the Kurds and the Shiites: television coverage. Baker admits that heavy media attention was the impetus for his seven-minute visit to one of the Kurdish refugee camps in the

mountains of northern Iraq.[109] Haass directly implicates television coverage as the decisive variable. He argues that "[t]elevision and press accounts
created public and congressional as well as international calls for a response
[to the Kurdish crisis].... As a result ... the United States overcame its
reluctance to get involved more directly."[110] Furthermore, Haass contends
that in northern Iraq "scenes of misery helped draw in the United States."[111]
The Shiah, while as miserable as the Kurds, did not have television to draw
the U.S. in and to help overcome its reluctance to intervene.

No Global Television, No Visibility, No Influence

George Bush and Western public opinion, which might have
demanded assistance for the Shiites, lay just beyond the reach of real-time
television and its potential ability to affect diplomatic outcomes. Shaw
concludes that the "unfilmability of Basra and the other southern cities was
the central difference in Western responses compared to Kurdistan. The
majority of Shiitic refugees fled to Iran, which media organizations
regarded largely as a no-go area."[112] Gowing argues that "Access to the
southern marshes by TV reporters and crews was impossible. As a result
there were no TV images and there was no pressure for western action."[113]
The absence of real-time global television was a primary difference between
these two crises and suggests the probable difference in their respective outcomes.

Although the Shiah uprisings occurred largely beyond the logistical
reach of global television, a few print journalists did make it into Southern Iraq and provided the bulk of what little information the outside world
had on the unfolding humanitarian emergency. However, these journalists were operating in areas not under the control of coalition troops, faced
significant personal danger, and were often subject to detention by Iraqi
government troops. John Simpson of the British Broadcasting Corporation (BBC) made a revealing admission: "By comparison with the Kurds,
the predicament of the Shi'ite people has had very little attention in the
outside world. That is not surprising: there have been no pictures of the
suffering of the Shi'ite refugees; the Iraqi government has seen to that,"
even though the Shiite rebellion "was far greater and cost many more lives
than the Kurdish uprising."[114] The Shiite uprising went unfilmed.[115]

The simple fact that Kurdish suffering could be visually displayed
marked a primary distinction between these two humanitarian emergencies. Bush himself underscored this fact when on August 16, while announcing the largest military relief operation in U.S. history, he conceded the

impact of the television pictures pouring out of Kurdistan.[116] Television put Western political leaders on the spot and linked them to the suffering of the Kurdish rebels. In Western public perception, the Kurds first became refugees from the Republican Guard's onslaught and then they became victims of Saddam's ruthlessness. Most importantly, the Kurds ultimately became victims of having believed Western political leaders' hollow encouragement. The Kurds' status as victims was further enhanced by the West's subsequent dallying in the face of the complex humanitarian emergency that unfolded nightly on our television screens. The Kurds had received the requisite visibility to transform them from rebels into victims.[117]

The Shiites, however, never enjoyed the high visibility that comes with real-time global television coverage. Video cameras and satellite dishes did not make it to southern Iraq. Consequently, knowledge about the uprisings in southern Iraq was severely limited, and the prevailing Western perception was that of the Shiah as rebels and insurgents. Unfortunately, the Shiites who fled to Iran before the Republican Guard's onslaught failed to achieve refugee status in the court of Western public opinion; never did the Shiah achieve victim status commensurate with that accorded the Kurds. The primary factor — real-time television — that transformed the Kurds from rebels into victims was not available for the arguably more brutalized Shiites.[118]

Alternative/Additional Causal Variables

This chapter has argued that real-time television coverage was the probable cause of the different outcomes in the Kurdish and Shiite cases. However, three alternative causes have also been advanced: the special U.S. relationship with Turkey, a North Atlantic Treaty Organization (NATO) ally; the impediments to helping rebels in southern Iraq, or the so-called "feasibility factor"; and U.N. Security Council Resolution 688. According to those who advance these alternative arguments, concrete national interests were responsible for the U.S. intervention on behalf of the Kurds. Likewise, the absence of such interests was also responsible for the lack of any intervention on behalf of the Shiites.[119]

Turkey, a staunch NATO ally, was unable to deal with the magnitude of the complex humanitarian emergency unfolding on its border with Iraq. Turkey also has a Kurdish minority of its own that would not have looked favorably on continued Turkish inaction. Furthermore, Turkey had concerns about fueling Kurdish separatist ambitions among its own Kurdish

population. Hence, when Turkish President Turgut Ozal called for safe
havens for the Iraqi Kurds, he called for them inside Iraq and not Turkey.
Certainly, Turkey's relationship with the U.S. and NATO contributed to
Western interest in solving the complex humanitarian emergency unfolding on Turkey's borders.[120]

The feasibility factor also affected efforts to intervene on behalf of the
Kurds: Turkey provided a major staging point for U.S. operations on behalf
of the Kurds in northern Iraq. In contrast, the coalition's Gulf State partners, such as Saudi Arabia, were dubious about hosting a military operation on behalf of the Shiah for fear of fanning the flames of Islamic
fundamentalism within their own countries.[121] These facts also contributed
to a Western inclination to help in matters involving Turkey.

U.S. relations with Iran were also different from those between the U.S.
and Turkey. The Bush Administration and Western governments had concerns about the Islamic fundamentalist government of Iran, concerns that
no doubt affected the West's calculus regarding the Shiites in 1991. At the
same time, the West recognized that Iran's role during the 1991 Gulf War
had generally been helpful to the allied coalition's efforts. Furthermore,
both the U.S. and Britain were working behind the scenes with Iran and
remained hopeful that Iranian good graces could help secure the release
of Western hostages from Lebanon. Iran also assisted significantly with the
Kurdish refugee crisis, even though it already had more refugees than any
other country in the world, including 600,000 Kurdish refugees from previous Iraqi repressions. Unlike Turkey, however, which had stopped the
fleeing Kurds at its border with Iraq, Iran opened its borders to an additional one million Kurdish refugees during the 1991 crisis.[122]

However, the Shiitic humanitarian emergency did not occur inside
Iran. Rather, it occurred in southern Iraq very near sizable U.S. and coalition military elements.[123] The city of Basra, the epicenter of the Shiitic
uprising, was just thirty-five miles from the furthest U.S. advance into
southern Iraq.[124] Much of the Republican Guard's worst repression of the
Shiites occurred in full view of American forces from across the armistice
military demarcation line, according to the U.S. Army's official history of
the Gulf War.[125] True, the war was over and the U.S. was strongly disposed
to bring the troops home. But had all other things been equal, this pre-
disposition should have operated with equal intensity in northern Iraq
where the Kurdish refugees were located.

However, subsequent history suggests that feasibility alone did not
preclude intervention on behalf of the Shiah. Within a year and a half the
Bush Administration had overcome its concerns about feasibility, Iran,
and Islamic fundamentalism. In August 1992, the U.S. extended protection

over southern Iraq. A no-fly zone was provided over southern Iraq to protect the Shiah against a new round of repression by Saddam. Operation "Southern Watch," as it was dubbed, was no small undertaking: it covered nearly seven million people and all of Iraq below the thirty-second parallel. Operation Southern Watch extended U.S. air coverage over thirty-five percent of Iraq's total territory.[126] Any Iraqi aircraft flying below the thirty-second parallel were to be shot down by U.S. aircraft.[127] The logistical feasibility that facilitated Southern Watch in August 1992 would have been equally available to provide protection during Saddam's 1991 repression of the Shiites. However, by August 1992, the official U.S. position toward the Shiah had been re-evaluated. The Shiites were now referred to as "Iraqis first, not separatists," and as "a persecuted people and not necessarily the precursor of a radical Islamic state that would align itself with Iran."[128] The feasibility of protecting the Shiites in 1991 appears to have been impeded primarily by previous policy, rather than logistical concerns.

Some have alleged that United Nations Security Council Resolution 688 effectively bound the U.S. to act inside Iraq on behalf of the Kurds.[129] Resolution 688 was passed on April 5, 1991, largely on the initiative of Turkey and France. This resolution paved the way for foreign interference in domestic Iraqi affairs. Although this resolution specifically condemned Iraq's repression of its Kurdish population, it also condemned the "repression of the Iraqi civilian population in many parts of Iraq" and insisted that Iraq allow immediate access "to all those in need of assistance in all parts of Iraq."[130] Therefore, nothing in Resolution 688 itself would have differentiated between involvement in northern Iraq on behalf of the Kurds and similar involvement in the predominantly Shiite south.

Resolution 688 may have provided welcome, official sanction for U.S. action in northern Iraq. However, it is doubtful that this resolution alone compelled the U.S. to undertake the largest military relief operation in the history of the republic. History suggests that U.S. military operations are determined by U.S. strategic interests, and not specific U.N. authorization or lack thereof. For example, the U.S. has, on prior occasions, chosen to violate a country's national sovereignty for humanitarian reasons, and it has done so without Security Council approval. Andrew Natsios, currently vice president of World/Vision and the Bush Administration's former assistant administrator of the U.S. Agency for International Development (USAID) and director of its Foreign Disaster Assistance Office, contends that on five separate occasions the administration "violated national sovereignty" to deliver relief commodities to those at risk: Iraq, Somalia, Angola, Sudan, and Ethiopia.[131] Only two of these five operations, Iraq and Somalia, were authorized under specific U.N. Security Council Resolutions.

Natsios concludes bluntly that interventions of the Kurdish type do not result from any "carefully fashioned doctrine, but out of practical necessity."[132]

Resolution 688 clearly contained language that would have allowed intervention on behalf of both the Kurds and the Shiah. However, focusing on Resolution 688 obscures two simple facts, given the history of U.S.-U.N. relations and U.S. willingness to violate national sovereignty as necessary for relief operations. First, it seems unlikely that Resolution 688 could have forced the U.S. to undertake any particular action on behalf of the Kurds, had the U.S. not been so inclined. Conversely, the resolution's lack of specific reference to the Shiites is not likely to have precluded U.S. intervention on their behalf, had the U.S. been so inclined.

Ironically, Resolution 688's language was ultimately invoked in August 1992 as legal justification for the U.S. to violate Iraqi sovereignty on behalf of the Shiah. Bush National Security Council staffer Haass cites Resolution 688 as the legal justification for the August 1992 no-fly zone imposed by the U.S. over southern Iraq.[133] In other words, the very language that is alleged to have precluded involvement on behalf of the Shiites in 1991 was, in fact, used to justify involvement when this decision suited U.S. purposes. Therefore, Security Council Resolution 688 may have been, in theory, a causal variable contributing to U.S. involvement on behalf of the Kurds. However, both history and events subsequent to 1991 confirm that Resolution 688 did not, in fact, preclude U.S. involvement on behalf of the Shiites.

Each of the three factors above may well have contributed to U.S. involvement on behalf of the Kurds: Turkey's status as an ally, feasibility, and Resolution 688. Admittedly, each of these factors did favor intervention on behalf of the Kurds. However, had there been no real-time television coverage of the Kurdish crisis, would the U.S. still have intervened as it did? The evidence presented in this chapter suggests that the U.S. probably would not have done so. Conversely, had the Shiah received extensive television exposure, would the outcome have been the same, given that none of the three factors discussed above precluded intervention on their behalf? This analysis concludes that the outcome may well have been different for the Shiites, had there been significant real-time coverage.

The weight of the evidence suggests that the presence of real-time global television was the necessary causal variable in Western intervention to protect the Kurds. Arguably, the absence of real-time media coverage of the Shiitic uprisings was a factor in the West's lack of intervention on their behalf in 1991; the similarity, simultaneity, and juxtaposition of these two crises supports such an argument. Real-time communications was probably a primary factor in the respective outcome of each crisis. In the case of the 1991 Kurdish crisis, communications exerted an effect on the diplomatic outcome. In the case of the Shiites, global television was notable by its absence. Thus, quite a different outcome befell the Shiah, something which still contributes to Shiah resentment "long after the end of the Gulf War."[134] Global communications had demonstrated its ability to influence policy.

However, there are limits to this ability, as events three years later in Rwanda would demonstrate. The same necessary causal variable that prompted intervention on behalf of the Kurds, global television, was also present during the 1994 Rwandan genocide. Yet, Rwanda experienced a markedly different outcome. Despite extensive media coverage, no international intervention was forthcoming on behalf of Rwandans; they were left to slaughter each other.

Rwanda: The Limits to Global Television's Ability to Drive Policy

Although the Kurdish and Shiitic cases suggest that communications now has the ability to affect diplomatic outcomes under certain conditions, the 1994 genocide in Rwanda demonstrates the limits of this ability. Unlike the case of the Kurdish refugees, no international intervention was forthcoming on behalf of the Rwandans. Each of the five conditions required for communications to influence policy were present. Yet, no discernible effect on policy occurred during the genocidal phase of Rwanda's humanitarian tragedy.

The Rwandan genocide continued apart from international intervention for two reasons. First, during the genocide Rwandans never achieved "living victim status" in Western public sentiment.[135] The subjects of humanitarian tragedies must become "living victims" if global television is to affect policy. However, the Rwandan genocide provided no such victims. The graphic pictures that emanated from Rwanda during the genocide largely portrayed dead corpses "clogging rivers and lakes."[136] Rwanda's genocide only provided dead victims.

Second, Rwanda was not perceived as "do-able" during the genocide, given the issues at stake and the risks involved. In other words, the leading members of the international community judged that intervening inside of Rwanda itself entailed risks that exceeded those justified by national interest or any reasonable degree of humanitarian concern. Any intervention by outside powers ultimately depends upon a cost-benefit analysis that weighs the potential risks against the potential national and/or strategic interests at stake.

The lack of perceived "do-ability" was especially true on the part of the U.S. government, according to former National Security Council staffer Richard Haass.[137] As a result, the U.S. equivocated. This hesitancy contributed to stalling the deployment of a largely African U.N. force to intervene in Rwanda during the genocide, according to former Assistant Secretary of State for African Affairs Herman Cohen.[138] Given the necessity of U.S. leadership for international intervention to occur in situations such as Rwanda, the balance of this section will focus largely on U.S. policy toward the Rwandan genocide.

Humanitarian benefits are secondary to considerations of national interest in intervention decisions. For the U.S., the risks in Rwanda were significantly greater than the perceived likelihood of any successful end to the genocide. And the U.S. had no perceived vital strategic or national interests at stake in Rwanda.[139] In other words, given the risks involved *vs.* the issues at stake, the U.S. determined that a successful intervention in Rwanda was not "do-able." Therefore, Rwanda's genocide went largely unaddressed by the U.S. and, subsequently, the international community. Ultimately, Rwanda illustrates that the absence of "victim status" or the "do-ability" factor will restrict, if not prevent, real-time television's ability to influence policy outcomes.

Communications failed to affect policy toward the 1994 Rwandan genocide because of these two limiting factors, even though the five conditions required for communications to do so were present. Rwanda was a complex humanitarian emergency that quickly became a global political crisis. Events in Rwanda unfolded with such speed that the international community, and the U.S. political leadership in particular, was left groping for a policy to address the genocide. Furthermore, Rwanda became the subject of significant and graphic media coverage. Yet, for all its potential susceptibility to communications' influence, Rwanda's genocide demonstrated the limits to global television's policy influence.

A Complex Humanitarian Emergency and a Global Political Crisis

On April 6, 1994, the presidents of Rwanda and Burundi were killed. The airplane in which they were riding was downed near the Rwandan capital, Kigali, by two shoulder-fired anti-aircraft missiles.[140] No one has ever claimed responsibility for the downing of the aircraft. All aboard were killed.

Both presidents had been members of the Hutu tribe. The Hutus constituted a majority of the Rwandan population as well as monopolizing state power.[141] The death of Rwandan President Juvenal Habyaramina became the trigger for what had apparently been a pre-planned, systematic campaign of genocide by Hutus against the minority tribe in Rwanda, the Tutsis. At least 800,000, and perhaps as many as 1,000,000, Tutsi and moderate Hutus were slaughtered in Rwanda in 100 days.[142] The killings were conducted at a rate that outstripped the abilities of history's most efficient murderers: Hitler's Jewish dead accumulated at only one-third the rate at which Rwandan killings were carried out, and Pol Pot had taken four years to accumulate similar numbers of Cambodian dead.[143] Panic set in, prompting a mass refugee flow. Within one two day at the end of April, 400,000 mostly Tutsi Rwandans fled into Taneonia.[144] The mass murders only stopped when a Tutsi army, called the Rwandan Patriotic Front (RPF), arrived to conquer the country and stem the tide of violence.[145] The RPF, and not any outside intervention, brought a conclusion to the genocide phase of the Rwandan tragedy.[146]

The succeeding phase of the Rwandan tragedy entailed a mass human exodus of equally historic proportions. As the Tutsi RPF consolidated its hold on power inside Rwanda, Hutus in Rwanda feared revenge from the army that had quelled the mass killing of Tutsis. As a result, Hutus began pouring over the border into neighboring countries. Zaire began receiving refugees at rates as high as 15,000 persons per hour. In one forty-eight hour period period during late July, 800,000 refugees fled into Zaire through the border town of Goma. Out of a total pre-April 1994 population of 8 million Rwandans, upwards of 1 million had been killed, some 2 million had become refugees, and a significant number of Rwandans were also displaced within their own country.[147]

The sheer number of refugees, and the speed with which they arrived, overwhelmed the host countries. People were forced to live in uninhabitable spaces. Refugees began dying at significant rates because of a lack of clean water and the resulting cholera and dysentery. Jim Wooten of ABC News described the horror of the refugee camps where tens of thousands died of cholera: "For seven days human beings were constantly falling all around us. In many cases, we and the lenses of our cameras were the very last things they saw in the very last moments of their lives. It was an excruciating dilemma."[148] The second phase of the Rwandan tragedy had begun: the refugee phase.[149]

Both phases in the Rwandan situation were obviously complex humanitarian emergencies. And, both phases also became global political crises. As is detailed in sections 4) and 5) below, Rwanda received sufficient coverage in the global media to afford it the visibility requisite to becoming a global political crisis.[150] Most of the global television coverage was of the something-must-be-done nature, with its implicit calls for international intervention.[151] Yet only the refugee phase of the Rwandan disaster prompted any significant international intervention. The calls for intervention to stop the genocide inside Rwanda went unheeded, despite extensive media coverage of the carnage.

The international community had had a presence in Rwanda prior to the beginning of the April 1994 genocide. A United Nations peacekeeping force arrived in October 1993 to maintain a fragile truce that had been negotiated between Hutus and Tutsis to quell a three-year-old Tutsi insurgency.[152] U.N. forces were initially reduced from 2,500 to 450 as the genocide began, with this remnant largely responsible for insuring the safe departure of the remaining westerners.[153]

However, calls from the international community for intervention mounted quickly as the genocide was unleashed. Non-governmental organizations (NGOs) made increased and repeated calls for U.S. leadership to stop the killing during the genocide, which the Clinton Administration refused to do.[154] In the midst of the genocide, the United Nations Security Council called for the deployment of troops to Rwanda.[155] The proposed U.N. force would have consisted of 5,500 troops composed of Africans who were willing to take on the difficult and dangerous assignment.[156] The African countries that had volunteered troops for the operation requested airlifts to move their troops to Rwanda along with armored personnel carriers.

Although the U.S. initially agreed to these requests, it subsequently dragged its feet for four months.[157] U.S. equivocation on the proposed troop deployments centered on whether U.N. troops should be given the strong mandate required to successfully operate in Rwanda. Ultimately, U.S. foot dragging resulted in the forces not being assembled and deployed until after the genocide phase was over. Catherine Newbury has argued that "in 1994, the United States decided not to support a United Nations proposal to intervene in strife-torn Rwanda. This inaction meant that state-sponsored genocide was allowed to run its course."[158] A lack of U.S. political leadership had largely prevented the organized international community from acting during the genocide in Rwanda.[159]

France was the only country to intervene inside of Rwanda. Two months into the genocide France launched a unilateral military operation in southwestern Rwanda to create a safe haven for the terrified population.[160] France's Operation *Turquoise* established a security zone in southern Rwanda that saved many lives, protected internally displaced persons, provided 10,000 tons of humanitarian supplies, and buried thousands of bodies.[161] Operation *Turquoise* demonstrated what could be accomplished on short notice with a highly professional and well motivated military force.[162] Civilian and military experts have concluded that a credible military force of 5,000 dispatched during the early, critical two weeks of the genocide from April 7-21 could have "squelched the violence [and] prevented its spread from the capital to the countryside."[163] Although international pressure for intervention was present, the will to do so was largely absent amongst the major powers, particularly the U.S. With the notable exception of France, no intervention was forthcoming to attempt to stem the genocide.

However, international assistance poured into Rwanda from governments and international aid agencies alike when the crisis shifted from one involving genocide to one involving refugees.[164] The "politics of pity" now moved international relief efforts into high gear. Rwandans had become living victims, which prompted an international response to the refugees that approached "ludicrous proportions."[165] During fiscal 1995, twelve international relief agencies each had budgets in excess of $10 million in Rwanda. CARE alone had $14 million to spend in a twelve-month period, a figure that surpassed the entire budget for the government of Rwanda.[166]

U.S. vacillation was, however, apparent even during the refugee phase. Once genocide gave way to a refugee crisis, the Clinton Administration dispatched 2,350 troops to Rwanda. The U.S. ordered a massive airlift to assist the U.N. and NGOs in stopping the dying in the refugee camps.[167] But U.S. troops were employed strictly for logistical purposes, transporting and assembling equipment and pipe to provide clean water for refugees in the Goma camps.[168] Furthermore, U.S. troops had to be withdrawn prematurely because their budgetary support was exhausted. The Administration had failed to ensure adequate funding for it to be able to deliver on even this modest offer of assistance.[169] Human Rights Watch consultant Kathi Austin contends that the U.S.'s late but sudden efforts were motivated by guilt:

> [Such efforts were] as much as a palliative for failed intervention during the genocide as [they were] to prevent a medical epidemic. Sending in the U.S. military and giving the humanitarian effort a 'new' military look was planned to gloss over the U.S. policy failure to prevent and stop the genocide.[170]

U.S. policy toward Rwanda suffered from a lack of clarity and consistency during both phases of the crisis.

Distinguishing between the genocide and the refugee phases of the Rwandan crisis is central to understanding the limits of global television's ability to influence policy. Julia Taft, president of InterAction, a coalition of 150 U.S.-based NGOs, has observed that when pictures were shown of Rwandans "being hacked to death," private relief groups received very little in the way of donations from the viewing public.[171] However, when Rwandan refugees flooded into Zaire, the pictures of "women and children, ... innocents in need" produced overwhelming financial responses, according to Taft.[172] The Rwandans who survived the genocide had achieved the status of living victims who presented the international community with relatively easy and "do-able" options for assistance.

Both phases of the Rwandan tragedy clearly met the criteria for a global political crisis. There was a "world-wide *perception*" of indiscriminately violating internationally accepted human rights norms.[173] And these violations resulted in significant calls for international intervention to redress the problems that quickly unfolded inside Rwanda.[174] Global television had afforded both crises high visibility. Yet the influence of real-time television was markedly different between the two phases. The Rwandan refugee crisis illustrated the ability of global television to affect diplomatic outcomes, while the genocide illustrated the limits to this ability. The balance of this chapter addresses the genocide phase of the Rwandan crisis and the reasons that communications failed to influence policy.

Fast-Breaking Events and a Lack of Leadership

As outlined above, this project contends that a policy lacking clarity and consistency suggests the type of confusion indicative of an absence of leadership. However, the sheer rush of events alone can be sufficient to create a leadership vacuum. The genocide inside Rwanda occurred with lightning speed; historic numbers of people were killed in equally unprecedented periods of time.[175] But factors in addition to the rush of events contributed to the leadership vacuum toward Rwanda: the "Somalia Syndrome" and the prospect that a Rwandan intervention would have required heavily armed combat troops.

In April 1994, the U.S. was operating in the backwash of the Somalia Syndrome. "Somalia Syndrome" has become shorthand in the defense and foreign policy establishments for a humanitarian mission that runs amok. Such a mission draws the U.S. ever deeper into political infighting within the host country, all without a precise objective that defines the mission's endpoint. In other words, the Somalia Syndrome involves U.S. troops being drawn into a neverending cycle of political reprisals, but without any clear exit strategy.

In December 1992 the U.S. undertook what was billed as a bold mission for a new world order. A U.S.-led military intervention was launched in Somalia to insure the delivery of humanitarian relief supplies to this drought-stricken and starving nation. However, Somalia was a failed state: its government had ceased to exist, as had the civil society and order that comes with government. In the wake of government's demise, humanitarian relief supplies had become hostage to feuding Somali warlords. These supplies were often prohibited from being unloaded at Somali docks, left to rot within sight of people starving to death; or were stolen by the bands of thugs who did the warlords' bidding. Although the U.S. mission was launched as part of a new world order (i.e., maintaining order in the post-Cold War world), its conclusion left U.S. policymakers dubious about future humanitarian military interventions.

In October 1993, 18 American Army Rangers were killed during a battle to capture Somali warlord Mohammed Farah Aidid. The Rangers' deaths prompted calls for the withdrawal of American troops from Somalia. Subsequently, the Clinton Administration announced its intention to withdraw all U.S. troops from Somalia by early 1994. This withdrawal had just been completed when the Rwandan genocide began.

John Prendergast, an international aid and development scholar, has argued that the "fruitless, violent hunt for Aidid in Somalia undoubtedly played" a role in the lack of political leadership to counter the genocide in Rwanda.[176] According to one Pentagon official, "exit strategy" became the mantra for U.S. interventions: "I can't overemphasize how those two words drove policy on intervention after Somalia."[177] And the Rwandan genocide provided no self-evident exit strategy. As a result, the Somalia Syndrome "inhibited further American participation in or leadership of humanitarian and peacekeeping missions, most noticeably during the crisis in Rwanda in 1994."[178] In other words, the perceived lessons of Somalia drove the Clinton Administration's policy toward Rwanda, including unwillingness to dispatch troops to Rwanda; unwillingness to take a leadership position in U.N. decision-making toward Rwanda; foot-dragging over the prospect of giving U.N. troops a strong mandate to operate in Rwanda; and U.S. equivocation and lack of follow-through on the limited, post-genocide commitments that it did finally make. Arguably, the U.S. relied upon the past in Somalia as prologue for Rwanda.

The Rwandan genocide posed the need for heavily armed combat troops similar to those required at the peak of violence in Somalia. This type of humanitarian intervention is sometimes referred to as an imposed intervention. In other words, at least one of the parties to the conflict does not welcome outside intervention and may be expected to oppose it. Therefore, the intervention must be imposed. A consensual intervention, however, occurs with the agreement of all parties to the conflict, and, therefore, requires only unarmed or lightly armed personnel.[179] The U.S. intervention to protect the Kurds in northern Iraq was and is an imposed intervention. Although this intervention has been successfully carried out since April 1991, the U.S. was reluctant to mount such an operation in Rwanda following the Somali debacle.[180] Former Bush Administration official Natsios has concluded that Rwanda was "a crisis where only military intervention could have stopped the genocide."[181] This was precisely the type of intervention the U.S. was reluctant to undertake.

Therefore, the absence of U.S. political leadership toward Rwanda stemmed from the Somalia syndrome, as well as the unprecedented rush of events. John Harriss has charged, with regard to Rwanda, that there was a lack of will amongst the great powers to "commit their military forces—their own citizens—to the pursuit of political objectives which [did] not have to do with their own immediate interests."[182] Strobel has argued that amongst the U.S. leadership, "[w]here the humanitarian and the military converged, caution prevailed."[183] U.S. policy toward Rwanda was to avoid another Somalia. Beyond that, the U.S. had no clear idea of what it wanted to do in Rwanda.

Some have suggested that this reluctance to intervene militarily was, in fact, indicative of U.S. leadership on Rwanda. According to this line of reasoning, U.S. political leaders were firmly against, rather than for, Rwandan involvement.[184] True, leadership can be demonstrated via policies for or against a particular option such as military intervention. And, given U.S. reluctance to intervene, one could plausibly suggest that this stemmed from a clear, consistent U.S. policy against involvement in Rwanda. In other words, some would contend that the reluctance to intervene militarily derived from a firm U.S. policy.

However, the weight of the evidence on Rwanda arguably suggests that the U.S. had no real Rwanda policy. A lack of policy consistency and clarity stems from a leadership vacuum in a particular situation. Several factors indicate that U.S. policy suffered from this lack of consistency and clarity. The U.S. equivocated over whether to allow the strong U.N. mandate that would have been required for African troops to intervene to stop the genocide. In addition, the U.S. initially agreed to provide airlift and armored personnel carriers for these African troops, but then delayed for four months before providing what it had agreed to. U.S. equivocation ultimately stymied the organized international community from acting, although no U.S. troops would have been part of international efforts to stop the genocide. Furthermore, U.S. policy was no more clear or consistent during the refugee phase of the crisis. U.S. troops were employed for logistical purposes only and had to be withdrawn early because of the administration's failure to secure funding sufficient to complete their mission.

This overall degree of equivocation, inconsistency, and lack of clarity arguably did not stem from firm U.S. leadership on Rwanda, even leadership against involvement. Rather, this degree of equivocation suggests that the U.S. had no Rwanda policy. In other words, there was a policy vacuum toward Rwanda in the U.S. political leadership.

High Visibility

The Rwandan genocide received the high visibility necessary for communications to influence policy. Although the media had access to Rwanda, conditions at the time of the genocide did pose significant danger for journalists attempting to cover the story.[185] Prior to April 1994 there was only limited print coverage of the political conditions inside Rwanda. However, as the situation exploded into deliberate genocide, media coverage began to increase.[186] In fact, numerous scholars have characterized the overall media coverage of the Rwandan genocide as extensive.[187]

In fact, Rwanda received more television coverage than did the Somali famine prior to U.S. military intervention. Network evening newscasts mentioned Rwanda more often each month during the genocide than mentioned the famine in Somalia during any single month prior to the U.S. military intervention there in December 1992. During the first two months of genocide, April and May 1994, Rwanda was mentioned in forty-three evening news stories each month. By May 1994 satellite broadcasting facilities were established in the Rwandan capital of Kigali. In June 1994, the final month of the genocide, the total mentions of Rwanda slipped to twenty-seven. By way of contrast, the maximum number of mentions that Somalia received during any one month prior to the U.S. military intervention was thirty-six in the month of August 1992. In fact, during the three months of the genocide, Rwanda received 113 mentions on the network evening newscasts. Somalia and its famine received only ninety-three mentions during the entire eleven-month period from January through November 1992. The result was that "Relentless coverage of inhumanity in ... Rwanda, matching the intensity of that directed toward Somalia in late 1992 and early 1993, failed ... to produce Somali-style interventions" in Rwanda.[188] Given that the Rwandan genocide received more television coverage than did the 1992 Somali famine, clearly it received the necessary coverage to achieve high visibility.[189]

However, coverage of the Rwandan refugee crisis far exceeded that given to the genocide. During the genocide Rwanda received a maximum of forty-three mentions during one month's network evening newscasts. Rwanda garnered sixty-five mentions during the first month of the refugee crisis, tapering off to thirty-eight during the second month. For the balance of 1994, Rwanda virtually dropped off the radar screen, when it garnered only five total mentions during the last four months of 1994.[190] As the crisis moved into the refugee phase there was increasing coverage on Rwanda, both in the electronic and the print media.[191] And this increase in coverage "helped pressure donor governments into acting and sparked a flood of monetary support for the relief agencies."[192] In contrast, the genocide phase elicited no similar response, "despite massive media coverage with scenes of such horror that all previous complex emergencies paled by comparison."[193] Communications had found the limits of its ability to affect diplomatic outcomes.

All of the Conditions; None of the Influence

In the Rwandan genocide, all five conditions necessary for communications to influence diplomatic outcomes were present. This project has established that, given certain conditions, global communications can affect diplomatic outcomes when 1) the situation involves certain high-interest subjects such as complex humanitarian emergencies or global political crises; 2) the events are fast-breaking and/or 3) there is a leadership vacuum; 4) global television has access to the events and relative autonomy of action 5) the situation acquires a high degree of visibility. The events surrounding Rwanda satisfied all five conditions. Yet, extensive television coverage resulted in virtually no international attempts at stopping Rwanda's genocide.

Rwanda demonstrates the limits to communications' ability to drive policy. Two primary limiting factors were identified above. Both of these factors inhibited communications' ability to influence diplomatic outcomes in the case of Rwanda. First, the subjects of media coverage in a global political crisis must be living victims for whom something can be done. And, second, the necessary policies for assisting these victims must be perceived by other governments as "do-able" within a reasonable assessment of risks *vs.* national interests and humanitarian benefits.

Rwanda suggests that apart from bestowing victim status on them, communications may be unable to affect the plight of those suffering in humanitarian crises.[194] Some sense of personal empathy and responsibility is required to move the viewing public to action. David Keen has argued that "A range of evidence — including firsthand accounts from Iraqi Kurds — suggests a powerful western responsibility for the Kurdish uprising in 1991."[195] The Rwandans never garnered the sense of Western responsibility for their plight that the Kurdish refugees were able to achieve.[196] Thus, Rwanda's genocide did not evoke a felt need to intervene among Western viewing publics.

Furthermore, it appeared as if nothing could be done for the hapless subjects of Rwanda's genocide. According to one American reporter, television needs "good people to whom bad things are happening," "innocents in hell" for whom something can be done.[197] The refugee phase of the Rwandan tragedy lent itself to this simplified and "irresistible" television story of "victims in flight."[198] In contrast, the genocide presented grotesque pictures of bodies that had been machetied and clubbed to death as a result of complex and little-understood political causes. Therefore, the genocide did not present the media with the simple, "striking image of helpless living victims."[199] And, lacking these images "needed to mobilize the public," the genocide of April through June "failed to galvanize the public."[200] Rwandans killed in the genocide failed to garner either a sense of Western responsibility or the status of living victims for whom something could be done, as had the Kurds. As result, unlike the Kurdish situation, communications' ability to influence policy toward Rwanda was limited.

However, Rwanda arguably posed less overt risk for those who would attempt to intervene than did the Kurdish case. As noted above, a decisive early Rwandan intervention that employed as few as 5,000 troops might have been successful in stopping the killing, especially given the "lightly armed character of the genocidists."[201] The Kurdish refugee rescue was the largest American humanitarian military relief operation to date, involving 10,000 troops (half of whom were U.S.) and sufficient air cover to ensure that no Iraqi aircraft could operate in the significant portion of Iraq that lay north of the 36th parallel.[202]

But Rwanda also did not possess the national and strategic interests that were present in the Kurdish case. The Rwandan and post-Gulf War Iraqi cases differed significantly on the question of U.S. strategic interests: A NATO ally did not lie just beyond the border of Rwanda, as did Turkey just north of Iraq; the genocidal forces inside Rwanda were not a known and recently vanquished opponent, as were those of Saddam Hussein; and a major U.N. military coalition was not already in place for Rwanda, as it had been in Iraq. Rwanda's lack of U.S. strategic and national interests explains why "the Clinton Administration ... actively resisted the flow of horrific pictures that documented the mass slaughter."[203] Tribal genocide that raged for twelve weeks and that featured terrifying "footage of scores of bodies floating down rivers and the hacking to death of a woman" failed to move the U.S. government to action.[204] The U.S. government had determined that the pictures' demand for action could "not be satisfied without exertions or risks that go well beyond those justified by any sense of national interest or even reasonable humanitarian concern."[205] The risk of humanitarian military intervention in Rwanda was not outweighed by any significant U.S. national interests. In other words, the U.S. determined that Rwanda was not "do-able" during the genocide phase of the tragedy. This lack of "do-ability" also operated to limit communications' ability to influence policy.

However, other factors may also have operated to inhibit communications' effect on diplomatic outcomes. The very nature of the coverage that a particular crisis receives can pose limits on communications' ability to influence policy. The overall media coverage of the genocide was largely devoid of the prolonged buildup from which the Kurdish refugees had benefited in post-Gulf War Iraq. Coverage of Rwanda exploded onto television screens apart from virtually any prior mention of potential problems. This type of coverage is often referred to as "parachute journalism," where journalists with little prior knowledge or background literally drop into a crisis that is already unfolding.[206] Rwanda suffered from such a lack of historical context.

The political context was also lacking. Serious, politically motivated fighting had been going on inside Rwanda since 1990.[207] In addition, warfare between the Hutus and the Tutsis had cost more than 50,000 lives in neighboring Burundi during 1993.[208] The politics of the situation were difficult at best, and virtually defied accurate portrayal on television. A reductionist medium, such as television, requires that the complex be simplified, and lends itself well to black-and-white portrayals of good and evil. Rwanda offered no simple, black-and-white distinctions. Hutu and Tutsis are nearly identical in appearance — at least to Western eyes. As a result, many Hutu genocidists found effective freedom from responsibility for their crimes by seeking safe haven in refugee camps that had been established for Tutsis fleeing the terror inside Rwanda. The genocide was largely committed by Hutus on Tutsis. Yet, some, especially moderate, Hutus also became victims of the genocide because of their failure to participate in the violence committed against the Tutsis. The RPF that halted the genocide was led by Tutsis, but it also contained Hutu. And in a final blurring of the distinctions between good and evil, soldiers of the post-genocide Tutsi-led government killed 3,000 Hutu refugees in a camp inside Rwanda. This same government was, however, officially committed to reconciliation between Hutus and Tutsis.[209] Rwanda did not lend itself to reductionist portrayals.

Rwanda's apparent incongruities defied explanation in most of television's coverage. Early coverage largely depicted the strife inside Rwanda as a "historical feud" between competing ethnic factions and was cast into a simplistic Hutu *vs.* Tutsi format. And, although ethnicity and civil war were both factors in the violence, its genocidal core was clouded during much of the early reporting.[210] Robert I. Rotberg, president of the World Peace Foundation, and Thomas G. Weiss, a former United Nations official, conclude that media coverage of the carnage in Rwanda was "essentially flawed."[211] As a result of global television's largely contextless coverage, the Rwandan crisis failed to achieve the simple identities with Western audiences and governments that might have prompted and sustained intervention.[212]

Some have also suggested that Rwanda was just too remote to elicit the type of Western concern required for intervention — too remote geographically, ethnically, and empathetically. Rwanda is, after all, a tiny central African state that few Americans had heard of prior to April 1994. Furthermore, the killing in Rwanda was committed by blacks against other blacks, which has been suggested as an additional reason for Americans' lack of interest. Alas, Rwanda presented yet another case of African murder and mayhem that suddenly explodes out of nowhere onto the evening news. Given the history of humanitarian crises in Africa, and apart from any historical or contextual build-up, viewers are tempted to regard this as just another in a long string of humanitarian tragedies from the dark continent. The "frantic and sporadic" nature of such coverage can lead to "compassion burnout" and viewer "fatigue."[213] The confusing, contextless events unfolding in Rwanda simply seemed too far removed from the concerns of most Western audiences.[214]

Although communications has the ability to affect diplomatic outcomes under telediplomacy, Rwanda illustrates the limits to that ability. A failure to achieve "living victim status," a lack of "do-ability," and the very nature of global television's coverage itself can mitigate communications' influence upon policy. However, when communications does affect diplomatic outcomes apart from these limiting factors, it exerts its influence through predictable means. The four mechanisms whereby global communications can drive policy are taken up in the following chapter.

Chapter 7

Global Television's Mechanisms for Driving Policy

"The television sets a great deal of the agenda [in foreign policy], and then the President and his Secretary of State have to deal with it."
— *Former U.S. Secretary of State Lawrence Eagleburger, 1994*

"[F]oreign policy does not rest upon a definition of the national interest. It rests on public opinion."
— *Former U.S. Secretary of Defense James Schlesinger, 1989*

The fact that television can potentially affect diplomatic outcomes is not a new proposition. Former White House counsel Lloyd Cutler argued in 1984 that "it came as a distinct surprise to me how much television news had intruded into both the timing and the substance of the policy decisions [especially foreign-policy decisions] that an American president is required to make ... and more than most experienced observers realize."[1] Barbara McDougall, Canadian External Affairs Minister during much of the Yugoslav crisis from 1991 to 1993 contends that, as with many ministers, she did modify foreign-policy because of television coverage. But, when asked specifically how this occurred, McDougall responded, "I am not sure. It is hard to know how our brains reacted."[2] Yet there are identifiable mechanisms whereby global communication exerts its influence on diplomatic outcomes.

Television has the potential to function as an independent actor in foreign policy. Its ability to do so has been enhanced markedly by the development of real-time global television.[3] Bernard C. Cohen pioneered scholarly work on how the media influences foreign policy, including his landmark 1963 work entitled *The Press and Foreign Policy* and his 1973 work, *The Public's Impact on Foreign Policy*. By 1994, Cohen was contending that "television itself has finally become a major force in the media-foreign-policy equation."[4] According to Cohen, "television alone, in pursuit of its own independent and unique norms, can ... force a different set of priorities on policy makers from those they themselves would otherwise prefer."[5] Such was the case with U.S. policymakers during the Kurdish refugee crisis.

Communications' ability to affect diplomatic outcomes is one of telediplomacy's distinguishing characteristics. Global television has the ability to do so both directly and indirectly. Real-time television can directly influence policymakers and the policymaking process by functioning as an agenda-setter, by providing the type of information that is unique to real-time media, and/or by acting as a diplomatic broker. Global television can indirectly affect policy by first influencing public opinion, which subsequently influences policy. This distinction between direct and indirect effects provides a useful framework for analyzing the mechanisms whereby real-time television influences foreign policy. However, in practice both direct and indirect influences are likely to operate at the same time. Thus, while the direct/indirect distinction is a useful analytical tool, both influences operate concurrently in cases where global television drives policy.

Global Television's Direct Effects on Diplomatic Outcomes

Real-Time Television as Agenda-Setter

Television's ability to function as an agenda-setter in foreign-policy was best described by Cohen: the press "may not be successful in telling its readers what to think, but it is stunningly successful in telling its readers what to think about."[6] Global television's instantaneous and pervasive coverage allows it to tell policymakers what events should be included on their agendas. Real-time television now functions as an electronic wire service for policymakers. This simple fact is the primary reason that many foreign-policy officials around the world keep their televisions tuned to CNN in their offices throughout the day.[7]

Communications theorists describe media effects in terms of agenda-setting and two closely related concepts, priming and framing. Agenda-setting is defined as the degree of importance attached to any particular issue. Communication theory usually separates agenda-setting from its closely related media effects, priming and framing, even though these are considered to be extensions of agenda-setting itself.

Priming addresses the relative weight that the media assigns to specific issues, and the effects of this on the criteria by which political leaders are judged. For example, a difference in the relative weight accorded Bush's handling of a particular foreign-policy issue, such as the Kurdish crisis, *vs.* Bush's handling of the economy, shapes the criteria by which the president's job performance will be judged. Framing refers to the angles from which the media present various issues. For example, how should the Shiites be characterized? As rebels, insurgents, refugees, or victims? How should the Kurds be characterized? There is a substantial difference in whether the Shiites and Kurds are respectively framed as rebels, insurgents, refugees, or victims. These frames of reference each provide a different context for media coverage, as well as different criteria for judging events. Priming and framing ultimately determine the degree of importance ascribed to any particular issue. Given this, agenda-setting will be dealt with as a macro principle that includes priming and framing, as well. In other words, agenda-setting as used in this chapter refers to the overall level of importance that is ultimately assigned to any particular issue.[8]

Television's role in agenda-setting was highlighted during a 1993 seminar by the Annenberg Communications Policy program. The seminar was designed to explore the relationship among television, presidents, and foreign crises. Seminar participants were former top-level U.S. government officials, including a president, secretary of defense, undersecretary of defense, deputy secretary of defense, and CIA director, as well as two former national security assistants to the president and other top foreign-policy officials. Two specific conclusions related to agenda-setting came from this seminar. First, television's ability to show unexpected events can influence the public's perception about foreign crises. Second, television can create an unexpected agenda, especially during the beginning and ending stages of a crisis.[9]

Global television exerts its agenda-setting influence in two different ways. The traditional understanding of agenda-setting implies the ability to put something on the agenda about which policymakers were not already aware. However, real-time television also has the power to quickly move an issue to a much higher level of policy consideration within the foreign-policy decision-making apparatus.[10] Gowing has argued that "Where they are deployed, TV news cameras do have a role in prioritizing crisis management both *within* a specific crisis and *between* different crises."[11] In addition, issues involving human rights and suffering or the environment, or those that touch Americans, are much more likely to be advanced on foreign-policy agendas than are such arcane issues as trade terms with Brunei. In other words, as has been noted before, television's ability to influence foreign-policy agendas is issue-specific.[12]

The Kurdish and Shiite case studies above illustrate television's ability to function as an agenda setter. Although U.S. policymakers were already aware of the Kurds' plight, global television forced the Kurdish issue onto foreign-policy agendas "against all the *realpolitik* wishes of Western governments."[13] And, during the two weeks after the Kurdish crisis had been placed on foreign-policy agendas, television continued to push the crisis up the agenda in terms of its priority. In addition, global television moved this issue to higher and higher levels of consideration within the foreign-policy establishment. The bottom-line was that

> Bush ... knew precisely what he did *not* want to do during the final stages of the 1991 Gulf War: He had no interest in becoming embroiled in Saddam Hussein's ongoing battle with the Kurds.... But news reports, particularly those with vivid television pictures, were a major factor in Bush's decision to change his policy.[14]

By April 16 the Kurdish crisis virtually commanded the full attention of the president, the nation's top foreign-policy official.

By way of comparison, the 1991 Shiitic crisis never received real-time coverage, so it never made it onto the foreign-policy agendas of Western governments. As one senior British official confirmed, "We are under no pressure to do something about crises that are not on TV."[15] Such was the case with the Shiites; television effectively functioned as an agenda-setter by virtue of its absence. Former Bush Administration official Natsios has argued that without television coverage of Somalia and Bosnia in the 1990s and Ethiopia in the 1980s, "the three [U.S.] presidents who ordered [troops to assist with humanitarian] interventions [in these three countries] might not have known about the catastrophic circumstances in the first place, given the lengthy formal process for getting information to the chief executive on events abroad."[16] Television coverage transformed the Kurds into victims meriting Western assistance, while the Shiah never made it onto the foreign-policy radar screen.[17]

Real-Time Television as a Unique Information Source

Real-time global television is also a provider of unique information. The uniqueness of this information derives from global television's immediacy and impact — its ability to provide graphic images and instantaneous and/or critical information. Real-time television's immediacy and impact can make policymakers feel as if it is demanding a policy response. As a result, "the emotional pressure of images is modifying the political decision-making process."[18] California Senator Diane Feinstein claims that graphic television images caused her to reverse her original vote in favor of lifting the weapons embargo against Bosnia in the former Yugoslavia. According to Feinstein, "One image punched through to me: That young woman hanging from a tree. That to me said it all."[19] Such brutal and shocking images cry out to policymakers to do something to stop the horror before viewers' eyes, especially when the horror involves "innocent civilians."[20] Likewise, assistant Secretary of State John Shattuck argues that there is a "genuine distinction between print and electronic media.... Nothing compares with the sheer intimacy of television ... to grab and galvanize the viewer and compel the public to shout: *do something!*"[21] Former State Department official Rozanne Ridgway has contended, "Sometimes the mind says 'no' to action, but politics says you must do something. It's very difficult to stand up before the public and say 'Let's do nothing.'"[22] In other words, the very nature of information provided by global television often eliminates the "do nothing" option, even when diplomatic prudence might suggest otherwise.

U.S. military involvement in Somalia between December 1992 and March 1994 illustrates the power of television as an information source. The U.S. decision to become involved in Somalia, as well as its subsequent decision to withdraw its troops, was almost certainly influenced by real-time images. Lee Hamilton (R-IN), Chairman of the U.S. House of Representatives Committee on International Relations charged that "Pictures of the starving children, not policy objectives, got us into Somalia in 1992. Pictures of U.S. casualties, not the completion of our objectives, led us to exit Somalia."[23] Shattuck and Gowing both concur with the congressman's conclusion.[24] Somalia stands as an example of global television's influence on policy via graphic imagery.

The U.S. had been part of an international effort providing relief supplies to Somalia since mid-1992. However, President Bush significantly increased American involvement by making the decision to send U.S. military troops into Somalia on December 9, 1992. The troops were to insure the delivery of relief supplies. Evidence suggests that the U.S. decision to intervene militarily was driven largely by the vivid television images of the unfolding Somali tragedy. U.N. Secretary General Boutros Boutros-Ghali argues that the media were central to the undertaking in Somalia: "The day that [the media] began to pay attention to Somalia, we began to receive the support of the member states. Then they were ready to give us planes for transport and to provide more humanitarian assistance and the forces to protect it."[25] Likewise, television pictures from Somalia probably moved George Bush to take military action, something that he had not originally intended to do.[26]

Bush was a lame duck president in December 1992. Yet, during the eleventh hour of his Administration, pictures coming out of Somalia played a role in the administration's last-minute decision to intervene militarily. When Bush's National Security Adviser, Brent Scowcroft, was asked whether the U.S. government's response to Somalia would have been the same without the television images he admitted, "I'd like to say, 'Yes, we would have done it anyway.' But I don't know."[27] According to Fitzwater, "[t]he President said, 'I just can't live with this for two months.' Television tipped us over the top at a time when the death rate [from starvation] was over 100 a day."[28] Bush's Secretary of State, Lawrence Eagleburger, confirms Fitzwater's account of television's effect:

> Television had a great deal to do with President Bush's decision to go in. I was one of those two or three that was strongly recommending he do it, and it was very much because of the television pictures of these starving kids, substantial pressures from the Congress that came from the same source, and my honest belief that we could do this ... at not too great a cost and, certainly, without any great danger of body bags coming home.[29]

Fitzwater, Eagleburger, and Scowcroft all contend that graphic television pictures pushed U.S. policymakers to intervene militarily in Somalia.

George F. Kennan agrees. Kennan has been a U.S. diplomat and foreign-policy expert for more than half a century. According to Kennan, U.S. policy in Somalia was "provoked by the commercial television industry" rather than the "deliberative organs of our government."[30] Kennan contends that the U.S. reaction to events in Somalia resulted from exposure "by the American media; above all, television. The reaction would have been unthinkable without this exposure. The reaction was an emotional one, occasioned by the sight of the suffering of the starving people in question ... not a thoughtful or deliberate one."[31] Kennan is arguing, of course, that communications drove U.S. policy to intervene militarily in Somalia.

However, on October 3, 1993, U.S. Army Rangers became engaged in a firefight with Somali "warlord" Mohammed Farah Aidid. This resulted in eighteen Rangers being killed. The body of one dead Ranger was dragged through the streets of the Somali capital, Mogadishu, an event that was picked up and broadcast by the media. Public reaction was swift and negative. Public opinion overwhelmingly supported U.S. withdrawal from Somalia. Images of starving children played a role in the U.S. decision to intervene militarily in Somalia. Likewise, the images of a dead U.S. serviceman being dragged through Mogadishu influenced the U.S. decision to withdraw its troops from Somalia.

Gowing concludes that these images of a dead Army Ranger "forced" President Bill Clinton to announce a phased withdrawal of troops from Somalia.[32] Policymakers tend to concur. Haass, a senior staffer on Bush's National Security Council at the time, agrees that the pictures created a public furor demanding that the Administration "do something."[33] Madeleine Albright, who was U.N. ambassador at the time, testified before the Senate Foreign Relations Committee shortly after the attack on U.S. Army Rangers. In her testimony, Albright lamented that television increased the pressure for "immediate disengagement when events do not go according to plan."[34] Anthony Lake, Clinton's then National Security Adviser, admitted that "[television] pictures helped us recognize that the military situation in Mogadishu had deteriorated in a way that we had not frankly recognized."[35] U.S. troops would not be completely withdrawn until six months after the Rangers' deaths. However, within three days of the fire fight Clinton felt compelled to address the nation. In his address, Clinton announced significant changes in U.S. policy in Somalia, including a firm troop withdrawal date of March 31, 1994.

Anthony Lake's statement above contains a telling admission. This statement suggests that Lake, Clinton's National Security Adviser, first realized the untenable nature of the military situation in Mogadishu via real-time television. But, Lake's admission should not be surprising. Global television can function as a singularly potent source for critical and instantaneous information about real-time events. The cases of Tiananmen Square and the Gulf War peace overture discussed above demonstrate television's ability to provide this type of information. Information about the 1989 Tiananmen Square events came to the president largely via this information source. And, according to the evidence above, global-television determined both the speed and the nature of the official U.S. response in the case of Tiananmen. Likewise, the U.S. response to Saddam Hussein's peace overture during the Gulf War was driven by the global media's ability to instantaneously provide critical information.

The abortive August 1991 coup attempt in the former Soviet Union also illustrates global television's unique ability as an information source. George Bush initially learned about the coup from CNN, not from an ambassador or a diplomatic cable.[36] Likewise, Bush's subsequent decision to oppose the coup plotters was cemented by powerful images broadcast on CNN. Bush watched as Russian President Boris Yeltsin defiantly read a statement of opposition to the coup plotters from atop a Soviet tank. According to a close Bush adviser, this imagery's powerful impact determined Bush's course of action: "When the President saw [Yeltsin], that was the key for us."[37] After seeing Yeltsin's defiance atop the tank, Bush decided to condemn the coup. Former Secretary Baker confirms this account: Bush decided to condemn the coup plotters based on information that he got from CNN.[38]

The Soviet putsch also provides examples of real-time television's effect on diplomacy's methods of practice and its pace. The event illustrates a recurring problem: diplomatic practice failed to recognize that the communication paradigm had already shifted, and, consequently, so had the diplomatic paradigm. Thus, diplomats were, yet again, attempting to operate according to outdated and obsolete methods. Former newspaper editor and author Michael F. O'Neill highlights the reality of diplomats attempting to operate under a previous communication paradigm:

> The U.S. Embassy in Moscow, which did not even have CNN, was little more than an occasional message center. The president and his top advisers were operating on facts they got from CNN and other media rather than reports from diplomats trailing behind events. And when [Bush] took action, he did so on television rather than through diplomatic channels. As one official put it, the first thought was not how to cable instructions to American diplomats but how to get a statement on CNN that would shape an allied response. "Diplomatic communications just can't keep up with CNN," he [Bush] said.[39]

In other words, the president's condemnation of the coup had been influenced by real-time information and imagery. And, according to Baker, once Bush decided to condemn the coup, the president "used the fastest source available for getting a message to Moscow: CNN."[40] The president had used a public broadcast over CNN to communicate his condemnation of the putsch, as well as to drum up allied support for this reaction — providing further evidence of traditional diplomacy's obsolescence in times of rapidly unfolding international crises. O'Neill concludes that communications "proved to be the final arbiter" in the diplomatic outcome.[41] New diplomacy had been displaced by the immediacy and impact of telediplomacy.

Real-Time Television as a Diplomatic Broker

Global television can also function as either an active or a passive diplomatic broker. Ted Koppel's *Nightline* news program on ABC has become famous for its on-air interviews between opposing national leaders. Such interviews are an example of television functioning as an active diplomatic broker between parties. Two specific examples of "on-the-air meetings" illustrate global television's ability to broker diplomatic outcomes: Walter Cronkite's role in the early stages of the Middle East peace process and the 1985 hijacking of TWA Flight 847.

In 1977 Cronkite conducted separate interviews via satellite with Egyptian President Anwar Sadat and Israeli Prime Minister Menachem Begin. The interviews were subsequently edited with images of the two leaders being combined onto one screen. Thus, Cronkite appeared to have conducted simultaneous interviews with the leaders. Even though the audience was told of the editing, the effect of the on-air product was dramatic, given the context of the times.[42] The resulting interview came to be known as "Cronkite diplomacy."

During the interview, Sadat told Cronkite that he was willing even to go to Jerusalem to discuss peace if it meant saving the life of one Egyptian soldier. Cronkite pressed Sadat as to what he would need to make such a trip. When Sadat said all that he needed was just a "proper invitation," Cronkite further asked how soon he would be willing to make such a trip. Sadat replied that he would be willing to go at "the earliest time possible." Cronkite pressed further: "That could be, say, within a week?"; to which Sadat responded, "You can say that, yes."[43]

Even before the interview concluded, CBS news producers began attempting to locate Begin. When they were successful in doing so six hours later, Cronkite recounted his exchange with Sadat to Begin. Begin promptly responded, "Tell him [Sadat] he's got an invitation." When pressed further, Begin told Cronkite that he would make a statement to the Israeli parliament the following day, would talk to the U.S. ambassador about forwarding the invitation, and would postpone a scheduled trip to Berlin to accommodate Sadat's trip within one week. Although Cronkite was less than sanguine at the time about any diplomatic role that he might have played, he reflected somewhat differently about his role some years later:

> The important point is that television journalism, in this case at least, speeded up the process, brought it into the open, removed a lot of possibly obstructionist middlemen, and made it difficult for principals to renege on their very public agreement.... Television as a means of communication

between heads of state outside the stodgy bureaucratic channels may be one of its great contributions. Professional diplomats may differ because it is their ox that is being gored.[44]

In the closing pages of his memoirs Cronkite talks again of television's role in writing history. According to Cronkite, the Israeli-Egyptian peace "resulted from the meeting of Anwar Sadat and Menachem Begin that was partly brought about by the separate interviews with them on the *CBS Evening News.*"[45] Whatever the ultimate effect upon policy may have been, Cronkite had functioned effectively as a diplomatic broker.[46]

The resolution of the TWA Flight 847 hijacking in 1985 also illustrates television's power to function as an active diplomatic broker. Flight 847 was hijacked while en route from Athens to Rome on June 14, 1985. The passengers included 104 Americans. After allowing some passengers to leave, the hijackers subsequently threatened to kill all remaining passengers if Israel refused to release Moslem prisoners that had been captured in Lebanon. As a show of their determination, the hijackers killed one American passenger while persisting in their demands.[47]

The U.S. response to the hijackers' demands was that there would be no concessions. President Reagan subsequently moved special U.S. military forces into the region in preparation for a rescue mission. However, on June 16 Palestinian leader Nabih Berri appeared on television as a principal negotiator for the terrorists' demands. Berri had removed thirty of the hostages from the aircraft and had control over them. On June 20 the American hostages themselves entered, via television, the negotiations between the U.S. government and the hijackers. The hostages asked that U.S. forces be withdrawn from the region and that no rescue mission be attempted. Now the terrorists, Berri, and the American hostages were regularly calling for the U.S. to meet the hijackers' demands and avoid any use of force.[48]

Although U.S. policy shifted several times during the crisis, the Reagan Administration's threat to use force in securing the hostages' release was dropped. Ultimately, all hostages were released on July 1. On July 3, Israel released three hundred Moslem prisoners, amidst disclaimers that Israel had made no concessions nor had it struck any deals. The terrorists were never apprehended.[49]

Two possible instances of a direct media-policy impact have been identified in connection with the outcome of the TWA 847 hijacking. First, television introduced the hostages themselves as parties to the negotiations. The hostages warned against any rescue attempt and any linkage of their fate to the fate of other American hostages held in the Middle East. Both of these policy options were under heavy consideration by the U.S. administration. However, in both cases the hostages' televised requests prevailed. Although the administration had spoken publicly about the use of force against the terrorists, as well as the requirement that all American hostages be released, the administration changed its strategy on both counts. Significant media coverage of the hostages' requests, followed by the subsequent change in policy, suggests that the administration may have been influenced by media pressure.[50]

Television also introduced Berri as one of the principals in the negotiations. Apart from the platform and influence afforded by television, Berri would have held no position from which to negotiate (as, indeed, neither would the terrorists themselves). Berri appeared on television with specific demands and a specific negotiating framework, both of which defined the negotiating process that ultimately led to the hostages' release. Berri was successful in securing his demands. Television had functioned as an active diplomatic broker in the TWA 847 crisis, and appears to have affected the ultimate outcome.[51]

Television can also serve as a passive diplomatic broker. Immediately following the 1991 Iraqi invasion of Kuwait, Kuwaiti government officials in exile began to market their government's image and objectives to the American public. This marketing effort provides an example of the media as passive diplomatic broker. Both print and electronic media factored heavily into Kuwait's public relations efforts. However, television's visual advantages over print operated in this case, as in others.

Bush decided to evict Iraq immediately after its invasion of Kuwait. However, he knew that doing so would require substantial persuasion for both the American people and our allies. Kuwait is an emirate, meaning that it is ruled by the emir, or head, of the Kuwaiti royal family. The Emir of Kuwait at the time of the Iraqi invasion, Sheikh Ahmad al-Sabah, succeeded to the throne in 1977. Prior to the invasion of Kuwait, no one in the West cared much about the oil-rich Arab emirate's sovereignty, or its supposed democracy — which was non-existent, since the emir of Kuwait ruled by personal decree. However, if necessary, Bush was willing to use the U.S. military to restore Kuwait's sovereignty and what he alleged to be Kuwaiti democracy.[52]

Bush began actively seeking a justification for his intended rescue of Kuwait. He was especially interested in a rationale that would play well with American public opinion. Ultimately, the President hoped to blunt the criticism that had arisen of any potential U.S. military involvement on behalf of the oil-rich kingdom. Bush did not want his intended rescue of Kuwait portrayed as an exercise in trading "blood-for-oil."[53]

However, Bush soon had a valuable ally in his effort to legitimize U.S. military involvement in the Gulf. The Kuwaiti royal family hired Hill and Knowlton, a major U.S. public relations firm, to head the family's campaign to market its image and objectives to the American people. The emir and his government provided $11.8 million of Hill and Knowlton's total budget of $12.0 million for the Kuwaiti campaign. A significant portion of this amount, $2.6 million, was paid to a polling firm, the Wirthlin Group, for extensive polling of the American public. Wirthlin began its polling on August 20 and followed up with daily tracking polls through late October. The firm continued with biweekly surveys until mid-December, when it became apparent that the Kuwaiti government's objectives had been achieved: the U.S. was committed to acting militarily on behalf of Kuwait. In addition, Wirthlin ran numerous focus groups and routinely briefed Citizens for a Free Kuwait, the Kuwaiti government's front-group that served as Hill and Knowlton's client. The polling firm also provided media training for Kuwaiti officials appearing on American television. And, as further proof of the power of televised images, Wirthlin produced videos in Saudi Arabia using members of the Kuwaiti resistance. The videos were destined for major news services and networks.[54]

Hill and Knowlton also orchestrated the now-famous baby incubator atrocity story. Exclusive televised hearings on Capitol Hill featured a fifteen-year-old Kuwaiti who identified herself only as Nayirah. She was introduced as a hospital worker and witness to Iraqi atrocities. Iraqi soldiers were alleged to have stolen pediatric incubators and left Kuwaiti newborns to die. Grainy photographs were circulated that depicted bayoneted and tortured victims. Television reported all of this in graphic detail. The Kuwaitis achieved victim status and hatred for Saddam was inspired.[55]

Hill and Knowlton was the original source for the story. But there was a different truth behind the story's imagery. Nayirah, the firsthand witness to the infamous "incubator atrocities," turned out to be the daughter of the Kuwaiti ambassador to the U.S. Hill and Knowlton had helped her prepare her testimony, which had been rehearsed before video cameras in the firm's offices. Subsequent investigations by Middle East Watch, a human rights group, concluded that the incident never happened. Likewise, the bayoneted and tortured victims in the grainy photographs turned out to be mannequins. Reality had succumbed to distortion and imagery.[56]

John R. MacArthur has made a study of the pro-Kuwait public relations campaign. In his book entitled *Second Front*, MacArthur concludes that "The perceived degree of violence and terror committed [against Kuwaitis] had everything to do with America's choice of war."[57] The baby-incubator atrocity story lent tangible credibility to the Saddam-Hussein-as-Hitler-analogy. This analogy served as one of the Bush Administration's primary political justifications for the use of force against Iraq.[58] Although the Bush Administration had no involvement in orchestrating Hill and Knowlton's activities, the firm's public-relations campaign did serve as a powerful broker on behalf of Kuwait's attempts to influence U.S. foreign policy.[59] Craig Fuller, a former top aide to Bush, was president of Hill and Knowlton. Fuller's access to the White House allowed Hill and Knowlton to push "all the right buttons" on Capitol Hill.[60] The extent of the Kuwaiti royal family's efforts through Hill and Knowlton illustrate the power of images on serious foreign-policy decisions.

Hill and Knowlton's survey research had indicated the potential success of a victimization strategy. Thus, Kuwait's objectives were marketed to the American public in the context of Kuwait-as-victim. The firm originally wanted to market Kuwait as the most democratic country in the region and the one that granted the greatest number of rights to women, although, such claims could only be made in relative terms via comparisons with other Persian Gulf States which were more highly autocratic and restrictive, states such as Bahrain, Oman, Qatar, and the United Arab Emirates. But the themes that resonated with the American public were victimization and anti-Saddam images. This strategy produced pro-Kuwait and anti-Iraq public opinion responses.[61] The Hill and Knowlton strategy was so successful that it prompted the coining of a special term, "strategic public diplomacy," to describe the effectiveness of this type of influence on U.S. foreign policy.[62]

Although Kuwait's victim status was certainly enhanced by Hill and Knowlton's strategic public diplomacy, the final policy outcome was probably not changed by this imagery. On August 8, Bush had announced a firm decision that he would intervene militarily, if necessary, to evict Iraq from Kuwait.[63] Nevertheless, the images were useful in blunting criticism of the impending U.S. military involvement in the Gulf. Between August 8 and January 3 the three major network evening newscasts devoted approximately one percent of their total coverage to views that opposed the military build-up. Out of 2,855 minutes of total coverage, only twenty-nine minutes were devoted to views opposing the government's intended military intervention.[64]

The Kuwaiti royal family's public relations campaign certainly reflects the belief that television can be an effective diplomatic broker. The Kuwaiti government willingly invested nearly $12 million in an extensive strategic public diplomacy initiative. The extent of this initiative begs an obvious question: What difference did this carefully orchestrated initiative have on U.S. foreign-policy toward the Iraqi invasion of Kuwait? Perhaps none, given Bush's early and unchanging decision to forcibly evict the Iraqis from Kuwait. If, however, the Hill and Knowlton undertaking made $12 million worth of difference to the emir and his government, one thing is certain: Television is perceived to be a highly influential diplomatic broker.[65]

Global Television's Indirect Effect on Diplomatic Outcomes

Real-time television can also exert an indirect influence on policy. Under this construction, global television's influence first shapes public opinion, which subsequently influences foreign policy. The traditional model of foreign policymaking, the elite model, saw policy as being crafted solely by professional diplomats and their masters.

Foreign-policy elites form a diverse but powerful group. Although there is no formal agreement on who qualifies as an "elite," in the U.S. the group surely includes top members of the State Department and other officials in the foreign-policy establishment; influential members of Congress; opinion leaders in the society at large, such as the major media outlets and their chief personalities; and members of think tanks and top academics. The elite model saw public opinion, at best, as something to be educated regarding elite policy preferences. Recall that the prevailing attitude toward public opinion among State Department officials in the 1960s was "to hell with public opinion"; what these officials expected was "public acquiescence." Such attitudes have traditionally characterized the elite model of foreign policymaking.[66]

However, as discussed above, recent advances in communication technology have increased public opinion's potential influence on foreign policymaking.[67] O'Neill has argued that in the case of the Kurdish refugees, "Snowballing public opinion, propelled by emotion-laden pictures, demanded a presidential response, sovereignty be damned. Bush finally buckled."[68] The bottom line is that "Massive audience intervention by way of the television screen has become a strategic item of war in the postmodern age."[69] Public opinion's increasing importance in foreign-policy decision-making stems from global television's erosion of the diplomat's former monopoly over knowledge.[70] Today, the American people and policymakers receive critical information at the same time, as the case studies above illustrate. Prior to the television age, mass media was thought to have only "minimal" effects on public opinion.[71] However, continuing research has shown that the mass media now have a significantly greater effect on public opinion than was previously recognized.[72]

The elitist theory of foreign-policy decision-making has also been called into question by recent research. The elitist paradigm argued that public opinion was "volatile," "unstructured," and that changes in mass attitude came from a top-down process.[73] These changes began with foreign-policy elites who then affected the attitudes of the attentive public, who subsequently influenced mass attitudes. Public opinion was not considered to be significant in foreign-policy or national-security decisions.[74]

In fact, public opinion has behaved differently toward foreign-policy than the elitist model recognized. The last fifty years of survey data provides "no evidence" to suggest that the public is "fundamentally ignorant, fickle, impulsive, erratic, or tempestuous in nature."[75] In fact, statistical analyses of this data reveal a rational public that "makes clear and coherent distinctions about which policies it favors and which it opposes."[76] The overall pattern that emerges is that of a public that displays rational, responsible, sensible, and "even sophisticated opinion about national security matters."[77]

Public opinion also has had a greater effect on foreign-policy decision-making than was recognized by the elitist model. According to scholars Shapiro and Page, a cynical view of public opinion's influence on foreign-policy "has never been correct, at least not during the fifty or sixty years for which systematic survey data are available."[78] Likewise, former U.S. foreign affairs officer Thomas W. Graham argues that "Over the last fifty years public opinion has played an important, but not adequately recognized role in U.S. foreign-policy decision making."[79]

Graham identifies five different levels of public opinion's impact on foreign-policy decision-making during the last half century.[80] He bases these levels on more than five hundred national surveys and the primary source documents of seven presidential administrations. When public opinion on a particular topic was less than 50 percent, the public "rarely" influenced decision-makers. However, at levels where a "majority" of the public (between 50 percent and 59 percent) held a particular position, some influence was apparent. At "consensus" levels (60 percent to 69 percent) public opinion became an important factor in decision-making, sufficiently important to defeat strong opponents within the foreign-policy establishment. When public opinion reaches overwhelming levels of influence, or "preponderant" levels (in the range of 70 percent to 79 percent), it "causes the political system to act according to its dictates" and also has the ability to prevent political opposition from challenging public opinion on a specific decision. "Nearly unanimous" levels of public opinion (those above 79 percent) bring with them an almost automatic conformity between foreign-policy and public opinion.[81]

According to Graham, public opinion can have a "substantial" impact on both foreign-policy formation and implementation.[82] However, four factors must be understood to appreciate public opinion's role in foreign policy.[83] The first factor relates to the magnitude of public opinion, as described above. If public opinion is to have a substantial effect on policy, it must exceed majority levels (greater than 59 percent).[84]

Second, public opinion's ultimate effect depends on the stage in the policy process where that effect is brought to bear. Graham divides the foreign-policy decision-making process into four distinct stages: 1) agenda-setting 2) policy negotiations 3) ratification of policy decisions 4) policy implementation. During policy negotiations (the second stage) or the implementation phase (the fourth and final stage), public opinion only exerts an indirect influence, if it exerts any influence at all during these stages. However, public opinion can directly affect policy during the first, agenda-setting phase, as well as the third phase, where policy decisions are ratified.[85]

Third, public opinion can still play a role in foreign-policy even when officials attempt to implement initiatives that face organized opposition. This third way in which public opinion can influence policy is complex and multidimensional. However, if government officials seek long-term policy success, they must understand and utilize public opinion's most politically relevant aspects in the formulation of policy. The need for this is greatest when officials seek to organize and implement significant policy initiatives that face general opposition. Ignoring public opinion's strongest and most politically relevant facets will almost surely lead to policy failure.[86]

Fourth, public opinion does establish the broad policy boundaries within which the foreign-policy establishment must operate. This applies even to the most popular presidents. Apart from exceptional circumstances, no president can expect to produce more than marginal effects (in the range of 10 percent to at most 15 percent) on the public's opinion toward specific policy initiatives. Public opinion does impose real limitations on elites' policymaking decisions.[87]

In the final analysis, if public opinion is strong, powerful bureaucratic players can be overridden. As the four factors above suggest, the cause-and-effect linkages between public opinion and policy are complex. However, public opinion can act as a powerful determinant of policy decisions.

Given the right conditions, public opinion can make certain foreign-policy decisions virtually automatic.[88]

Several models have been offered to explain the complex cause-effect linkages between public opinion and policy. A so-called "recoil effect" has been offered as one model for public opinion's influence upon policy. According to this model, officials take anticipated public opinion into consideration in the policymaking process. By doing so, officials preempt the possibility of a public backlash and subsequent policy reversals.[89]

Definitive cause-effect linkages are always difficult to prove, however. Statistical studies can establish that a relationship does exist between two variables such as foreign-policy and public opinion. However, statistical studies cannot definitively establish which variable is cause and which is effect. In other words, statistical analysis cannot completely rule out the possibility for a reverse effect where policy influences public opinion.

Furthermore, it is virtually impossible to determine those decisions where politicians effectively hid behind public opinion. In other words, it is nearly impossible to distinguish between those decisions that were truly affected by public opinion and those where policymakers claim such an effect but where, in fact, the policy was actually shaped by other forces. Such political maneuvering further complicates the establishment of meaningful cause-and-effect linkages.[90]

The policy–public opinion relationship is inherently complex.[91] Leaders often launch policy initiatives that may, at least initially, appear unpopular. Such initiatives are undertaken as a preemptive measure by leaders who believe that the public would judge government's performance unfavorably in retrospect, were certain policies not pursued. As a result, a complex interplay emerges between elites and public opinion where "elites attempt to lead and to follow at the same time."[92] In other words, elites always have some ideas of their own, but at the same time are "always looking back to see whether the public is following" and always trying to anticipate which policy the public will say that it wanted, once the dust has settled.[93] For example, President Lyndon Johnson feared a potential future backlash for "losing Vietnam" if he failed to escalate the war in Southeast Asia. Given this, LBJ led the public into a war that "neither he nor the public wanted."[94]

Public opinion can and does influence foreign-policy to a greater degree than has historically been suggested by the elite model. Even in situations where elites are leading public opinion, the public can have a substantial reciprocal influence upon its leaders, if from no other source than the threat of exacting retribution at the next election.[95] The extremes to which officials go in attempts to manipulate public opinion suggest something about its potential for influence. "Spin-doctors"—individuals who publicize favorable interpretations of their political masters' words or actions—have now become part of the U.S. political process. The existence of spin-doctoring suggests that public opinion is something deserving of significant attention.

Recent research indicates at least a two-thirds congruence between changes in public opinion and subsequent changes in foreign policy.[96] In other words, when public opinion changes on a specific policy, that policy will change to align with public opinion two out of three times. One data set, which analyzed more than two hundred case studies, indicated a 92 percent congruence between majority opinion and subsequent policy.[97] Overall, such data tend to indicate approximately a 90 percent congruence between foreign-policy and majority (greater than 59 percent) public opinion.[98] Suffice it to say that public opinion can exert a significant influence upon foreign-policy decisions.[99]

The media's ability to influence public opinion stems primarily from its agenda-setting functions. The media is effective at telling the public what to think about. In addition, the media can effectively frame the issues presented to the public. Framing the issue involves the slant or angle given to a story by, for example, the distinction between victims and rebels. Finally, the media can establish the criteria by which the public will judge its political leaders, a practice that is referred to as priming.[100] Iyengar, a pioneer in researching the media's influence upon public opinion, concludes that by the time of the 1991 Persian Gulf War it was "well established that television news has a significant impact on public opinion."[101] Former Assistant Secretary of State Shattuck argues that television drives domestic public opinion, particularly in the context of humanitarian crises.[102] Such was certainly the case in the Kurdish refugee crisis.

The media drove policy during the Kurdish crisis by first influencing public opinion, which in turn influenced U.S. policy toward the crisis. As the crisis first began to unfold, the Bush Administration quietly argued that helping the Kurds would be a public opinion "loser." Furthermore, the administration believed that its policy of bringing the troops home was what the public really wanted. At the end of March 1991, senior presidential advisors were still dismissing events in Northern Iraq as unimportant. Bush officials argued that "there is no political downside to our policy" and that "the only pressure for the U.S. to intervene is coming from columnists and commentators."[103] Yet, within two weeks, television had created what Daniel Schorr refers to as an "unofficial plebiscite" on the subject of U.S. policy towards the Kurds.[104] And, "public opinion turned out to be overriding."[105] An independent actor, the media, had influenced American public opinion. And public opinion subsequently forced an about-face in U.S. foreign policy.[106]

Communications had affected a diplomatic outcome. Real-time television can influence policy by functioning as an agenda-setter, by virtue of its nature as a unique information source, and/or by acting as a diplomatic actor. Whether directly, or indirectly via public opinion, communications now has the potential to drive policy.

Three

COMMUNICATIONS AND DIPLOMACY: FUTURE POTENTIAL

Chapter 8

Today's Communications, Tomorrow's Diplomacy

"In this changed environment, the media, in turn, assumes a greater importance than in the past."
— *Peter Young and Peter Jesser, 1997;* The Media and the Military: From the Crimea to Desert Strike

By 1995, diplomatic scholars could conclude that the technological revolution had "facilitated the transformation, and in some instances the transcendence, of traditional methods of diplomacy."[1] Diplomatic practitioners tended to agree. Former U.N. Secretary General, Boutros Boutros-Ghali, has observed that "Today the media do not simply report the news. Television has become part of the event it covers."[2] The U.N./European Union negotiating team for the former Yugoslavia in Geneva contends that "television and CNN have become the sixth permanent member of the U.N. Security Council [which only has five permanent members]."[3]

Global television made its first appearance in 1980. Twenty years ago, real-time television's ultimate role in world politics was not foreseen. Global television had yet to become part of the event that it was covering. Likewise, real-time television was not yet perceived of as being the sixth permanent member of the U.N. Security Council. However, by 1980 history had already established the defining linkage between communications and diplomacy: major changes in today's communications will result in major changes in tomorrow's diplomacy.

The link between communications and diplomacy was first established by the change to mass printing, especially the mass printing of newspapers. This linkage's defining effect on diplomacy was apparent in the run-up to the Spanish-American War. Ultimately, the change to mass printing resulted in the subsequent change to new diplomacy immediately following World War I. However, by the time of the Vietnam era, another major change in communications was occurring. By 1963, more Americans were getting their news from television than from newspapers. The Vietnam War brought mounting evidence of television's influence as a diplomatic actor. Television's subsequent transformation into a real-time, global medium has resulted in yet another major change in diplomacy—telediplomacy. History has established this fact: by studying today's communications we will be better able to understand tomorrow's diplomacy.

The historic linkage between communications and diplomacy has defined different methods of diplomatic practice. Historically, communications has exerted three specific effects on diplomatic practice. First, communications has displaced the existing diplomatic paradigm's methods of practice. Second, communications has accelerated diplomacy's pace. And, third, communications has increased the diplomatic influence of non-traditional actors. Furthermore, each succeeding shift in the communications paradigm has, in turn, brought succeeding shifts in paradigms of diplomatic practice. Shifts in the communications paradigm resulted in the move from old to new diplomacy. And the latest paradigm of diplomatic practice, telediplomacy, is just emerging in the wake of recent communications developments, specifically real-time global television. Communications has, for the second time in history, defined different methods of diplomatic practice. This is communications' historic role in diplomacy.

However, under telediplomacy communications has acquired the potential to influence diplomatic outcomes, as well. Under certain conditions, communications can now drive policy. However, global television's ability to influence diplomatic outcomes is limited to certain specific issues, such as global political crises; events that are unfolding rapidly and/or events where there is an absence of political leadership; and situations where the media have both the access and autonomy to provide the required visibility. Telediplomacy is characterized by its immediacy and impact. However, telediplomacy's primary difference from its predecessors is the unique potential for global communications to drive policy.

Such was the case in the 1991 Kurdish refugee crisis. Ultimately, real-time television forced a change in the Bush Administration's policy toward the Kurds. After ten days of categorically denying help for the Kurds, Bush was moved to launch the largest humanitarian relief effort in U.S. history. The Kurdish refugee crisis met all five conditions for global television to drive policy, and the Bush Administration changed its policy. By way of contrast, the 1991 Shiite refugee crisis failed to meet a required condition: it did not receive the necessary high visibility for communications to drive policy. As a result, no intervention was forthcoming on behalf of the Shiites.

However, as the case of genocide in Rwanda demonstrates, there are limits to communications' ability to influence diplomatic outcomes. Although Rwanda was a global political crisis, two primary limiting factors were identified. First, Rwanda failed to present living victims for whom something could reasonably be done. Second, the potential risks of intervention exceeded the potential benefits for any would-be interveners.

Two additional factors may also serve to limit communications' influence on policy: 1) real-time television's simplistic, contextless coverage; 2) viewers' emotional distance from the tragedies unfolding on their television screens. This emotional distance can result from geographic isolation, cultural differences, and/or simple viewer fatigue. Therefore, as the case of Rwanda demonstrates, global television's ability to influence diplomatic outcomes is neither automatic nor is it without certain limitations.

When conditions do allow communications to affect policy, it does so through identifiable mechanisms. Real-time television can directly drive policy by functioning as an agenda setter, a unique source of information, or as a diplomatic broker. Global television can also indirectly affect policy outcomes: By first influencing public opinion, global television can influence foreign policy decision-makers. When global television does affect policy outcomes, it does so through a combination of these mechanisms. The Kurdish refugees were saved by global television's combined effects, both direct and indirect.

The fact that a connection exists between communications and diplomacy is reasonably well understood. What is *not* well understood is the specific effects of this connection. This project offers an alternative to the stereotypical conclusion that "[t]echnology changes everything and nothing in international affairs."[4] Communications' role in world politics is definite and specific: it has historically defined diplomacy's practice; today, it can also affect diplomacy's outcome. Differentiating between diplomatic practice and diplomatic outcomes clarifies communications' effect on world politics.

The historic linkage between diplomacy and communications also has implications for the future: tomorrow's diplomacy can be better understood by studying today's communications. History has established that communications will continue to define diplomatic practice. However, communications' future effect on diplomatic outcomes is less well established. Global television's ability to drive policy is a recent development. Consequently, there are a limited number of such cases available for analysis. Ultimately, the extent of global television's ability to drive policy can only be determined by studying future foreign-policy decisions.

However, history does suggest that communications will play an increasing role in shaping world politics. Today's increasing reliance upon global television suggests its increasing influence over tomorrow's policy outcomes. Young and Jesser concluded a 1997 study on the media's role in military operations by observing that

> There should be no doubt that the global reach and immediacy of the new media and communications technologies, and the ability of those technologies to shape both national and international public opinion, has made the media a major player in limited conflict and peacekeeping deployments.... The media can be expected to become increasingly influential in the future.[5]

Two facts are certain. First, by studying today's communications we will better understand tomorrow's policy outcomes. Second, whatever global television's future influence may be, it will be better understood by distinguishing between communications' historic ability to influence diplomatic practice, and communications' more recent ability to influence diplomatic outcomes. On these two points history is clear.

Notes

Chapter 1. The Communication-Diplomacy Link

1. Hans J. Morgenthau, *Politics Among Nations: The Struggle for Power and Peace* (New York: Alfred A. Knopf, 1949), 425; emphasis added.

2. Henry A. Kissinger, *Diplomacy* (New York: Simon & Schuster, 1994), 808.

3. Quoted in Larry Minear, Colin Scott, and Thomas G. Weiss, *The News Media, Civil War, and Humanitarian Action* (Boulder, CO: Lynne Rienner, 1996), 4.

4. John Hohenberg, *Free Press/Free People: The Best Cause* (New York: Columbia University Press, 1971), 470.

5. Patricia A. Karl, "Media Diplomacy," *The Proceedings of the Academy of Political Science* 34, number 4, 1982, 152.

6. Timothy J. McNulty, "Television's Impact on Executive Decisionmaking and Diplomacy," *The Fletcher Forum of World Affairs* 17, number 1 (Winter 1993), 82.

7. Keith Hamilton and Richard Langhorne, *The Practice of Diplomacy: Its Evolution, Theory and Administration* (London: Routledge, 1995), 234.

8. James A. Baker, III with Thomas M. DeFrank, *The Politics of Diplomacy: Revolution, War and Peace, 1989–1992* (New York: G.P. Putnam's Sons, 1995), 103.

9. Nik Gowing, "Real-Time Television Coverage of Armed Conflicts and Diplomatic Crises," Working Paper 94–1, Joan Shorenstein Barone Center, John F. Kennedy School of Government, Harvard University, June 1994, 3. Richard Parker, "Technology and the Future of Global Television," in Pippa Norris, ed., *Politics and the Press: The News Media and Their Influences* (Boulder, CO: Lynne Rienner, 1997), 21–23.

10. *Webster's New World Dictionary of the American Language* (New York: Simon and Schuster, 1980), 287.

11. Ibid., 287.

12. Michael G. Roskin and Nicholas O. Berry, *The New World of International Relations* (Englewood Cliffs, NJ: Prentice Hall, 1993), 313–14.

13. Donald M. Snow and Eugene Brown, *The Contours of Power: An Introduction to Contemporary International Relations* (New York: St. Martin's Press, 1996), 468.

14. Snow and Brown, *The Contours of Power*, 468. Jack C. Plano and Milton Greenberg, *The American Political Dictionary* (Ninth Edition) (Fort Worth, TX: Harcourt, Brace, Jovanovich, College Publishers; 1993), 526–527.

15. Theodore A. Couloumbis and James H. Wolfe, *Introduction to International Relations:*

155

Power and Justice (Englewood Cliffs, NJ: Prentice Hall, 1990), 143. Roskin and Berry, *The New World of International Relations*, 314.

16. Daniel S. Papp, *Contemporary International Relations: Frameworks for Understanding* (New York: MacMillan Publishing Company, 1991), 503. Couloumbis and Wolfe, *Introduction to International Relations*, 143. Kingdon B. Swayne, "Reporting Function," in Elmer Plischke, ed., *Modern Diplomacy: The Art and the Artisans* (Washington, DC: American Enterprise Institute for Public Policy Research, 1979), 350.

17. Papp, *Contemporary International Relations*, 503.

18. Papp, *Contemporary International Relations*, 503. John T. Rourke, *International Politics on the World Stage* (Guilford, CT: The Dushkin Publishing Group, Inc., 1993), 281–82.

19. Papp, *Contemporary International Relations*, 505.

20. Papp, *Contemporary International Relations*, 503. Couloumbis and Wolfe, *Introduction to International Relations*, 151.

21. Papp, *Contemporary International Relations*, 504. Rourke, *International Politics on the World Stage*, 303.

22. Rourke, *International Politics on the World Stage*, 280.

23. Bruce Russett and Harvey Starr, *World Politics: The Menu for Choice*, (New York: W. H. Freeman and Company, 1989), 157.

24. Tran Van Dinh, *Communication and Diplomacy in a Changing World* (Norwood, NJ: Ablex Publishing Corporation, 1987), xiii.

25. Wilbur Schramm, "The Process of Communication: How Communication Works," in Wilbur Schramm, ed., *The Process and Effects of Mass Communication* (Urbana, IL: University of Illinois Press, 1954), 12–18.

26. J. T. Klapper, *The Effects of Mass Communication* (New York: The Free Press, 1960), 98.

27. Stephen Kern, *The Culture of Time and Space, 1880–1918* (Cambridge, MA: Harvard University Press, 1983), 4.

28. Morgenthau, *Politics Among Nations*, 437; emphasis added.

29. Harold Adams Innis, *Empire and Communication* (Oxford: Oxford University Press, 1950), 7–13.

30. Ibid., 7.

31. Ibid., 6–13.

32. Ibid., 172.

33. Ibid., 165–172.

34. Harold Adams Innis, *The Bias of Communication* (Toronto, Canada: University of Toronto Press, 1951), 31.

35. Ibid., 4.

36. Ibid., 33.

37. Thomas Kuhn, *The Structure of Scientific Revolutions* (Chicago: The University of Chicago Press, 1970).

Chapter 2. Paradigms, Communication, and Diplomacy

1. Kuhn, *The Structure of Scientific Revolutions*.

2. Ibid., 10 & 111–135.

3. Ibid., 6.

4. Ibid., 10.

5. Ibid., 97.

6. Ibid., 62.

7. Ibid., 85.

8. Ibid., 20.

9. Ibid., 64

10. Quoted in Ibid., 151.

11. Ibid., 62.

12. Ithiel de Sola Pool, *Technologies of Freedom* (Cambridge, MA: The Belknap Press of Harvard University Press, 1983), 24.

13. Kuhn, *The Structure of Scientific Revolutions*, 111–135, 6–11.

14. Ibid., 20.

15. Pool, *Technologies of Freedom*, 20.

16. J. M. Roberts, *History of the World* (New York: Oxford University Press, 1993), 148, 167.

17. Innis, *Empire and Communication*, 68.

18. Ibid., 70.

19. Quoted in Ibid., 68.

20. Walter J. Ong, *Orality and Literacy: The Technologizing of the Word* (London: Methuen, Inc., 1982), 80.

21. Innis, *Empire and Communication*, 7–8.

22. Pool, *Technologies of Freedom*, 24.

23. Carolyn Marvin, *When Old Technologies Were New: Thinking About Electric Communication in the Late Nineteenth Century* (New York: Oxford University Press, 1988), 3.

24. Kern, *The Culture of Time and Space, 1880–1918*, 81.

25. Kuhn, *The Structure of Scientific Revolutions*, 62, 92, 151.

26. Ibid., 20.

27. Ronald Berkman, *Politics in the Media Age* (New York: McGraw-Hill, Inc., 1986), 20.

28. Francis MacDonald Cornford, *The Republic of Plato* (New York: Oxford University Press, 1980), xix.

29. Bruce Wetterau, *World History: A Dictionary of Important People, Places, and Events, from Ancient Times to the Present* (New York: Henry Holt and Company, 1994), 977.

30. Hohenberg, *Free Press/Free People*, 10.

31. Ibid., 12.

32. Kuhn, *The Structure of Scientific Revolutions*, 20.

33. Pool, *Technologies of Freedom*, 13.

34. Ibid., 14.

35. Thomas C. Leonard, *The Power of the Press: The Birth of American Political Reporting* (New York: Oxford University Press, 1986), 14.

36. Pool, *Technologies of Freedom*, 13.

37. Frank Luther Mott, *American Journalism, A History: 1690–1960* (New York: The MacMillan Company, 1968), 8.

38. Hohenberg, *Free Press/Free People*, 17. Richard M. Brace, "Cardinal Richelieu," in *World Book Encyclopedia*, Volume 16 (Chicago: Field Enterprises Educational Corporation, 1968), 306–307.

39. Pool, *Technologies of Freedom*, 15.

40. Hohenberg, *Free Press/Free People*, 17–18.

41. Tim Harris, "Propaganda and Public Opinion in Seventeenth-Century England," in Jeremy D. Popkin, ed., *Media and Revolution: Comparative Perspectives* (Lexington, KY: The University Press of Kentucky, 1995), 51.

42. Jeffrey A. Smith, *Printers and Press Freedom: The Ideology of Early American Journalism* (New York: Oxford University Press, 1988), 32–33.

43. Ibid., 31.

44. Hohenberg, *Free Press/Free People*, 38.

45. Ibid., 38–39.

46. Ibid., 38–40.

47. Ibid., 45.

48. Ibid., 38–45.

49. Quoted in Smith, *Printers and Press Freedom*, 164.

50. Ibid., 162–164.

51. Innis, *The Bias of Communication*, 138.

52. Hohenberg, *Free Press/Free People*, 43–44.

53. James Melvin Lee, *History of American Journalism* (Garden City, NY: The Garden City Publishing Co., Inc., 1923), 8–9.

54. Mott, *American Journalism, A History*, 9–10.

55. Ibid., 11.

56. Lee, *History of American Journalism*, 27.

57. Mott, *American Journalism, A History*, 59.

58. Hohenberg, *Free Press/Free People*, 44.

59. Mott, *American Journalism, A History*, 159, 216.

60. Thomas C. Leonard, *The Power of the Press*, 56.

61. Ibid., 54.

62. Ibid., 4.

63. Innis, *The Bias of Communication*, 138.

64. Ibid., 156–162. Pool, *Technologies of Freedom*, 18.

65. Innis, *Empire and Communication*, 26–7.

66. Berkman, *Politics in the Media Age*, 20.

67. Innis, *The Bias of Communication*, 160.

68. Pool, *Technologies of Freedom*, 18.

69. Innis, *The Bias of Communication*, 160.

70. Pool, *Technologies of Freedom*, 18.

71. Innis, *The Bias of Communication*, 161–162.

72. Menahem Blondheim, *News Over the Wires: The Telegraph and the Flow of Public Information in America, 1844–1897* (Cambridge, MA: Harvard University Press, 1994), 25.

73. Ibid., 48.

74. Pool, *Technologies of Freedom*, 251.

75. Quoted in Smith, *Printers and Press Freedom*, 164.

76. Quoted in Jeremy D. Popkin, "Media and Revolutionary Crisis," in Jeremy D. Popkin, ed., *Media and Revolution: Comparative Perspectives* (Lexington, KY: The University Press of Kentucky, 1995), 15.

77. Ibid., 19.

78. Berkman, *Politics in the Media Age*, 20.

79. Blondheim, *News Over the Wires*, 29.

80. Mott, *American Journalism, A History*, 524–526, 539.

81. Ibid., 538–539.

82. Hohenberg, *Free Press/Free People*, 147.

83. Mott, *American Journalism, A History*, 550.

84. Ibid., 549.

85. Hohenberg, *Free Press/Free People*, 199.

86. Ibid., 199.

87. Daniel R. Headrick, *The Invisible Weapon: Telecommunications and International Politics, 1851–1945* (New York: Oxford University Press, 1991), 12.

88. Ibid., 12.

89. Pool, *Technologies of Freedom*, 20–21.

90. Blondheim, *News Over the Wires*, 30.

91. Ibid., 30.

92. Ibid., 11.

93. Quoted in Ibid., 28.

94. Kern, *The Culture of Time and Space, 1880–1918*, 6.

95. Ibid., 6.

96. Ibid., 6.

97. Marvin, *When Old Technologies Were New*, 3. Pool, *Technologies of Freedom*, 24.

98. Pool, *Technologies of Freedom*, 6.

99. Headrick, *The Invisible Weapon*, 4, 73.

100. Ibid., 17.

101. Ibid., 17–18.
102. Oliver Gramling, *AP: The Story of News* (Port Washington, NY: Kennikat Press, 1969), 32.
103. Ibid., 32–35.
104. Ibid., 34–35.
105. Headrick, *The Invisible Weapon*, 18–19.
106. Ibid., 32.
107. Hamilton and Langhorne, *The Practice of Diplomacy*, 131.
108. Irving E. Fang, *A History of Mass Communication: Six Information Revolutions* (Boston: Focal Press, 1997), 79.
109. Headrick, *The Invisible Weapon*, 73.
110. Blondheim, *News Over the Wires*, 32–33.
111. Marvin, *When Old Technologies Were New*, 217.
112. Kern, *The Culture of Time and Space, 1880–1918*, 69.
113. Marvin, *When Old Technologies Were New*, 218.
114. Ibid., 219–221.
115. Ibid., 222.
116. Ibid., 222.
117. Ibid., 223–226
118. Ibid., 231
119. Pool, *Technologies of Freedom*, 32.
120. Marvin, *When Old Technologies Were New*, 227–231.
121. Ibid., 231.
122. Ibid., 221.
123. Ibid., 227–231.
124. Kern, *The Culture of Time and Space, 1880–1918*, 81.
125. Quoted in Ibid., 81.
126. Headrick, *The Invisible Weapon*, 116–118.
127. Ibid., 121–122.
128. Hohenberg, *Free Press/Free People*, 160.
129. Kern, *The Culture of Time and Space, 1880–1918*, 69.
130. Ibid.
131. Headrick, *The Invisible Weapon*, 202–203.
132. Innis, *The Bias of Communication*, 59.
133. Headrick, *The Invisible Weapon*, 116.
134. Ibid.
135. Innis, *The Bias of Communication*, 81.
136. Headrick, *The Invisible Weapon*, 138.
137. Pool, *Technologies of Freedom*, 31.
138. Headrick, *The Invisible Weapon*, 116.
139. Pool, *Technologies of Freedom*, 31.
140. Smith, *Printers and Press Freedom*, 164.
141. Pool, *Technologies of Freedom*, 47.
142. Ibid.
143. Hohenberg, *Free Press/Free People*, 161.
144. Ibid., 237.
145. Fang, *A History of Mass Communication*, 154.
146. Hohenberg, *Free Press/Free People*, 280.
147. Innis, *Empire and Communication*, 12–13.
148. Ibid., 13.
149. Pool, *Technologies of Freedom*, 33.
150. Jack Gould, "Television," in *The World Book Encyclopedia*, Volume 18 (Chicago, IL: Field Enterprises Educational Corporation, 1968), 100–101.
151. Hohenberg, *Free Press/Free People*, 279–280.

152. Susan Welch, John Gruhl, Michael Steinman, and John Comer, *American Government* (St. Paul, MN: West Publishing Company, 1992), 216–218.

153. Berkman, *Politics in the Media Age*, 39.

154. Ibid., 40.

155. James M. Freeman, "Telephone," in *The World Book Encyclopedia*, Volume 18 (Chicago, IL: Field Enterprises Educational Corporation, 1968), 84.

156. Gladys D. Ganley, *The Exploding Political Power of Personal Media* (Norwood, NJ: Ablex Publishing Corporation, 1992), xv.

157. Ibid., 3–4.

158. Ibid., 13–24.

159. Ibid., 29.

160. Ibid., 44–45.

161. Ibid.

162. Ibid., 97–100.

163. Ibid., 50.

164. Ibid.

165. Ibid., 49–51.

166. Ted Koppel, Testimony before the U.S. House of Representatives Committe on International Relations, chaired by Lee Hamilton, R-IN; April 26, 1994; recorded and aired on C-SPAN.

167. Ganley, *The Exploding Political Power of Personal Media*, 49–51.

168. Ibid., 51.

169. Jeremy D. Popkin and Jack R. Censer, "Lessons from a Symposium," in Jeremy D. Popkin, ed., *Media and Revolution: Comparative Perspectives* (Lexington, KY: The University Press of Kentucky, 1995), 11.

170. Quoted in Michael J. O'Neill, *The Roar of the Crowd: How Television and People Power are Changing the World* (New York: Time Books, 1993), 95.

171. For example, see the following sources: Morgenthau, "The Permanent Values in the Old Diplomacy," in Stephen D. Kertesz and M.A. Fitzsimons, eds., *Diplomacy in a Changing World* (Notre Dame, IN: University of Notre Dame Press, 1959); James L. McCamy, *Conduct of the New Diplomacy* (New York: Harper & Row, Publishers, 1964); Sir Harold Nicolson, *The Evolution of Diplomacy* (New York: Collier Books, 1966); Geoffrey McDermott, *The New Diplomacy and Its Apparatus* (London: The Plume Press Limited, 1973); Elmer Plischke, "The New Diplomacy," in Elmer Plischke, ed., *Modern Diplomacy: The Art and the Artisans* (Washington: American Enterprise Institute, 1979); Abba Eban, *The New Diplomacy: International Affairs in the Modern Age* (New York: Random House, 1983); M. S. Anderson, *The Rise of Modern Diplomacy, 1450–1919* (New York: Longman Publishing, 1993); and Hamilton and Langhorne, *The Practice of Diplomacy*.

172. Kuhn, *The Structure of Scientific Revolutions*, 111–135, 6–11.

173. Ibid., 62, 151.

174. Ibid., 20.

175. Hamilton and Langhorne, *The Practice of Diplomacy*, 89.

176. Eban, *The New Diplomacy*, 339.

177. Anderson, *The Rise of Modern Diplomacy*, 2–3.

178. Eban, *The New Diplomacy*, 337.

179. Sir Harold Nicolson, *Diplomacy* (New York: Oxford University Press, 1965), 13.

180. Anderson, *The Rise of Modern Diplomacy*, 7–8.

181. Ibid.

182. Hamilton and Langhorne, *The Practice of Diplomacy*, 34–35.

183. Nicolson, *The Evolution of Diplomacy*, 100–104.

184. Eban, *The New Diplomacy*, 343–345. Nicolson, *The Evolution of Diplomacy*, 100–104. Nicolson, *Diplomacy* (London: Thornton Butterworth, Ltd; 1939), 73.

185. Alan Brinkley, *The Unfinished Nation: A Concise History of the American People* (New York: McGraw-Hill, Inc., 1993), 187. Eban, *The New Diplomacy*, 343–345. Henry Kissinger,

A World Restored: Metternich, Castlereagh and the Problems of Peace, 1812–1822 (Boston: Houghton Mifflin Co.) 1994; 61 & 165. Livingston Merchant, "New Techniques in Diplomacy," in E.A.J. Johnson, ed., *The Dimensions of Diplomacy* (Baltimore: Johns Hopkins Press, 1964), 122. Nicolson, *The Evolution of Diplomacy*, 100–104.

186. Eban, *The New Diplomacy*, 343–345. Nicolson, *The Evolution of Diplomacy*, 100–104.

187. Eban, *The New Diplomacy*, 343–345. Nicolson, *The Evolution of Diplomacy*, 100–104.

188. Eban, *The New Diplomacy*, 341–345. K.J. Holsti, "Governance Without Government: Polyarchy in Nineteenth Century European International Politics," pp. 30–57 in James N. Rosenau and Ernst-Otto Czempiel (eds.), *Governance Without Government: Order and Change in World Politics* (Cambridge: Cambridge University Press), 54. Kern, *The Culture of Time and Space*, 274. Kissinger, *A World Restored*, 5 & 323. Nicolson, *The Evolution of Diplomacy*, 100–104.

189. Eban, *The New Democracy*, 331.

190. Kissinger, *A World Restored*, 323.

191. Ibid., 61.

192. Ibid., 63.

193. Ibid., 5–83.

194. Nicolson, *Diplomacy* (1939), 73.

195. Merchant, "New Techniques In Diplomacy," 122.

196. Brinkley, *The Unfinished Nation*, 187.

197. Merchant, "New Techniques In Diplomacy," 122.

198. Hamilton and Langhorne, *The Practice of Diplomacy*, 131.

199. Brinkley, *The Unfinished Nation*, 171, 187–188.

200. Nicolson, *The Evolution of Diplomacy*, 85, 103.

201. Anderson, *The Rise of Modern Diplomacy*, 292.

202. Eban, *The New Diplomacy*, 345.

203. Quoted in Ibid., 345.

204. Morgenthau, *Politics Among Nations*, 428.

205. Eban, *The New Diplomacy*, 345.

206. Nicolson, *The Evolution of Diplomacy*, 113.

207. Morgenthau, *Politics Among Nations*, 426.

208. Ibid., 427.

209. Eban, *The New Diplomacy*, 345.

210. Ibid., 369.

211. Nicolson, *The Evolution of Diplomacy*, 122–124. Nicolson, *Diplomacy* (1939), 92.

212. Robert D. Putnam, "Diplomacy and Domestic Politics: The Logic of Two-Level Games," *International Organization* 42, number 3 (Summer 1988), 459–460.

213. Eban, *The New Diplomacy*, 367–369.

214. Ibid., 367.

215. Kern, *The Culture of Time and Space, 1880–1918*, 274.

216. Nicolson, *Diplomacy* (1965), 144.

217. James Der Derian, *On Diplomacy: A Genealogy of Western Estrangement* (Oxford, England: Basil Blackwell, Ltd., 1987), 208.

218. Ibid.

219. Adam Watson, *Diplomacy: The Dialogue Between States* (New York: New Press, McGraw-Hill Book Company, 1983), 142.

220. Eban, *The New Diplomacy*, 366.

221. Ibid., 367.

222. Merchant, "New Techniques In Diplomacy," 120–121.

Chapter 3. Diplomacy and Communication: The Results of Linkage

1. Quoted in Hamilton and Langhorne, *The Practice of Diplomacy*, 132.

2. Ibid., 135.
3. Ibid., 137.
4. Anderson, *The Rise of Modern Diplomacy*, 12–13.
5. Hamilton and Langhorne, *The Practice of Diplomacy*, 32–33.
6. Nicolson, *The Evolution of Diplomacy*, 55.
7. Ibid.
8. Nicolson, *Diplomacy* (1965), 55.
9. Innis, *The Bias of Communication*, 60.
10. Kissinger, *A World Restored*, 165–68.
11. Ibid., 323.
12. Holsti, "Governance Without Government," 54.
13. Ibid.
14. Sir Geoffrey Jackson, *Concorde Diplomacy* (London: Hamish Hamilton, Ltd., 1981), 135.
15. Hamilton and Langhorne, *The Practice of Diplomacy*, 132.
16. Headrick, *The Invisible Weapon*, 4.
17. Ibid., 73–4.
18. Kern, *The Culture of Time and Space, 1880–1914*, 316.
19. Ibid., 262.
20. Ibid., 268.
21. Headrick, *The Invisible Weapon*, 139.
22. Kern, *The Culture of Time and Space, 1880–1914*, 259–261.
23. Ibid., 263.
24. Ibid., 276.
25. Ibid.
26. Headrick, *The Invisible Weapon*, 138.
27. Kern, *The Culture of Time and Space, 1880–1914*, 275–76.
28. Hamilton and Langhorne, *The Practice of Diplomacy*, 133.
29. Eban, *The New Diplomacy*, 367.
30. Hamilton and Langhorne, *The Practice of Diplomacy*, 133.
31. Ibid., 131–136.
32. Headrick, *The Invisible Weapon*, 68.
33. Ibid., 68.
34. Kern, *The Culture of Time and Space*, 274.
35. Quoted in Headrick, *The Invisible Weapon*, 74.
36. Anderson, *The Rise of Modern Diplomacy*, 173.
37. Quoted in Ibid., 137.
38. Quoted in Kern, *The Culture of Time and Space*, 274.
39. Quoted in Anderson, *The Rise of Modern Diplomacy*, 136.
40. Kern, *The Culture of Time and Space*, 260.
41. Headrick, *The Invisible Weapon*, 111.
42. Peter Young and Peter Jesser, *The Media and the Military: From the Crimea to Desert Strike* (New York: St. Martin's Press, 1997), 20.
43. Nicolson, *Diplomacy* (1965), 92.
44. Young and Jesser, *The Media and the Military*, 20; emphasis in the original.
45. Anderson, *The Rise of Modern Diplomacy*, 136.
46. Quoted in Young and Jesser, *The Media and the Military*, 20.
47. Eban, *The New Diplomacy*, 345.
48. Morgenthau, *Politics Among Nations*, 431–32.
49. Hamilton and Langhorne, *The Practice of Diplomacy*.
50. Kern, *The Culture of Time and Space*, 260.
51. Girija K. Mookerjee, *Diplomacy* (New Delhi, India: Trimurti Publications Private Limited, 1973), 103.
52. Nicolson, *Diplomacy* (1939), 37.
53. Quoted in Nicolson, *Diplomacy* (1939), 168.

54. Quoted in Anderson, *The Rise of Modern Diplomacy*, 137.

55. Quoted in Nicolson, *Diplomacy* (1965), 37.

56. Quoted in Innis, *The Bias of Communication*, 79.

57. Philip M. Seib, *Headline Diplomacy: How News Coverage Affects Foreign Policy* (Westport, CT: Praeger Publishers, 1997), 5.

58. Mott, *American Journalism, A History*, 529.

59. Seib, *Headline Diplomacy*, 1–13. Mott, *American Journalism, A History*, 529. Hohenberg, *Free Press/Free People*, 146–49.

60. Mott, *American Journalism, A History*, 532.

61. Hohenberg, *Free Press/Free People*, 148.

62. Seib, *Headline Diplomacy*, 1–3. Hohenberg, *Free Press/Free People*, 148–49. Mott, *American Journalism, A History*, 532.

63. Mott, *American Journalism, A History*, 531.

64. Hohenberg, *Free Press/Free People*, 148.

65. Ibid., 146.

66. Mott, *American Journalism, A History*, 532. Warren P. Strobel, *Late-Breaking Foreign Policy: The News Media's Influence on Peace Operations* (Washington, D.C.: United States Institute of Peace Press, 1997), 21–23.

67. Hohenberg, *Free Press/Free People*, 148.

68. Seib, *Headline Diplomacy*, 2.

69. Ibid., 12.

70. Seib, *Headline Diplomacy*, 1–13. Mott, *American Journalism, A History*, 529–539. Hohenberg, *Free Press/Free People*, 146–149.

71. Seib, *Headline Diplomacy*, 12–13.

72. Ibid., 5.

73. Welch, et al., *American Government*, 218.

74. Seib, *Headline Diplomacy*, 107.

75. Daniel C. Hallin, *The "Uncensored War": The Media and Vietnam* (Berkley, CA: The University of California Press, 1989).

76. Berkman, *Politics in the Media Age*, 39.

77. James Aronson, *The Press and the Cold War* (New York: Monthly Review Press, 1970), 199.

78. Ibid., 199–201.

79. Hallin, *The "Uncensored War": The Media and Vietnam*, 108.

80. Ibid.

81. Robert Dallek, *Flawed Giant: Lyndon Johnson and His Times, 1961–1973* (New York: Oxford University Press, 1998), 506.

82. Ibid., 527–529.

83. Noel Cohen, *Media Diplomacy: The Foreign Office in the Mass Communications Age* (London, England: Frank Cass and Company, Limited, 1986), 156.

84. Eban, *The New Diplomacy*, 345.

85. Tran Van Dinh, *Communication and Diplomacy in a Changing World*, 37.

Chapter 4. The Persian Gulf War and Telediplomacy: The Next Diplomatic Paradigm

1. Johanna Neuman, *Lights, Camera, War: Is Media Technology Driving International Politics?* (New York: St. Martin's Press, 1996), 225.

2. Lawrence Freedman and Efraim Karsh, *The Gulf Conflict, 1990–1991: Diplomacy and War in the New World Order* (Princeton, NJ; Princeton University Press, 1993), xxxiii.

3. E.D. Sheppard and D. Bawden, "More News, Less Knowledge? An Information Content Analysis of Television and Newspaper Coverage of the Gulf War," *International Journal of Information Management* 17, number 3 (June 1997), 212.

4. Seib, *Headline Diplomacy*, 53.

5. Quoted in Michael R. Beschloss, *Presidents, Television and Foreign Crises* (Northwestern University: The Annenberg Washington Program in Communications Policy Studies, 1993), 24–5.

6. Quoted in Tom Engelhardt, "The Gulf War as Total Television," in Susan Jeffords and Lauren Rabinovitz, eds., *Seeing Through the Media* (New Brunswick, NJ: Rutgers University Press, 1994), 89.

7. Quoted in Beschloss, *Presidents, Television and Foreign Crises*, 25.

8. Gowing, "Real-Time Television Coverage of Armed Conflicts and Diplomatic Crises," 14.

9. Neuman, *Lights, Camera, War*, 16.

10. Seib, *Headline Diplomacy*, 70.

11. Ibid., 69.

12. Ibid.

13. Ibid., 53.

14. Strobel, *Late-Breaking Foreign Policy*, 234.

15. Strobel, *Late-Breaking Foreign Policy*, 234. Philip M. Taylor, *Global Communications, International Affairs and the Media Since 1945* (London: Routledge, 1997), 124–25.

16. Quoted in Patrick O'Heffernan, *Mass Media and Foreign Policy* (Norwood, NJ: Ablex Publishing Corporation, 1991), 1.

17. O'Neill, *The Roar of the Crowd*, 195.

18. Ibid.

19. John W. Tuthill, "Conclusions," in Dacor Bacon House Foundation *American Diplomacy in the Information Age* (Lanham, MD: University Press of America, 1991), 131.

20. Bosah Ebo, "Media Diplomacy and Foreign Policy: Toward a Theoretical Framework," in Abbas Malek, ed., *News Media and Foreign Relations* (Norwood, NJ: Ablex Publishing Corporation, 1997), 43.

21. Walter R. Roberts, "The Media Dimension II: Diplomacy in the Information Age," *The World Today* 47, number 7 (July 1991), 112–13.

22. Etyan Gilboa, "Media Diplomacy: Conceptual Divergence and Applications," *The Harvard International Journal of Press/Politics* 3, number 2 (Summer 1998), 72.

23. Quoted in Hamilton and Langhorne, *The Practice of Diplomacy*, 23–32.

24. Bernard C. Cohen, "A View from the Academy," in W. Lance Bennett and David L. Paletz, eds., *Taken by Storm: The Media, Public Opinion, and U.S. Foreign Policy in the Gulf War* (Chicago: The University of Chicago Press, 1994), 9.

25. Quoted in Christer Jönsson, "Diplomatic Signaling in the Television Age," *The Harvard International Journal of Press/Politics* 1, number 3 (Summer 1996), 24–40.

26. Fang, *A History of Mass Communication*, 167.

27. Ibid., xxxii.

28. Patrick O'Heffernan, "A Mutual Exploitation Model of Media Influence in U.S. Foreign Policy," in W. Lance Bennett and David L. Paletz, eds., *The Media, Public Opinion, and U.S. Foreign Policy in the Gulf War* (Chicago: The University of Chicago Press, 1994), 234.

29. Ibid.

30. Fang, *A History of Mass Communication*, xxxiii & 168.

31. Lloyd N. Cutler, "Foreign Policy on Deadline," *The Atlantic Community Quarterly* 22, number 3 (Fall 1984), 223.

32. Quoted in Neuman, *Lights, Camera, War*, 14–15.

33. Baker, *The Politics of Diplomacy*, 384.

34. Quoted in David D. Pearce, *Wary Partners: Diplomats and the Media* (Washington, DC: Congressional Quarterly, Inc., 1995), 18.

35. Nicholas Burns, "Talking to the World about American Foreign Policy," *The Harvard International Journal of Press/Politics* 1, number 4 (Fall 1996), 13.

36. Fang, *A History of Mass Communication*, 168 & 202.

37. Taylor, *Global Communications*, 95.

38. Daniel C. Hallin and Todd Gitlin, "The Gulf War as Popular Culture and Television Drama," In W. Lance Bennett and David L. Paletz, eds., *Taken by Storm: The Media, Public Opinion, and U.S. Foreign Policy in the Gulf War* (Chicago: The University of Chicago Press, 1994), 149.

39. Fang, *A History of Mass Communication*, 202.

40. Stephen Hess, *International News and Foreign Correspondents* (Washington, DC: The Brookings Institution, 1996), 64.

41. Sheppard and Bawden, "More News, Less Knowledge?," 212.

42. Ibid.

43. Armand Mattelart and Michèle Mattelart, "On New Uses of Media in Time of Crisis," in Marc Raboy and Bernard Dagenais, eds., *Media Crisis, and Democracy: Mass Communication and the Disruption of Social Order* (London: Sage Publications, 1992), 177.

44. Taylor, *Global Communications*, 95.

45. Linda Jo Calloway, "High Tech Comes to War Coverage: Uses of Information and Communications Technology for Television Coverage in the Gulf War," in Thomas A. McCain and Leonard Shyles, eds., *The 1,000 Hour War: Communication in the Gulf* (Westport, CT: Greenwood Publishing Group, Inc., 1994), 56.

46. Ed Turner, Testimony before the U.S. House of Representatives Committee on International Relations; Chaired by Lee Hamilton, R-IN, April 26, 1994; recorded and aired on C-SPAN.

47. Taylor, *Global Communications*, 95.

48. Quoted in The Freedom Forum Media Studies Center Research Group, *The Media and Foreign Policy in the Post-Cold War World* (New York: Columbia University Press, 1993), 16.

49. Hess, *International News and Foreign Correspondents*, 3 & 64.

50. Quoted in Pearce, *Wary Partners*, 48. Mustapha Masmoudi, "Media and the State in Periods of Crisis," in Marc Raboy and Bernard Dagenais, eds., *Media Crisis, and Democracy: Mass Communication and the Disruption of Social Order* (London: Sage Publications, 1992), 40.

51. Pearce, *Wary Partners*, 48.

52. Hess, *International News and Foreign Correspondents*, 64.

53. Gadi Wolfsfeld, *Media and Political Conflict: News from the Middle East* (Cambridge, England: Cambridge University Press, 1997), 59.

54. Taylor, *Global Communications*, 96.

55. Ibid., 95.

56. Baker, *The Politics of Diplomacy*, 364.

57. Pool, *Technologies of Freedom*, 20–21.

58. Quoted in Beschloss, *Presidents, Television and Foreign Crises*, 6.

59. Lawrence K. Grossman, *The Electronic Republic: Reshaping Democracy in the Information Age* (New York: Penguin Group, 1995), 101.

60. Donald L. Shaw and Shannon E. Martin, "The Natural, and Inevitable, Phases of War Reporting: Historical Shadows, New Communication in the Persian Gulf," in Robert E. Denton, Jr., ed., *The Media and the Persian Gulf War* (Westport, CT: Praeger Press, 1993), 34.

61. Freedman and Karsh, *The Gulf Conflict, 1990–1991*, 78.

62. O'Heffernan, "A Mutual Exploitation Model," 236.

63. Ibid.

64. McNulty, "Television's Impact on Executive Decisionmaking and Diplomacy," 82.

65. Quoted in Frank J. Stech, "Winning CNN Wars," *Parameters* 24, number 3 (Autumn 1994), 39.

66. Quoted in O'Heffernan, *Mass Media and Foreign Policy*, 41.

67. Ibid., 42.

68. Quoted in Rourke, *International Politics on the World Stage*, 281.

69. Baker, *The Politics of Diplomacy*, 367.

70. Ibid., 363.

71. David D. Newsom, ed., *The Diplomatic Record, 1990–1991* (Westview Press, 1992), 14.

72. Baker, "Report First, Check Later: Former Secretary of State James A. Baker, III, Interview with Marvin Kalb," *Press/Politics* 1, number 2 (Spring 1996), 7.

73. Newsom, ed., *The Diplomatic Record, 1990–1991*, 14.

74. Don M. Flournoy, *CNN World Report: Ted Turner's International News Coup* (London: John Libbey & Company, Ltd., 1992), 66.

75. Baker, *The Politics of Diplomacy*, 284–5.

76. Neuman, *Lights, Camera, War*, 246.

77. Karl, "Media Diplomacy," 152.

78. Ibid., 149.

79. Quoted in Rourke, *International Politics on the World Stage*, 293.

80. O'Heffernan, "A Mutual Exploitation Model," 236.

81. Quoted in Shaw and Martin, "The Natural, and Inevitable," 34.

82. Strobel, *Late-Breaking Foreign Policy*, 44.

83. Quoted in Gannett Foundation Media Center, *The Media at War: The Press and the Persian Gulf Conflict*, (New York: Columbia University Press, 1991), 74.

84. Ibid.

85. O'Heffernan, "A Mutual Exploitation Model," 237.

86. Quoted in O'Heffernan, *Mass Media and Foreign Policy*, 55.

87. David D. Newsom, *The Public Dimension of Foreign Policy*, (Bloomington and Indianapolis, IN: Indiana University Press, 1996), 95.

88. Quoted in Taylor, *Global Communications*, 93–4.

89. Gowing, "Real-Time Television Coverage," 14–15.

90. Quoted in Ibid.

91. Eban, *The New Diplomacy*, 345.

92. McNulty, "Television's Impact," 82.

93. Taylor, *Global Communications*, 97.

94. Quoted in McNulty, "Television's Impact," 71.

95. Quoted in Walter B. Wriston, "Bits, Bytes, and Diplomacy," *Foreign Affairs* 76, number 5 (September/October 1997), 174; ellipses in the original.

96. Quoted in McNulty, "Television's Impact," 71.

97. Quoted in Ibid.

98. Wriston, "Bits, Bytes, and Diplomacy," 174.

99. Hamilton and Langhorne, *The Practice of Diplomacy*, 134.

100. Bruce Wetterau, *World History*, 1139.

101. Wriston, "Bits, Bytes, and Diplomacy," 174.

102. Ibid.

103. Morgenthau, *Politics Among Nations*, 437.

104. Eric Clark, *Diplomat: The World of International Diplomacy* (New York: Taplinger Publishing Company, 1973), 1.

105. William Hachten and Marva Hachten, "Reporting the Gulf War," in Doris A. Graber, ed., *Media Power in Politics* (Washington, DC: CQ Press, 1994), 340.

106. Seib, *Headline Diplomacy*, 104.

107. Quoted in O'Neill, *The Roar of the Crowd*, 95.

108. Seib, *Headline Diplomacy*, 105–106.

109. Quoted in McNulty, "Television's Impact," 74–75; emphasis added.

110. Quoted in Beschloss, *Presidents, Television and Foreign Crises*, 21.

111. Ibid.

112. Wriston, "Bits, Bytes, and Diplomacy," 174.

113. Quoted in Pearce, *Wary Partners*, 23.

114. Baker, "Report First, Check Later," 7.

115. Quoted in Jönsson, "Diplomatic Signaling," 31.

116. Quoted in Gowing, "Real-Time Television Coverage," 84–5.

117. Taylor, *Global Communications*, 96.

118. Baker, "Report First, Check Later," 7.

119. O'Heffernan, *Mass Media and Foreign Policy*, 90.

120. Ibid.

121. Quoted in Seib, *Headline Diplomacy*, 108.

122. Quoted in Pearce, *Wary Partners*, 22.

123. Brenda M. Seaver, "The Public Dimension of Foreign Policy," *The Harvard International Journal of Press/Politics* 3, number 1 (Winter 1998), 78.

124. Baker, *The Politics of Diplomacy*, 103.

125. Sir Harold Nicolson, *Diplomacy* (Washington, DC: Institute for the Study of Diplomacy, School of Foreign Service, Georgetown University, 1988), 52–53.

126. Quoted in Neuman, *Lights, Camera, War*, 5.

127. Quoted in McNulty, "Television's Impact," 77.

128. O'Neill, *The Roar of the Crowd*, 179.

129. Newsom, *The Public Dimension of Foreign Policy*, 96.

130. O'Neill, *The Roar of the Crowd*, 178.

131. Tom Rosenstiel, "The Myth of CNN," *The New Republic* volume 211, numbers 8 & 9 (August 22 & 29, 1994), 28.

132. O'Heffernan, *Mass Media and Foreign Policy*, 91.

133. Koppel, Testimony before the House International Relations Committee (1994).

134. Dom Bonafede, "The President, Congress, and the Media in Global Affairs," in Abbas Malek, ed., *News Media and Foreign Relations: A Multifaceted Perspective* (Norwood, NJ: Ablex Publishing Company, 1997), 96.

135. Quoted in Rourke, *International Politics on the World Stage*, 293.

136. David R. Gergen, "Diplomacy in a Television Age: The Dangers of Teledemocracy," in Simon R. Serfaty, ed., *The Media and Foreign Policy* (New York: St. Martin's, 1990), 48–9.

137. Ronald H. Hinckley, *People, Polls, and Policymakers* (New York: Lexington Books, 1992), 140.

138. Bernard C. Cohen, *The Public's Impact on Foreign Policy* (Boston: Little, Brown, 1973).

139. Ibid.

140. Baker, "Report First, Check Later," 8.

141. Ibid.

142. Bernard C. Cohen, *The Public's Impact on Foreign Policy*, 62–64.

143. Seaver, "The Public Dimension of Foreign Policy," 65–66.

144. Philip J. Powlick, "The Attitudinal Bases for Responsiveness to Public Opinion Among American Foreign Policy Officials," *The Journal of Conflict Resolution* 35, number 4 (December 1991), 612. Seaver, "The Public Dimension of Foreign Policy," 75–78.

145. Seaver, "The Public Dimension of Foreign Policy," 66.

146. Powlick, "The Attitudinal Bases," 634–35.

147. Donald J. Jordan and Benjamin I. Page, "Shaping Foreign Policy Opinions: The Role of TV News," *The Journal of Conflict Resolution* 36, number 2 (June 1992), 227.

148. Ibid.

149. Taylor, *Global Communications*, 59.

150. Nicolson, *Diplomacy* (1988), 43.

151. Baker, *The Politics of Diplomacy*, 103.

Chapter 5. Global Television's Ability to Drive Policy

1. Cutler, "Foreign Policy on Deadline," 223.

2. Quoted in The Freedom Forum, *The Media and Foreign Policy in the Post-Cold War World*, 27.

3. Quoted in Neuman, *Lights, Camera, War*, 269–70.

4. James F. Hoge, Jr., "Media Pervasiveness," *Foreign Affairs* 73, number 4 (July/August 1994), 136.

5. Cited in McNulty, "Television's Impact," 74–75.

6. Baker, *The Politics of Diplomacy*, 103; emphasis added.

7. Ibid.

8. Andrew S. Natsios, *U.S. Foreign Policy and the Four Horsemen of the Apocalypse: Humanitarian Relief in Complex Emergencies* (Westport, CT: Praeger Press, 1997), 124–139.

9. Ibid., 1.

10. Rourke, *International Politics on the World Stage*, 303.

11. Martin Shaw, *Civil Society and Media in Global Crises: Representing Distant Violence* (London: Pinter Printers, 1996), 4; emphasis in the original.

12. Ibid., 2–4.

13. Ibid., 2–4 & 156.

14. Peter Shiras, "Big Problems, Small Print: A Guide to the Complexity of Humanitarian Emergencies and the Media," in Robert I. Rotberg and Thomas G. Weiss, eds., *From Massacres to Genocide: The Media, Humanitarian Crises, and Policy-Making* (Washington, DC: The Brookings Institution, 1996), 93–94.

15. Natsios, *U.S. Foreign Policy and the Four Horsemen of the Apocalypse*, 7.

16. Karl, "Media Diplomacy," 144. McNulty, "Television's Impact," 82. Natsios, *U.S. Foreign Policy and the Four Horsemen of the Apocalypse*, 7. O'Heffernan, *Mass Media and Foreign Policy*, 79.

17. Karl, "Media Diplomacy," 152. O'Heffernan, *Mass Media and Foreign Policy*, 42.

18. Strobel, *Late-Breaking Foreign Policy*, 220–22 & 225.

19. Koppel, Testimony before the House International Relations Committee (1994).

20. Neuman, *Lights, Camera, War*, 21.

21. Robert J. Lieber, ed. *Eagle Adrift: American Foreign Policy at the End of the Century* (New York: Longman, 1997).

22. Seib, *Headline Diplomacy*, 137.

23. Hoge, "Media Pervasiveness." Michael Mandelbaum, "The Reluctance to Intervene," *Foreign Policy* 95 (Summer 1994).

24. Strobel, *Late-Breaking Foreign Policy*, 56.

25. Neuman, *Lights, Camera, War*, 9.

26. Ibid., 21.

27. Strobel, *Late-Breaking Foreign Policy*, 5.

28. Seib, *Headline Diplomacy*, 38.

29. Strobel, *Late-Breaking Foreign Policy*, 130.

30. Gowing, "Real-Time Television Coverage," 14–15.

Chapter 6. Global Television and Diplomatic Outcomes

1. Shaw, *Civil Society and Media in Global Crises*, 23.

2. Shiras, "Big Problems, Small Print," 99.

3. Quoted in John Bulloch and Harvey Morris, *No Friends But the Mountains: The Tragic History of the Kurds* (New York: Oxford University Press, 1992), 30.

4. Ibid., 38.

5. Freedman and Karsh, *The Gulf Conflict*, 424. Minear, Scott, and Weiss, *The News Media, Civil War, and Humanitarian Action*, 51. Richard N. Haass, *Intervention: The Use of American Military Force in the Post-Cold War World* (Washington, DC: The Carnegie Endowment for International Peace, 1994), 36.

6. Yitzhak Nakash, *The Shi'is of Iraq* (Princeton, NJ: Princeton University Press, 1994), 277. David McDowall, *A Modern History of the Kurds* (New York: I.B. Tauris and Company, Ltd., 1996), 373–388.

7. Daniel Schorr, "Ten Days that Shook the White House," *Columbia Journalism Review* (July/August 1991), 23.

8. Martin Shaw, "TV's Finest Hour," *New Statesman and Society* 9, number 399 (April 1996), 23.

9. Steve A. Yetiv, *The Persian Gulf Crisis* (Westport, CT: Greenwood Press, 1996), xx.

10. Daniel P. Bolger, *Savage Peace: Americans at War in the 1990s* (Novato, CA: Presidio Press, 1995), 226. Sauri P. Battacharya, "The Situation of the Kurds in the Post-Gulf War Period and U.S. Policy Toward It," *Asian Profile* 22, no. 2 (April 1994), 154.

11. Bulloch and Morris, *No Friends But the Mountains*, 15 & 25.

12. Bolger, *Savage Peace*, 231–33. Freedman and Karsh, *The Gulf Conflict*, 420.

13. Baker, *The Politics of Diplomacy*, 431–33.

14. Cited in Shaw, *Civil Society and Media in Global Crises*, 93. Bulloch and Morris, *No Friends But the Mountains*, 29. Bolger, *Savage Peace*, 232.

15. Ibid.

16. John Mueller, *Policy and Opinion in the Gulf War* (Chicago: The University of Chicago Press, 1994), 85 & 158.

17. Freedman and Karsh, *The Gulf Conflict*, 411.

18. Bulloch and Morris, *No Friends But the Mountains*, 26.

19. Quoted in Ibid., 11–12.

20. McDowall, *A Modern History of the Kurds*, 372.

21. Ibid., 373.

22. Bulloch and Morris, *No Friends But the Mountains*, 30–31.

23. David Keen, "Short-Term Interventions and Long–Term Problems: The Case of the Kurds in Iraq," in John Harriss, ed., *The Politics of Humanitarian Intervention* (London: Pinter Publishers, 1995), 169.

24. Quoted in McDowall, *A Modern History of the Kurds*, 372.

25. Quoted in Freedman and Karsh, *The Gulf Conflict*, 417.

26. Freedman and Karsh, *The Gulf Conflict*, 420.

27. Michael M. Gunter, *The Kurds in Iraq* (New York: St. Martin's Press, 1992), 54–55.

28. Quoted in Bulloch and Morris, *No Friends But the Mountains*, 12.

29. Bulloch and Morris, *No Friends But the Mountains*, 12.

30. Freedman and Karsh, *The Gulf Conflict*, 420.

31. Quoted in Shaw, *Civil Society and Media in Global Crises*, 85.

32. Ibid., 22.

33. Ibid.

34. Quoted in Ibid.

35. Quoted in Freedman and Karsh, *The Gulf Conflict*, 421.

36. Freedman and Karsh, *The Gulf Conflict*, 421.

37. James Mayall, "Non-Intervention, Self-Determination and the 'New World Order,'" *International Affairs* 67, number 3 (July 1991), 22.

38. Cited in Schorr, "Ten Days that Shook the White House," *Columbia Journalism Review*, 23.

39. Shaw, *Civil Society and Media in Global Crises*, 156.

40. Minear, Scott, and Weiss, *The News Media, Civil War, and Humanitarian Action*, 51.

41. O'Neill, *The Roar of the Crowd*, 160.

42. Gowing, "Real-Time Television Coverage," 111.

43. Taylor, *Global Communications, International Affairs and the Media Since 1945*, 125.

44. Shaw, *Civil Society and Media in Global Crises*, 79. Philip M. Taylor, *War and the Media: Propaganda and Persuasion in the Gulf War* (Manchester, England: Manchester University Press, 1992), 15.

45. Deborah Amos, "Foreign Policy by Public Outrage," *Nieman Reports* XLVIII no. 2 (Summer 1994), 74.

46. Gowing, "Real-Time Television Coverage," 38. Bulloch and Morris, *No Friends But the Mountains*, 28.

47. Taylor, *War and the Media*, 277.

48. Ibid., 15.

49. Shaw, *Civil Society and Media in Global Crises*, 86–88.

50. Walter B. Wriston, *The Twilight of Sovereignty: How the Information Revolution is Transforming Our World* (New York: Charles Scribner's Sons, 1992), 139.

51. Shaw, *Civil Society and Media in Global Crises*, 88.

52. Bulloch and Morris, *No Friends But the Mountains*, 13.

53. Taylor, *Global Communications, International Affairs and the Media Since 1945*, 92.

54. Gowing, "Real-Time Television Coverage," 38.

55. Ibid., 38–39.

56. Freedman and Karsh, *The Gulf Conflict*, 423.

57. Strobel, *Late-Breaking Foreign Policy*, 128.

58. Quoted in Schorr, "Ten Days the Shook the White House," *Columbia Journalism Review*, 23.

59. Ibid.

60. Quoted in Beschloss, *Presidents, Television and Foreign Crises*, 25.

61. Haass, *Intervention*, 36.

62. Quoted in Beschloss, *Presidents, Television and Foreign Crises*, 25.

63. Strobel, *Late-Breaking Foreign Policy*, 128.

64. Jönsson, "Diplomatic Signaling," 29.

65. Lionel Rosenblatt, "The Media and the Refugee," in Robert I. Rotberg and Thomas G. Weiss, eds., *From Massacres to Genocide: The Media, Humanitarian Crises, and Policy-Making* (Washington, DC: The Brookings Institution, 1996), 141.

66. Keen, "Short-Term Interventions and Long-Term Problems," 183.

67. Pearce, *Wary Partners*, 22.

68. Wolfsfeld, *Media and Political Conflict*, 135.

69. Gladys Engel Lang and Kurt Lang, "The Press as Prologue: Media Coverage of Saddam's Iraq, 1979–1990," in W. Lance Bennett and David L. Paletz, eds., *The Media, Public Opinion, and U.S. Foreign Policy in the Gulf War* (Chicago: The Chicago University Press, 1994), 54–56.

70. Wolfsfeld, *Media and Political Conflict*, 135.

71. Gowing, "Real-Time Television Coverage," 38.

72. Quoted in Jonathan Benthall, *Disasters, Relief, and the Media* (London: I.B. Taurist & Co. Ltd. Publishers, 1993), 132.

73. David L. Paletz, "Just Deserts?" in *Taken by Storm: The Media, Public Opinion, and U.S. Foreign Policy in the Gulf War* (Chicago: The University of Chicago Press, 1994), 284.

74. Shaw, *Civil Society and Media in Global Crises*, 156 & 180.

75. Ibid., 180.

76. Quoted in Gowing, "Real-Time Television Coverage," 39.

77. Quoted in Frank J. Stech, "Winning CNN Wars," 39.

78. Shaw, *Civil Society and Media in Global Crises*, 95.

79. *The Economist*, 27 April 1991, 46.

80. Shaw, *Civil Society and Media in Global Crises*, 23.

81. Gowing, "Real-Time Television Coverage," 38–39.

82. Nakash, *The Shi'is of Iraq*, 7. Bolger, *Savage Peace*, 228–29.

83. Nakash, *The Shi'is of Iraq*, 274. Bolger, *Savage Peace*, 228.

84. Freedman and Karsh, *The Gulf Conflict*, 410. Benthall, *Disasters, Relief, and the Media*, 34. Nakash, *The Shi'is of Iraq*, 274–277. Geoff Simons, *Iraq: From Sumer to Saddam* (New York: St. Martin's Press, 1994), 25–26.

85. Bolger, *Savage Peace*, 228–230.

86. Bolger, *Savage Peace*, 230–231. Freedman and Karsh, *The Gulf Conflict*, 419–20. Nakash, *The Shi'is of Iraq*, 278–79. Shaw, "TV's Finest Hour," 22–23. Shaw, *Civil Society and Media in Global Crises*, 21. Mueller, *Policy and Opinion in the Gulf War*, 85.

87. Cited in Bolger, *Savage Peace*, 231.

88. Quoted in Taylor, *Global Communications*, 92.
89. Ibid.
90. Shaw, *Civil Society and Media in Global Crises*, 157.
91. Bulloch and Morris, *No Friends But the Mountains*, 12. Nakash, *The Shi'is of Iraq*, 275.
92. Stephen E. Ambrose, *Rise to Globalism: American Foreign Policy Since 1938* (New York: Penguin Group, 1993). Warren I. Cohen, *Empire Without Tears: America's Foreign Relations, 1921–1933* (New York: Alfred A. Knopf, 1987). John Lewis Gaddis, *Strategies of Containment* (Oxford, England: Oxford University Press, 1982). Charles W. Kegley, Jr. and Eugene R. Wittkopf, *American Foreign Policy: Pattern and Process* (Fifth Edition) (New York: St. Martin's, 1996), 37–43. Richard H. Immerman, *The CIA in Guatemala* (Austin, TX: University of Texas Press, 1990). Kenneth A. Oye, Robert J. Lieber, and Donald Rothchild, eds., *Eagle Resurgent? The Reagan Era in American Foreign Policy* (Boston: Little, Brown and Company, 1987). Guy E. Poitras, *The Ordeal of Hegemony: The United States and Latin America* (Boulder, CO: Westview Press, 1990). Bonnie Szumski, ed.,*Latin America and U.S. Foreign Policy: Opposing Viewpoints* (San Diego, CA: Greenhaven Press, 1988). R.W. Van Alstyne, *The Rising American Empire* (New York: W.W. Norton and Company, 1975).
93. Nakash, *The Shi'is of Iraq*, 274–279.
94. Ibid.
95. Nakash, *The Shi'is of Iraq*, 277. Freedman and Karsh, *The Gulf Conflict*, 420. McDowall, *A Modern History of the Kurds*, 370–77.
96. Quoted in Simons, *Iraq*, 28.
97. Ibid., 28.
98. Quoted in Nakash, *The Shi'is of Iraq*, 275.
99. Bolger, *Savage Peace*, 230–31.
100. Freedman and Karsh, *The Gulf Conflict*, 426.
101. Nakash, *The Shi'is of Iraq*, 276.
102. Shaw, *Civil Society and Media in Global Crises*, 22.
103. Baker, *The Politics of Diplomacy*, 431–439.
104. Ibid., 431 & 435.
105. Ibid., 434–435.
106. Haass, *Intervention*, 35.
107. Ibid., 36.
108. Ibid., 13.
109. Baker, *The Politics of Diplomacy*, 431.
110. Haass, *Intervention*, 36.
111. Ibid., 85.
112. Shaw, *Civil Society and Media in Global Crises*, 157.
113. Gowing, "Real-Time Television Coverage," 39.
114. Quoted in Shaw, *Civil Society and Media in Global Crises*, 95.
115. Shaw, *Civil Society and Media in Global Crises*, 81 & 119–20. Seib, *Headline Diplomacy*, 38.
116. Seib, *Headline Diplomacy*, 40.
117. Shaw, *Civil Society and Media in Global Crises*, 86 & 90. Benthall, *Disasters, Relief, and the Media*, 33–34.
118. Shaw, *Civil Society and Media in Global Crises*, 86–91.
119. Bolger, *Savage Peace*, 233.
120. Ibid., 233–34.
121. Bulloch and Morris, *No Friends But the Mountains*, 12.
122. Freedman and Karsh, *The Gulf Conflict*, 422. Baker, *The Politics of Diplomacy*, 435–39.
123. Bolger, *Savage Peace*, 232.
124. Shaw, *Civil Society and Media in Global Crises*, 38.
125. Cited in Bolger, *Savage Peace*, 231.

126. Simons, *Iraq*, 42.
127. Ibid.
128. Quoted in Nakash, *The Shi'is of Iraq*, 280.
129. Bolger, *Savage Peace*, 234–35.
130. Quoted in A.G. Noorani, *The Gulf Wars: Documents and Analysis* (Delhi, India: Konark Publishers, Private, Ltd., 1991), 392–93.
131. Natsios, *U.S. Foreign Policy*, 135.
132. Ibid.
133. Haass, *Intervention*, 36.
134. Gowing, "Real-Time Television Coverage," 39.
135. John C. Hammock and Joel R. Charny, "Emergency Response as Morality Play: The Media, the Relief Agencies, and the Need for Capacity Building," in Robert I. Rotberg and Thomas G. Weiss, eds., *From Massacres to Genocide: The Media, Public Policy, and Humanitarian Crises* (Washington, D.C.: The Brookings Institution, 1996), 122.
136. Ibid., 120.
137. Haass, *Intervention*, 136.
138. Quoted in Donald Rothchild, "Conclusion: Responding to Africa's Post-Cold War Conflicts," in Edmond J. Keller and Donald Rothchild, eds., *Africa in the New International Order: Rethinking State Sovereignty and Regional Security* (Boulder, CO: Lynne Rienner, 1996), 238–39.
139. Rothchild, "Conclusion," 238–39. Shaw, *Civil Society and Media in Global Crises*, 173. Hammock and Charny, "Emergency Response," 120.
140. Walter S. Clarke, "Waiting for 'The Big One,': Confronting Complex Humanitarian Emergencies and State Collapse in Central Africa," in Max G. Manwaring and John T. Fishel, eds., *Toward Responsibility in the New World Order*, 76.
141. Ibid., 75 & 76.
142. Clarke, "Waiting for 'The Big One,'" *Toward Responsibility*, 76. Seib, *Headline Diplomacy*, 94.
143. Ibid.
144. Larry Minear and Thomas G. Weiss, *Mercy Under Fire: War and the Global Humanitarian Community* (Boulder, CO: Westview Press, 1995), 223.
145. Shaw, *Civil Society and Media in Global Crises*, 172.
146. Clarke, "Waiting for 'The Big One,'" *Toward Responsibility*, 76. Shaw, *Civil Society and Media in Global Crises*, 172.
147. Hammock and Charny, "Emergency Response as Morality Play," 121–22. Minear and Weiss, *Mercy Under Fire*, 223–24.
148. Quoted in Seib, *Headline Diplomacy*, 95.
149. Hammock and Charny, "Emergency Response as Morality Play," 122–23.
150. John Seaman, "The International System of Humanitarian Relief in the 'New World Order,'" in *The Politics of Human Intervention* (London: Pinter Publishers, 1995), 19.
151. Shaw, *Civil Society and Media in Global Crises*, 172.
152. Clarke, "Waiting for 'The Big One,'" 75–6.
153. Duane Bratt, "Assessing the Success of UN Peacekeeping Operations," in Michael Pugh, ed., *The UN, Peace and Force* (London: Frank Cass, 1997), 78.
154. Andrew Natsios, "Illusions of Influence: The CNN Effect in Complex Emergencies," pp. 169–168 in Robert I. Rotberg and Thomas G. Weiss (eds.), *From Massacres to Genocide*, 162. Bratt, "Assessing the Success," 78.
155. Donald C.F. Daniel and Brad C. Hayes, "Securing Observance of UN Mandates through the Employment of Military Force," in Michael Pugh, ed., *The UN, Peace and Force* (London: Frank Cass, 1997), 115.
156. Rothchild, "Conclusion," 238–39.
157. Natsios, "Illusions of Influence," 162.
158. Quoted in Clarke, "Waiting for 'The Big One,'" 85.
159. Strobel, *Late-Breaking Foreign Policy*, 146. Rothchild, "Conclusion," 238–39.

160. Shaw, *Civil Society and Media in Global Crises*, 172. Clarke, "Waiting for 'The Big One,'" 76.

161. Tonny Brems Knudsen, "Humanitarian Intervention Revisited: Post-Cold War Responses to Classical Problems," pp. 146–165 in Michael Pugh (ed.), *The UN, Peace and Force* (London: Frank Cass, 1997), 157. Stephen P. Kinloch, "Utopian or Pragmatic? A UN Permanent Military Volunteer Force," in Michael Pugh, ed., *The UN, Peace and Force* (London: Frank Cass, 1997), 180.

162. Kinloch, "Utopian or Pragmatic?," 180.

163. Quoted in Clarke, "Waiting for 'The Big One,'" 81.

164. Minear, Scott, and Weiss, *The News Media, Civil War, and Humanitarian Action*, 63.

165. John Prendergast, *Frontline Diplomacy: Humanitarian Aid and Conflict in Africa* (Boulder, CO: Lynne Rienner, 1996), 5.

166. Ibid., 14.

167. Strobel, *Late-Breaking Foreign Policy*, 146.

168. Clarke, "Waiting for 'The Big One,'" 76–77.

169. Natsios, "Illusions of Influence," 162. Prendergast, *Frontline Diplomacy*, 14.

170. Quoted in Prendergast, *Frontline Diplomacy*, 8.

171. Quoted in Strobel, *Late-Breaking Foreign Policy*, 144.

172. *Ibid.*, 144.

173. Shaw, *Civil Society and Media in Global Crises*, 4; emphasis in the original.

174. Ibid., 2–4.

175. Seib, *Headline Diplomacy*, 94.

176. Prendergast, *Frontline Diplomacy*, 72.

177. Quoted in Strobel, *Late-Breaking Foreign Policy*, 146.

178. Carolyn J. Logan, "U.S. Public Opinion and the Intervention in Somalia: Lessons for the Future of Military-Humanitarian Interventions," *The Fletcher Forum of World Affairs* 20, number 2 (Summer/Fall 1996), 155.

179. Haass, *Intervention*, 62.

180. Ibid., 63.

181. Natsios, "Illusions of Influence," 161.

182. John Harriss, "Introduction: A Time of Troubles— Problems of International Humanitarian Assistance in the 1990s," in John Harriss, ed., *The Politics of Humanitarian Intervention* (London: Pinter Publishers, 1995), 7.

183. Strobel, *Late-Breaking Foreign Policy*, 152.

184. Strobel, *Late-Breaking Foreign Policy*, 146; see for example.

185. Steven Livingston, "Clarifying the CNN Effect: An Examination of Media Effects According to Type of Military Intervention," research paper R-18 (June), The Joan Shorenstein Barone Center on the Press, Politics and Public Policy, John F. Kennedy School of Government, Harvard University (Cambridge, MA: Harvard University), 14. Minear, Scott, and Weiss, *The News Media, Civil War, and Humanitarian Action*, 63. Rosenblatt, "The Media and the Refugee," 138.

186. Edward R. Girardet, "Reporting Humanitarianism: Are the New Electronic Media Making a Difference?" in Robert I. Rotberg and Thomas G. Weiss, eds., *From Massacres to Genocide: The Media, Public Policy, and Humanitarian Crises* (Washington, D.C.: The Brookings Institution, 1996), 57.

187. Hammock and Charny, "Emergency Response," 120. Natsios, "Illusions of Influence," 161. Shiras, "Big Problems, Small Print," 99. Strobel, *Late-Breaking Foreign Policy*, 144. Shaw, *Civil Society and the Media in Global Crises*, 170–72.

188. Minear, Scott, and Weiss, *The News Media, Civil War, and Humanitarian Action*, 3.

189. Strobel, *Late-Breaking Foreign Policy*, 133 & 145. Minear, Scott, and Weiss, *The News Media, Civil War, and Humanitarian Action*, 64.

190. Strobel, *Late-Breaking Foreign Policy*, 145.

191. Minear, Scott, and Weiss, *The News Media, Civil War, and Humanitarian Action*, 64.

192. Girardet, "Reporting Humanitarianism," 61.
193. Natsios, "Illusions of Influence," 162. Shiras, "Big Problems, Small Print," 99.
194. Rosenblatt, "The Media and the Refugee," 138–39.
195. Keen, "Short-Term Interventions," 169.
196. Shaw, Civil Society and the Media in Global Crises, 173.
197. Quoted in Minear Scott, and Weiss, The News Media, Civil War, and Humanitarian Action, 64–65.
198. Minear, Scott, and Weiss, The News Media, Civil War, and Humanitarian Action, 64–65.
199. Hammock and Charny, "Emergency Response," 122.
200. Ibid.
201. Shaw, Civil Society and the Media in Global Crises, 173.
202. Freedman and Karsh, The Gulf Conflict, 424. Minear, Scott, and Weiss, The News Media, Civil War, and Humanitarian Action, 51. Haass, Intervention, 36.
203. Taylor, Global Communications, 90.
204. Ibid.
205. Ibid.
206. Seib, Headline Diplomacy, 96.
207. Clarke, "Waiting for 'The Big One,'" 74–75.
208. Seib, Headline Diplomacy, 96.
209. Shaw, Civil Society and the Media in Global Crises, 172–73.
210. Minear, Scott, and Weiss, The News Media, Civil War, and Humanitarian Action, 64–65.
211. Robert I Rotberg and Thomas G. Weiss, eds., From Massacres to Genocide: The Media, Humanitarian Crises, and Policy-Making. (Washington, DC: The Brookings Institution, 1996), 182.
212. Minear, Scott, and Weiss, The News Media, Civil War, and Humanitarian Action, 64.
213. Seib, Headline Diplomacy, 96.
214. Ibid., 90–92 & 94–96.

Chapter 7. Global Television's Mechanisms for Driving Policy

1. Cutler, "Foreign Policy on Deadline," 223.
2. Quoted in Gowing, "Real-Time Television Coverage," 23.
3. Burns, "Talking to the World about American Foreign Policy." Gilboa, "Media Diplomacy." Rosenstiel, "The Myth of CNN." Seaver, "The Public Dimension of Foreign Policy." Seib, Headline Diplomacy. Strobel, Late-Breaking Foreign Policy.
4. Bernard C. Cohen, "A View from the Academy," 9–10.
5. Ibid.
6. Bernard C. Cohen, The Press and Foreign Policy (Princeton: Princeton University Press, 1963).
7. Burns, "Talking to the World about American Foreign Policy," 13.
8. Shanto Iyengar and Adam Simon, "News Coverage of the Gulf Crisis and Public Opinion: A Study of Agenda-Setting, Priming, and Framing," in W. Lance Bennett and David L. Paletz, eds., Taken by Storm: The Media, Public Opinion, and U.S. Foreign Policy in the Gulf War (Chicago: The University of Chicago Press, 1994), 168–172. Seaver, "The Public Dimension of Foreign Policy," 79–83.
9. Beschloss, Presidents, Television and Foreign Crises, 30.
10. O'Heffernan, Mass Media and Foreign Policy, 45.
11. Gowing, "Real-Time Television Coverage," 11; emphasis in the original.

12. O'Heffernan, "A Mutual Exploitation Model," 240.

13. Jönsson, "Diplomatic Signaling," 29.

14. Seib, *Headline Diplomacy*, 38; emphasis in the original.

15. Gowing, "Real-Time Television Coverage," 18.

16. Natsios, *U.S. Foreign Policy and the Four Horsemen of the Apocalypse*, 137.

17. Rosenblatt, "The Media and the Refugee," 138–39. Benthall, *Disasters, Relief, and the Media*, 33–34 & 49–50.

18. Mattelart and Mattelart, "On New Uses of Media in Time of Crisis," 176.

19. Quoted in Rotberg and Weiss, *From Massacres to Genocide*, 1.

20. Taylor, *Global Communications, International Affairs and the Media Since 1945*, 148.

21. John Shattuck, "Human Rights and Humanitarian Crises: Policy-Making and the Media," in Robert I. Rotberg and Thomas G. Weiss, eds., *From Massacres to Genocide: The Media, Humanitarian Crises, and Policy-Making* (Washington, DC: The Brookings Institution, 1996), 174; emphasis in the original.

22. Quoted in the Freedom Forum, 28.

23. Lee Hamilton, Testimony before the U.S. House of Representatives Committee on International Relations (1994); Chaired by Lee Hamilton, R-IN; April 26; Recorded and aired on C-SPAN.

24. Shattuck, "Human Rights and Humanitarian Crises," 174. Gowing, "Real-Time Television Coverage," 68 & 27.

25. Quoted in Mark D. Alleyne, *News Revolution: Political and Economic Decisions About Global Information* (New York: St. Martin's Press, 1997), 2.

26. Seib, *Headline Diplomacy*, 43–44.

27. Quoted in Strobel, *Late-Breaking Foreign Policy*, 142.

28. Quoted in Seib, *Headline Diplomacy*, 44.

29. Quoted in Minear, Scott, and Weiss, *The News Media, Civil War, and Humanitarian Action*, 55.

30. George F. Kennan, *At A Century's Ending: Reflections 1982–1995* (New York: W. W. Norton and Company, Inc., 1996), 294–97.

31. Ibid., 297.

32. Gowing, "Real-Time Television Coverage," 66.

33. Haass, *Intervention*, 46 & 85–86.

34. Quoted in Neuman, *Lights, Camera, War*, 14–15.

35. Quoted in Minear, Scott, and Weiss, *The News Media, Civil War, and Humanitarian Action*, 55.

36. Baker, *The Politics of Diplomacy*, 515. Michael R. Beschloss and Strobe Talbot, *At the Highest Levels: The Inside Story of the End of the Cold War* (Boston: Little, Brown and Company, 1993), 422.

37. Quoted in McNulty, "Television's Impact," 75–76.

38. Baker, *The Politics of Diplomacy*, 520.

39. O'Neill, *The Roar of the Crowd*, 20–21.

40. Baker, *The Politics of Diplomacy*, 520.

41. O'Neill, *The Roar of the Crowd*, 20.

42. Seib, *Headline Diplomacy*, 111. Gilboa, "Media Diplomacy," 69–70.

43. Walter Cronkite, *A Reporter's Life* (New York: Alfred A. Knopf, 1996), 314.

44. Ibid., 354–55.

45. Ibid., 383

46. Gilboa, "Media Diplomacy," 69–72.

47. O'Heffernan, *Mass Media and Foreign Policy*, 20.

48. Ibid., 19–26.

49. Ibid., 27–28 & 159–75.

50. Ibid., 27.

51. Ibid., 27–8.

52. Seib, *Headline Diplomacy*, 51.

53. Ibid., 49–50.

54. Jarol B. Manheim, "The Press as Prologue: Managing Kuwait's Image During the Gulf Conflict," in W. Lance Bennett and David L. Paletz, eds., *The Media, Public Opinion, and U.S. Foreign Policy in the Gulf War* (Chicago: The University of Chicago Press, 1994), 138–141. Seib, *Headline Diplomacy*, 51–52.

55. Jönsson, "Diplomatic Signaling," 34. Seib, *Headline Diplomacy*, 51–2.

56. Manheim, "The Press as Prologue," 138–145. Alleyne, *News Revolution*, 54–55.

57. John R. MacArthur, *Second Front* (New York: Hill and Wang, 1992), 69.

58. Seib, *Headline Diplomacy*, 52. Hallin and Gitlin, "The Gulf War as Popular Culture and Television Drama," 160–61.

59. Seib, *Headline Diplomacy*, 51–2.

60. O'Neill, *The Roar of the Crowd*, 130.

61. Seaver, "The Public Dimension of Foreign Policy," 81.

62. Manheim, "The Press as Prologue," 132.

63. Seib, *Headline Diplomacy*, 50.

64. Ibid., 53.

65. Manheim, "The Press as Prologue," 138–145.

66. Bernard C. Cohen, *The Public's Impact on Foreign Policy*, 62–64.

67. Baker, "Report First, Check Later." Bonafede, "The President, Congress, and the Media in Global Affairs," Gergen, "Diplomacy in a Television Age." Jordan and Page, "Shaping Foreign Policy Opinions." Powlick, "The Attitudinal Bases for Responsiveness." Seaver, "The Public Dimension of Foreign Policy."

68. O'Neill, *The Roar of the Crowd*, 158.

69. Mattelart and Mattelart, "On New Uses of Media in Time of Crisis," 177.

70. Hinckley, *People, Polls, and Policymakers*, 6–7. W. Lance Bennett, "The Media and the Foreign Policy Process," in David A. Deese, ed., *The New Politics of American Foreign Policy* (New York: St. Martin's Press, 1994), 170.

71. Hinckley, *People, Polls, and Policymakers*, 133.

72. Ibid.

73. Thomas W. Graham, "Public Opinion and U.S. Foreign Policy Decision Making," in David A. Deese, ed., *The New Politics of American Foreign Policy* (New York: St. Martin's Press, 1994), 190–191.

74. Ibid.

75. Hinckley, *People, Polls, and Policymakers*, 130.

76. Robert Y. Shapiro and Benjamin I. Page, "Foreign Policy and Public Opinion," in David A. Deese, ed., *The New Politics of American Foreign Policy* (New York: St. Martin's Press, 1994), 221.

77. Hinckley, *People, Polls, and Policymakers*, 139. Seaver, "The Public Dimension of Foreign Policy," 76–77.

78. Shapiro and Page, "Foreign Policy and Public Opinion," 216.

79. Graham, "Public Opinion and U.S. Foreign Policy Decision Making," 208.

80. Ibid., 195–197.

81. Ibid., 195–197.

82. Ibid., 195.

83. Ibid.

84. Ibid., 195–196.

85. Ibid., 197.

86. Ibid., 198–199.

87. Ibid., 199.

88. Ibid., 190–209.

89. Seaver, "The Public Dimension of Foreign Policy," 77. Shapiro and Page, "Foreign Policy and Public Opinion," 230–34.

90. Ibid.

91. John Zaller, "Elite Leadership of Mass Opinion: New Evidence from the Gulf War,"

and "Strategic Politicians, Public Opinion, and the Gulf Crisis," in W. Lance Bennett and David L. Paletz, eds., *Taken by Storm: The Media, Public Opinion, and U.S. Foreign Policy in the Gulf War* (Chicago: The University of Chicago Press, 1994).

   92. Zaller, "Elite Leadership of Mass Opinion," 204.

   93. Ibid.

   94. Zaller, "Strategic Politicians, Public Opinion, and the Gulf Crisis," 250.

   95. Ibid.

   96. Shapiro and Page, "Foreign Policy and Public Opinion," 230.

   97. Ibid.

   98. Jordan and Page, "Shaping Foreign Policy Opinions," 227.

   99. Seaver, "The Public Dimension of Foreign Policy," 76.

  100. Ibid., 69.

  101. Iyengar and Simon, "News Coverage of the Gulf Crisis and Public Opinion," 183.

  102. Shattuck, "Human Rights and Humanitarian Crises," 174.

  103. Quoted in Schorr, "Ten Days that Shook the White House," 22.

  104. Ibid., 23.

  105. Freedman and Karsh, *The Gulf Conflict*, 423.

  106. Minear, Scott, and Weiss, *The News Media, Civil War, and Humanitarian Action*, 50. Bulloch and Morris, *No Friends But the Mountains*, 2 & 30. Edward Girardet, "Public Opinion, the Media, and Humanitarianism," in Thomas G. Weiss and Larry Minear, eds., *Humanitarianism Across Borders: Sustaining Civilians in Times of War* (Boulder, CO: Lynne Rienner Publishers, Inc., 1993) 39–40. Shaw, *Civil Society and Media in Global Crises*, vii. Sheri Laizer, *Martyrs, Traitors and Patriots* (London: Zed Books, Ltd., 1996), 26.

Chapter 8. Today's Communications, Tomorrow's Diplomacy

   1. Hamilton and Langhorne, *The Practice of Diplomacy*, 244–45.

   2. Quoted in Gowing, "Real-Time Television Coverage," 16.

   3. Ibid.

   4. Neuman, *Lights, Camera, War*, 265.

   5. Young and Jesser, *The Media and the Military*, 271.

Bibliography

Alleyne, Mark D. (1997) *News Revolution: Political and Economic Decisions About Global Information.* New York: St. Martin's Press.

Ambrose, Stephen E. (1993) *Rise to Globalism: American Foreign Policy Since 1938.* New York: Penguin Group.

Amos, Deborah (1994) "Foreign Policy by Public Outrage," *Nieman Reports* XLVIII, number 2 (Summer): 74–75.

Anderson, M.S. (1993) *The Rise of Modern Diplomacy, 1450–1919.* New York: Longman Publishing.

Aronson, James. (1970) *The Press and the Cold War.* New York: Monthly Review Press.

Baker, James A., III. (1996) "Report First, Check Later: Former Secretary of State James A. Baker, III Interview with Marvin Kalb," *Press/Politics* 1, number 2 (Spring): 3–9.

_____, with Thomas M. DeFrank. (1995) *The Politics of Diplomacy: Revolution, War and Peace, 1989–1992.* New York: G.P. Putnam's Sons.

Battacharya, Sauri P. (1994) "The Situation of the Kurds in the Post-Gulf War Period and U.S. Policy Toward It," *Asian Profile* 22, number 2 (April): 151–160.

Bennett, W. Lance. (1994a) "The Media and the Foreign Policy Process," pp.168–188 in David A. Deese (ed.), *The New Politics of American Foreign Policy.* New York: St. Martin's Press.

_____. (1994b) "The News About Foreign Policy," pp. 12–40 in W. Lance Bennett and David L. Paletz (eds.), *Taken by Storm: The Media, Public Opinion, and U.S. Foreign Policy in the Gulf War.* Chicago: The University of Chicago Press.

Benthall, Jonathan. (1993) *Disasters, Relief, and the Media.* London: I.B. Tauris & Co. Ltd. Publishers.

Berkman, Ronald. (1986) *Politics in the Media Age.* New York: McGraw-Hill, Inc.

Beschloss, Michael R. (1993) *Presidents, Television and Foreign Crises.* Northwestern University: The Annenberg Washington Program in Communications Policy Studies.

_____, and Strobe Talbot. (1993) *At the Highest Levels: The Inside Story of the End of the Cold War.* Boston: Little, Brown and Company.

Blondheim, Menahem. (1994) *News Over the Wires: The Telegraph and the Flow of Public Information in America, 1844–1897.* Cambridge, MA: Harvard University Press.

Bolger, Daniel P. (1995) *Savage Peace: Americans at War in the 1990s.* Novato, CA: Presidio Press.

Bonafede, Dom. (1997) "The President, Congress, and the Media in Global Affairs," pp.

95–119 in Abbas Malek (ed.), *News Media and Foreign Relations: A Multifaceted Perspective*. Norwood, NJ: Ablex Publishing Company.

Brace, Richard M. (1968) "Cardinal Richelieu," pp. 306–07 in *World Book Encyclopedia*, Volume 16. Chicago: Field Enterprises Educational Corporation.

Bratt, Duane. (1997) "Assessing the Success of UN Peacekeeping Operations," pp. 64–81 in Michael Pugh (ed.), *The UN, Peace and Force*. London: Frank Cass.

Brinkley, Alan. (1993) *The Unfinished Nation: A Concise History of the American People*. New York: McGraw-Hill, Inc.

Bulloch, John, and Harvey Morris. (1992) *No Friends But the Mountains: The Tragic History of the Kurds*. New York: Oxford University Press.

Burns, Nicholas. (1996) "Talking to the World about American Foreign Policy," *The Harvard International Journal of Press/Politics* 1, number 4 (Fall): 10–14.

Calloway, Linda Jo. (1994) "High Tech Comes to War Coverage: Uses of Information and Communications Technology for Television Coverage in the Gulf War," pp. 55–72 in Thomas A. McCain and Leonard Shyles (eds.), *The 1,000 Hour War: Communication in the Gulf*. Westport, CT: Greenwood Publishing Group, Inc.

Clark, Eric. (1973) *Diplomat: The World of International Diplomacy*. New York: Taplinger Publishing Company.

Clarke, Walter S. (1998) "Waiting for 'The Big One': Confronting Complex Humanitarian Emergencies and State Collapse in Central Africa," pp. 72–101 in Max G. Manwaring and John T. Fishel (eds.), *Toward Responsibility in the New World Order: Challenges and Lessons of Peace Operations*. London: Frank Cass.

Cohen, Bernard C. (1963) *The Press and Foreign Policy*. Princeton: Princeton University Press.

_____. (1973) *The Public's Impact on Foreign Policy*. Boston: Little, Brown.

_____. (1994) "A View from the Academy," pp. 8–11 in W. Lance Bennett and David L. Paletz (eds.), *Taken by Storm: The Media, Public Opinion, and U.S. Foreign Policy in the Gulf War*. Chicago: The University of chicago Press.

Cohen, Noel. (1986) *Media Diplomacy: The Foreign Office in the Mass Communications Age*. London, England: Frank Cass and Company, Limited.

Cohen, Warren I. (1987) *Empire Without Tears: America's Foreign Relations, 1921–1933*. New York: Alfred A. Knopf.

Cornford, Francis MacDonald. (1980) *The Republic of Plato*, translated with introduction and notes by Francis MacDonald Cornford. New York: Oxford University Press.

Couloumbis, Theodore A., and James H. Wolfe. (1990) *Introduction to International Relations: Power and Justice*. Englewood Cliffs, NJ: Prentice Hall, Inc.

Cronkite, Walter. (1996) *A Reporter's Life*. New York: Alfred A. Knopf.

Cutler, Lloyd N. (1984) "Foreign Policy on Deadline," *The Atlantic Community Quarterly* 22, number 3 (Fall): 223–232.

Dallek, Robert. (1998) *Flawed Giant: Lyndon Johnson and His Times, 1961–1973*. New York: Oxford University Press.

Daniel, Donald C.F., and Brad C. Hayes. (1997) "Securing Observance of UN Mandates through the Employment of Military Force," pp. 105–125 in Michael Pugh (ed.) *The UN, Peace and Force*. London: Frank Cass.

Der Derian, James. (1987) *On Diplomacy: A Genealogy of Western Estrangement*. Oxford, UK: Basil Blackwell, Ltd.

Eagleburger, Lawrence. (1994) As quoted in Nik Gowing, "Real Time Television Coverage of Armed Conflicts and Diplomatic Crises: Does It Pressure or Distort Foreign Policy Decisions," p. 17; working paper 94–1; The Joan Shorenstein Barone Center on the Press, Politics and Public Policy; John F. Kennedy School of Government, Harvard University. Cambridge, MA: Harvard University.

Eban, Abba. (1983) *The New Diplomacy: International Affairs in the Modern Age*. New York: Random House.

Ebo, Bosah. (1997) "Media Diplomacy and Foreign Policy: Toward a Theoretical Framework," pp. 43–57 in Abbas Malek (ed.), *News Media and Foreign Relations: A Multifaceted Perspective.* Norwood, NJ: Ablex Publishing Corporation.

The Economist (1991) "God helps, so does Iran," April 27 (volume 319, number 7704): 46–47.

Engelhardt, Tom. (1994) "The Gulf War as Total Television," pp. 81–95 in Susan Jeffords and Lauren Rabinovitz (eds.), *Seeing Through the Media: The Persian Gulf War.* New Brunswick, NJ: Rutgers University Press.

Fang, Irving E. (1997) *A History of Mass Communication: Six Information Revolutions.* Boston: Focal Press.

Flournoy, Don M. (1992) *CNN World Report: Ted Turner's International News Coup* (Academic Research Monograph series: 9; Series editor: Manuel Alvarado). London: John Libbey & Company, Ltd.

Foa, Sylvana. (1994) As quoted in Nik Gowing, "Real-Time Television Coverage of Armed Conflicts and Diplomatic Crises: Does It Pressure or Distort Foreign Policy Decisions," p. 30; working paper 94–1; The Joan Shorenstein Barone Center on the Press, Politics and Public Policy; John F. Kennedy School of Government, Harvard University. Cambridge, MA: Harvard University.

Freedman, Lawrence, and Efraim Karsh. (1993) *The Gulf Conflict, 1990–1991: Diplomacy and War in the New World Order.* Princeton, NJ: Princeton University Press.

Freedom Forum Media Studies Center Research Group, The. (1993) *The Media and Foreign Policy in the Post-Cold War World.* New York: Columbia University Press.

Freeman, James M. (1968) "Telephone," pp. 80–84 in *The World Book Encyclopedia*, Volume 18. Chicago, IL: Field Enterprises Educational Corporation.

Gaddis, John Lewis. (1982) *Strategies of Containment.* Oxford, England: Oxford University Press.

Ganley, Gladys D. (1992) *The Exploding Political Power of Personal Media.* Norwood, NJ: Ablex Publishing Corporation.

Gannett Foundation Media Center. (1991) *The Media at War: The Press and the Persian Gulf Conflict.* New York: Columbia University Press.

Gergen, David R. (1990) "Diplomacy in a Television Age: The Dangers of Teledemocracy," pp. 47–63 in Simon R. Serfaty (ed.), *The Media and Foreign Policy.* New York: St. Martin's.

Gilbert, Richard. (1990) "How Much Should the Public Know?" *Foreign Service Journal* 67, number 5 (May): 19–23.

Gilboa, Etyan. (1998) "Media Diplomacy: Conceptual Divergence and Applications," *The Harvard International Journal of Press/Politics* 3, number 2 (Summer): 56–75.

Girardet, Edward R. (1993) "Public Opinion, the Media, and Humanitarianism," pp. 39–55 in Thomas G. Weiss and Larry Minear (eds.), *Humanitarianism Across Borders: Sustaining Civilians in Times of War.* Boulder, CO: Lynne Rienner Publishers, Inc.

_____. (1996) "Reporting Humanitarianism: Are the New Electronic Media Making a Difference?" pp. 45–67 in Robert I. Rotberg and Thomas G. Weiss (eds.), *From Massacres to Genocide: The Media, Public Policy, and Humanitarian Crises.* Washington, D.C.: The Brookings Institution.

Gould, Jack (1968) "Television," pp. 88–102 in *The World Book Encyclopedia*, Volume 18. Chicago, IL: Field Enterprises Educational Corporation.

Gowing, Nik. (1994) "Real-Time Television Coverage of Armed Conflicts and Diplomatic Crises: Does It Pressure or Distort Foreign Policy Decisions?" working paper 94–1, The Joan Shorenstein Barone Center on the Press, Politics and Public Policy, John F. Kennedy School of Government, Harvard University. Cambridge, MA: Harvard University.

Graham, Thomas W. (1994) "Public Opinion and U.S. Foreign Policy Decision Making," pp. 190–215 in David A. Deese (ed.), *The New Politics of American Foreign Policy.* New York: St. Martin's Press.

Gramling, Oliver. (1969) *AP: The Story of News.* Port Washington, NY: Kennikat Press.

Grossman, Lawrence K. (1995) *The Electronic Republic: Reshaping Democracy in the Information Age.* New York: Penguin Group.

Gunter, Michael M. (1992) *The Kurds in Iraq.* New York: St. Martin's Press.

Gutman, Roy. (1997) As quoted in Warren P. Strobel, *Late Breaking Foreign Policy: The News Media's Influence on Peace Operations*, p. 91. Washington, D.C.: United States Institute of Peace.

Haass, Richard N. (1994) *Intervention: The Use of American Military Force in the Post-Cold War World*. Washington, DC: The Carnegie Endowment for International Peace.

Hachten, William, with the collaboration of Marva Hachten. (1994) "Reporting the Gulf War," pp. 337–345 in Doris A. Graber (ed.), *Media Power in Politics*, 3rd ed. Washington, DC: CQ Press.

Hallin, Daniel C. (1986) *The "Uncensored War": The Media and Vietnam*. Berkeley, CA: University of California Press.

_____, and Todd Gitlin. (1994) "The Gulf War as Popular Culture and Television Drama," pp. 149–163 in W. Lance Bennett and David L. Paletz (eds.), *Taken by Storm: The Media, Public Opinion, and U.S. Foreign Policy in the Gulf War*. Chicago: The University of Chicago Press.

Hamilton, Keith, and Richard Langhorne. (1995) *The Practice of Diplomacy: Its Evolution, Theory and Administration*. London: Routledge.

Hamilton, Lee (R-IN). (1994) Testimony before the U.S. House of Representatives Committee on International Relations, Chaired by Lee Hamilton, R-IN, April 26, 1994, Recorded and aired on C-SPAN.

Hammock, John C., and Joel R. Charny. (1996) "Emergency Response as Morality Play: The Media, the Relief Agencies, and the Need for Capacity Building," pp. 115–135 in Robert I. Rotberg and Thomas G. Weiss (eds.), *From Massacres to Genocide: The Media, Public Policy, and Humanitarian Crises*. Washington, D.C.: The Brookings Institution.

Harris, Tim. (1995) "Propaganda and Public Opinion in Seventeenth-Century England," pp. 48–73 in Jeremy D. Popkin (ed.), *Media and Revolution: Comparative Perspectives*. Lexington, KY: The University Press of Kentucky.

Harriss, John. (1995) "Introduction: A Time of Troubles—Problems of International Humanitarian Assistance in the 1990s," pp. 1–16 in John Harriss (ed.), *The Politics of Humanitarian Intervention*. London: Pinter Publishers.

Headrick, Daniel R. (1991) *The Invisible Weapon: Telecommunications and International Politics, 1851–1945*. New York: Oxford University Press.

Hess, Stephen. (1996) *International News and Foreign Correspondents*. Washington, DC: The Brookings Institution.

Hinckley, Ronald H. (1992) *People, Polls, and Policymakers: American Public Opinion and National Security*. New York: Lexington Books.

Hoge, James F., Jr. (1994) "Media Pervasiveness," *Foreign Affairs* 73, number 4 (July/August): 136–44.

Hohenberg, John. (1971) *Free Press/Free People: The Best Cause*. New York: Columbia University Press.

Holsti, K.J. (1992). "Governance Without Government: Polyarchy In Nineteenth-Century European International Politics," pp. 30–57 in James N. Rosenau and Ernst-Otto Czempiel (eds.), *Governance Without Government: Order and Change in World Politics*. Cambridge: Cambridge University Press.

Immerman, Richard H. (1990) *The CIA in Guatemala*. Austin, TX: University of Texas Press.

Innis, Harold Adams. (1951) *The Bias of Communication*. Toronto, Canada: University of Toronto Press.

_____. (1950) *Empire and Communication*. Oxford, England: Oxford University Press.

Iyengar, Shanto and Adam Simon. (1994) "News Coverage of the Gulf Crisis and Public Opinion: A Study of Agenda-Setting, Priming, and Framing," pp. 167–185 in W. Lance Bennett and David L. Paletz (eds.), *Taken by Storm: The Media, Public Opinion, and U.S. Foreign Policy in the Gulf War*. Chicago: The University of Chicago Press.

Jackson, Sir Geoffrey. (1981) *Concorde Diplomacy*. London: Hamish Hamilton, Ltd.

Jönsson, Christer. (1996) "Diplomatic Signaling in the Television Age," *The Harvard International Journal of Press/Politics* 1, number 3 (Summer): 24–40.

Jordan, Donald L., and Benjamin I. Page. (1992) "Shaping Foreign Policy Opinions: The Role of TV News," *The Journal of Conflict Resolution* 36, number 2 (June): 227–241.

Karl, Patricia A. (1982) "Media Diplomacy," *The Proceedings of the Academy of Political Science* 34, number 4: 143–152.

Keen, David. (1995) "Short-Term Interventions and Long-Term Problems: The Case of the Kurds in Iraq," pp. 167–186 in John Harriss (ed.), *The Politics of Humanitarian Intervention*. London: Pinter Publishers.

Kegley, Charles W., Jr., and Eugene R. Wittkopf. (1996) *American Foreign Policy: Pattern and Process* (Fifth Edition). New York: St. Martin's.

Kennan, George F. (1996) *At a Century's Ending: Reflections 1982–1995*. New York: W. W. Norton and Company, Inc.

Kern, Stephen. (1983) *The Culture of Time and Space, 1880–1918*. Cambridge, MA: Harvard University Press.

Kinloch, Stephen P. (1997) "Utopian or Pragmatic? A UN Permanent Military Volunteer Force," pp. 166–190 in Michael Pugh (ed.), *The UN, Peace and Force*. London: Frank Cass.

Kissinger, Henry A. (1994) *Diplomacy*. New York: Simon & Schuster.

_____. (1973) *A World Restored: Metternich, Castlereagh and the Problems of Peace, 1812–1822*. Boston: Houghton Mifflin Company.

Klapper, J.T. *The Effects of Mass Communication*. New York: The Free Press. (1960).

Knudsen, Tonny Brems. (1997) "Humanitarian Intervention Revisited: Post-Cold War Responses to Classical Problems," pp. 146–165 in Michael Pugh (ed.), *The UN, Peace and Force*. London: Frank Cass.

Koppel, Ted. (1994) Testimony before the U.S. House of Representatives Committee on International Relations, chaired by Lee Hamilton, R-IN, April 26, 1994; recorded and aired on C-SPAN.

Kuhn, Thomas. (1970) *The Structure of Scientific Revolutions*. Chicago: The University of Chicago Press.

Laizer, Sheri. (1996) *Martyrs, Traitors and Patriots*. London: Zed Books, Ltd.

Lake, Anthony. (1994) As quoted in James F. Hoge, Jr., "Media Pervasiveness," *Foreign Affairs* 73, number 4 (July/August): 138–139.

Lang, Gladys Engel, and Kurt Lang. (1994) "The Press as Prologue: Media Coverage of Saddam's Iraq, 1979–1990," pp. 43–62 in W. Lance Bennett and David L. Paletz (eds.), *Taken by Storm: The Media, Public Opinion, and U.S. Foreign Policy in the Gulf War*. Chicago: The University of Chicago Press.

Lee, James Melvin. (1923) *History of American Journalism*. Garden City, NY: The Garden City Publishing Co., Inc.

Leonard, Thomas C. (1986) *The Power of the Press: The Birth of American Political Reporting*. New York: Oxford University Press.

Lieber, Robert J. (ed.) (1997) *Eagle Adrift: American Foreign Policy at the End of the Century*. New York: Longman.

Livingston, Steven. (1997) "Clarifying the CNN Effect: An Examination of Media Effects According to Type of Military Intervention," research paper R-18 (June). The Joan Shorenstein Barone Center on the Press, Politics and Public Policy, John F. Kennedy School of Government, Harvard University. Cambridge, MA: Harvard University.

Logan, Carolyn J. (1996) "U.S. Public Opinion and the Intervention in Somalia: Lessons for the Future of Military-Humanitarian Interventions," *The Fletcher Forum of World Affairs* 20, number 2 (Summer/Fall): 155–180.

MacArthur, John R. (1992) *Second Front*. New York: Hill and Wang.

Mandelbaum, Michael. (1994) "The Reluctance to Intervene," *Foreign Policy* 95 (Summer): 3–18.

Manheim Jarol B. (1994) "The Press as Prologue: Managing Kuwait's Image During the Gulf Conflict," pp. 131–148 in W. Lance Bennett and David L. Paletz (eds.), *Taken by Storm: The Media, Public Opinion, and U.S. Foreign Policy in the Gulf War*. Chicago: The University of Chicago Press.

Marvin, Carolyn. (1988) *When Old Technologies Were New: Thinking About Electric Communication in the Late Nineteenth Century.* New York: Oxford University Press.

Masmoudi, Mustapha. (1992) "Media and the State in Periods of Crisis," pp. 34–43 in Marc Raboy and Bernard Dagenais (eds.), *Media Crisis, and Democracy: Mass Communication and the Disruption of Social Order.* London: Sage Publications.

Mattelart, Armand, and Michèle Mattelart. (1992) "On New Uses of Media in Time of Crisis," pp. 162–180 in Marc Raboy and Bernard Dagenais (eds.), *Media Crisis, and Democracy: Mass Communication and the Disruption of Social Order.* London: Sage Publications.

Mayall, James. (1991) "Non-Intervention, Self-Determination and the `New World Order,'" *International Affairs* 67, number 3 (July): 421–429.

McCamy, James L. (1964) *Conduct of the New Diplomacy.* New York: Harper & Row, Publishers.

McDermott, Geoffrey. (1973) *The New Diplomacy and Its Apparatus.* London: The Plume Press Limited.

McDowall, David. (1996) *A Modern History of the Kurds.* New York: I.B. Tauris and Company, Ltd.

McNulty, Timothy J. (1993) "Television's Impact on Executive Decisionmaking and Diplomacy," *The Fletcher Forum of World Affairs* 17, number 1 (Winter): 49–83.

Merchant, Livingston. (1964) "New Techniques In Diplomacy," pp. 117–135 in E.A.J. Johnson (ed.), *The Dimensions of Diplomacy.* Baltimore, MD: The Johns Hopkins Press.

Minear, Larry, Colin Scott, and Thomas G. Weiss. (1996) *The News Media, Civil War, and Humanitarian Action.* Boulder, CO: Lynne Rienner Publishers.

Minear, Larry, and Thomas G. Weiss. (1995) *Mercy Under Fire: War and the Global Humanitarian Community.* Boulder, CO: Westview Press.

Mookerjee, Girija K. (1973) *Diplomacy: Theory and History.* New Delhi, India: Trimurti Publications Private Limited.

Morgenthau, Hans J. (1959) "The Permanent Values in the Old Diplomacy," pp. 10–20 in Stephen D. Kertesz and M.A. Fitzsimons (eds.), *Diplomacy in a Changing World.* Notre Dame, IN: University of Notre Dame Press.

_____. (1949) *Politics Among Nations: The Struggle for Power and Peace.* New York: Alfred A. Knopf, Inc.

Mott, Frank Luther. (1968) *American Journalism, A History: 1690–1960.* New York: The MacMillan Company.

Mueller, John. (1994) *Policy and Opinion in the Gulf War.* Chicago: The University of Chicago Press.

Nakash, Yitzhak. (1994) *The Shi'is of Iraq.* Princeton, NJ: Princeton University Press.

Natsios, Andrew S. (1996) "Illusions of Influence: The CNN Effect in Complex Emergencies," pp. 169–168 in Robert I. Rotberg and Thomas G. Weiss (eds.), *From Massacres to Genocide: The Media, Public Policy, and Humanitarian Crises.* Washington, D.C.: The Brookings Institution.

_____. (1997) *U.S. Foreign Policy and the Four Horsemen of the Apocalypse: Humanitarian Relief in Complex Emergencies.* Westport, CT: Praeger Press.

Neuman, Johanna. (1996) *Lights, Camera, War: Is Media Technology Driving International Politics?* New York: St. Martin's Press.

Newsom, David D. (1996) *The Public Dimension of Foreign Policy.* Bloomington and Indianapolis, IN: Indiana University Press.

_____ (ed.) (1992) *The Diplomatic Record, 1990–1991.* Boulder, CO: Westview Press.

Nicolson, Sir Harold. (1988) *Diplomacy.* Washington, DC: Institute for the Study of Diplomacy, School of Foreign Service, Georgetown University.

_____. (1939) *Diplomacy.* London: Thornton Butterworth, Ltd.

_____. (1965) *Diplomacy.* New York: Oxford University Press.

_____. (1966) *The Evolution of Diplomacy.* New York: Collier Books.

Noorani, A.G. (1991) *The Gulf Wars: Documents and Analysis.* Delhi, India: Konark Publishers, Private, Ltd.

O'Heffernan, Patrick. (1991) *Mass Media and Foreign Policy*. Norwood, NJ: Ablex Publishing Corporation.

_____. (1994) "A Mutual Exploitation Model of Media Influence in U.S. Foreign Policy," pp. 231–249 in W. Lance Bennett and David L. Paletz (eds.), *Taken by Storm: The Media, Public Opinion, and U.S. Foreign Policy in the Gulf War*. Chicago: The University of Chicago Press.

O'Neill, Michael J. (1993) *The Roar of the Crowd: How Television and People Power Are Changing the World*. New York: Times Books.

Ong, Walter J. (1982) *Orality and Literacy: The Technologizing of the Word*. London: Methuen, Inc.

Oye, Kenneth A., Robert J. Lieber, and Donald Rothchild. (eds.) (1987) *Eagle Resurgent? The Reagan Era in American Foreign Policy*. Boston: Little, Brown and Company.

Paletz, David L. (1994) "Just Deserts?" pp. 277–292 in W. Lance Bennett and David L. Paletz (eds.), *Taken by Storm: The Media, Public Opinion, and U.S. Foreign Policy in the Gulf War*. Chicago: The University of Chicago Press.

Papp, Daniel S. (1991) *Contemporary International Relations: Frameworks for Understanding*. New York: Macmillan Publishing Company.

Parker, Richard. (1997) "Technology and the Future of Global Television," pp. 21–44 in Pippa Norris (ed.), *Politics and the Press: The News Media and Their Influences*. Boulder, CO: Lynne Rienner.

Pearce, David D. (1995) *Wary Partners: Diplomats and the Media*. Washington, DC: Congressional Quarterly, Inc.

Planck, Max. (1949) *Scientific Autobiography and Other Papers*, translated by F. Gaynor. New York. As quoted in Kuhn, Thomas. (1970) *The Structure of Scientific Revolutions*. Chicago: The University of Chicago Press.

Plano, Jack C., and Milton Greenberg. (1993) *The American Political Dictionary* (Ninth Edition). Fort Worth, TX: Harcourt Brace Jovanovich College Publishers.

Plischke, Elmer. (1979) "The New Diplomacy," pp. 54–72 in Elmer Plischke (ed.), *Modern Diplomacy: The Art and the Artisans*. Washington: American Enterprise Institute.

Poitras, Guy E. (1990) *The Ordeal of Hegemony: The United States and Latin America*. Boulder, CO: Westview Press.

Pool, Ithiel de Sola. (1983) *Technologies of Freedom*. Cambridge, MA: The Belknap Press of Harvard University Press.

Popkin, Jeremy D., (1995) "Media and Revolutionary Crisis," pp. 12–30 in Jeremy D. Popkin (ed.), *Media and Revolution: Comparative Perspectives*. Lexington, KY: The University Press of Kentucky.

_____, and Jack R. Censer. (1995) "Lessons from a Symposium," pp. 1–11 in Jeremy D. Popkin (ed.), *Media and Revolution: Comparative Perspectives*. Lexington, KY: The University Press of Kentucky.

Powlick, Philip J. (1991) "The Attitudinal Bases for Responsiveness to Public Opinion Among American Foreign Policy Officials," *The Journal of Conflict Resolution* 35, number 4 (December): 611–641.

Prendergast, John. (1996) *Frontline Diplomacy: Humanitarian Aid and Conflict in Africa*. Boulder, CO: Lynne Rienner.

Putnam, Robert D. (1988) "Diplomacy and Domestic Politics: The Logic of Two-Level Games," *International Organization* 42, number 3 (Summer): 427–460.

Roberts, J.M. (1993) *History of the World*. New York: Oxford University Press.

Roberts, Walter R. (1991) "The Media Dimension II: Diplomacy in the Information Age," *The World Today* 47, number 7 (July): 112–115.

Rosenblatt, Lionel. (1996) "The Media and the Refugee," pp. 136–146 in Robert I. Rotberg and Thomas G. Weiss (eds.), *From Massacres to Genocide: The Media, Humanitarian Crises, and Policy-Making*. Washington, DC: The Brookings Institution.

Rosenstiel, Tom. (1994) "The Myth of CNN," *The New Republic*, August 22 & 29, 1994; volume 211 (numbers 8 & 9): 27–33.

Roskin, Michael G., and Nicholas O. Berry. (1993) *The New World of International Relations*. Englewood Cliffs, NJ: Prentice Hall.

Rotberg, Robert I., and Thomas G. Weiss. (eds.) (1996) *From Massacres to Genocide: The Media, Humanitarian Crises, and Policy-Making*. Washington, DC: The Brookings Institution.

Rothchild, Donald. (1996) "Conclusion: Responding to Africa's Post-Cold War Conflicts," pp. 227–242 in Edmond J. Keller and Donald Rothchild (eds.), *Africa in the New International Order: Rethinking State Sovereignty and Regional Security*. Boulder, CO: Lynne Rienner.

Rourke, John T. (1993) *International Politics on the World Stage*. Guilford, CT: The Dushkin Publishing Group, Inc.

Russett, Bruce, and Harvey Starr. (1989) *World Politics: The Menu for Choice*. New York: W. H. Freeman and Company.

Schlesinger, James. (1989) As quoted in Charles W. Kegley, Jr., and Eugene R. Wittkopf, *American Foreign Policy: Pattern and Process* (Fifth Edition), p. 294. New York: St. Martin's Press.

Schorr, Daniel. (1991) "Ten Days that Shook the White House," *Columbia Journalism Review* (July/August): 21–23.

Schramm, Wilbur. (1954) "The Process of Communication: How Communication Works," pp. 3–26 in Wilbur Schramm (ed.), *The Process and Effects of Mass Communication*. Urbana, IL: University of Illinois Press.

Seaman, John. (1995) "The International System of Humanitarian Relief in the 'New World Order,'" pp. 17–32 in John Harriss (ed.), *The Politics of Human Intervention*. London: Pinter Publishers.

Seaver, Brenda M. (1998) "The Public Dimension of Foreign Policy," *The Harvard International Journal of Press/Politics* 3, number 1 (Winter): 65–91.

Seib, Philip M. (1997) *Headline Diplomacy: How News Coverage Affects Foreign Policy*. Westport, CT: Praeger Publishers.

Shapiro, Robert Y., and Benjamin I. Page. (1994) "Foreign Policy and Public Opinion," pp. 216–235 in David A. Deese (ed.) *The New Politics of American Foreign Policy*. New York: St. Martin's Press.

Shattuck, John. (1996) "Human Rights and Humanitarian Crises: Policy-Making and the Media," pp. 169–175 in Robert I. Rotberg and Thomas G. Weiss (eds.), *From Massacres to Genocide: The Media, Humanitarian Crises, and Policy-Making*. Washington, DC: The Brookings Institution.

Shaw, Donald L., and Shannon E. Martin. (1993) "The Natural, and Inevitable, Phases of War Reporting: Historical Shadows, New Communication in the Persian Gulf," pp. 43–70 in Robert E. Denton, Jr. (ed.), *The Media and the Persian Gulf War*. Westport, CT: Praeger Press.

Shaw, Martin. (1996a) *Civil Society and Media in Global Crises: Representing Distant Violence*. London: Pinter Printers.

_____. (1996b) "TV's Finest Hour," *New Statesman and Society* 9, number 399 (April): 22–23.

Sheppard, E.D., and D. Bawden. (1997) "More News, Less Knowledge? An Information Content Analysis of Television and Newspaper Coverage of the Gulf War," *International Journal of Information Management* 17, number 3 (June): 211–227.

Shiras, Peter. (1996) "Big Problems, Small Print: A Guide to the Complexity of Humanitarian Emergencies and the Media," pp. 93–114 in Robert I. Rotberg and Thomas G. Weiss (eds.), *From Massacres to Genocide: The Media, Humanitarian Crises, and Policy-Making*. Washington, DC: The Brookings Institution.

Simons, Geoff. (1994) *Iraq: From Sumer to Saddam*. New York: St. Martin's Press.

Smith, Jeffery A. (1988) *Printers and Press Freedom: The Ideology of Early American Journalism*. New York: Oxford University Press.

Snow, Donald M., and Eugene Brown. (1996) *The Contours of Power: An Introduction to*

Contemporary International Relations. New York: St. Martin's Press.

Solomon, Richard H. (1997), "The Information Revolution and International Conflict Management," keynote address, *Virtual Diplomacy* Conference, United States Institute of Peace; Peaceworks No. 18, pp. v. and 1–5. Washington, D.C.: United States Institute of Peace.

Stech, Frank J. (1994) "Winning CNN Wars," *Parameters* 24, number 3 (Autumn): 37–56.

Strobel, Warren P. (1997) *Late-Breaking Foreign Policy: The News Media's Influence on Peace Operations.* Washington, D.C.: United States Institute of Peace Press.

Sullivan, William H. (1984) "The Transformation of Diplomacy," *The Fletcher Forum* 8, number 2 (Summer): 291–294.

Swayne, Kingdon B. (1979) "Reporting Function," pp. 350–363 in Elmer Plischke (ed.), *Modern Diplomacy: The Art and the Artisans.* Washington, DC: American Enterprise Institute for Public Policy Research.

Szumski, Bonnie. (ed.) (1988) *Latin America and U.S. Foreign Policy: Opposing Viewpoints.* San Diego, CA: Greenhaven Press.

Tarnoff, Peter. (1991) As quoted by Matthew Cooper in "The Very Nervy Win of CNN," *U.S. News & World Report,* January 28, 1991, 44. Cited in Robert E. Denton, Jr. (1993), "Television as an Instrument of War," pp. 27–42 in Robert E. Denton, Jr. (ed.) *The Media and the Persian Gulf War.* Westport, CT: Praeger Publishers.

Taylor, Philip M. (1997) *Global Communications, International Affairs and the Media Since 1945.* London: Routledge.

_____. (1992) *War and the Media: Propaganda and Persuasion in the Gulf War.* Manchester, England: Manchester University Press.

Turner, Ed. (1994) Testimony before the U.S. House of Representatives Committee on International Relations, Chaired by Lee Hamilton, R-IN, April 26, 1994; recorded and aired on C-SPAN.

Tuthill, John W. (1991) "Conclusions," pp. 131–135 in Dacor Bacon House Foundation *American Diplomacy in the Information Age* (Herbert Wilson Griffin Seminar in International Affairs). Lanham, MD: University Press of America.

Van Alstyne, R.W. (1975) *The Rising American Empire.* New York: W.W. Norton and Company.

Van Dinh, Tran. (1987) *Communication and Diplomacy in a Changing World.* Norwood, NJ: Ablex Publishing Corporation.

Watson, Adam. (1983) *Diplomacy: The Dialogue Between States.* New York: New Press, McGraw-Hill Book Company.

Webster's New World Dictionary of the American Language. (1980) Second College Edition. New York: Simon and Schuster.

Welch, Susan, John Gruhl, Michael Steinman, and John Comer. (1992) *American Government.* St. Paul, MN: West Publishing Company.

Wetterau, Bruce. (1994) *World History: A Dictionary of Important People, Places, and Events, from Ancient Times to the Present.* New York: Henry Holt and Company.

Wolfsfeld, Gadi. (1997) *Media and Political Conflict: News From the Middle East.* Cambridge, England: Cambridge University Press.

Wriston, Walter B. (1997) "Bits, Bytes, and Diplomacy," *Foreign Affairs* 76, number 5 (September/October): 172–182.

_____. (1992) *The Twilight of Sovereignty: How the Information Revolution is Transforming Our World.* New York: Charles Scribner's Sons.

Yetiv, Steve A. (1996) *The Persian Gulf Crisis.* Westport, CT: Greenwood Press.

Young, Peter and Peter Jesser. (1997) *The Media and the Military: From the Crimea to Desert Strike.* New York: St. Martin's Press.

Zaller, John. (1994) "Elite Leadership of Mass Opinion: New Evidence from the Gulf War," pp. 186–209, and "Strategic Politicians, Public Opinion, and the Gulf Crisis," pp. 250–276 in W. Lance Bennett and David L. Paletz (eds.), *Taken by Storm: The Media, Public Opinion, and U.S. Foreign Policy in the Gulf War.* Chicago: The University of Chicago Press.

Index

ABC (American Broadcasting Company) 70, 84, 119

agenda-setting 132; *see also* television, global, as a foreign policy agenda-setter

Aidid, Mohammed Farah 123, 135

Albright, Madeline 69, 136; and television as the 16th member of the U.N. Security Council 68; and the problem with "non-CNN wars" 106

ambassador: first permanent 39; resident 40

Amnesty International 105–106

Anderson, M. S. 39

Aquino, Corazon 35

Aristotle 15

Arnett, Peter 75

Ash, Timothy Garton 37, 79

Associated Press 27

Austin, Kathi 121

Austria 41

Austro-Hungarian Empire 51–52, 78

Baghdad, Iraq 66, 69, 73, 75, 82, 107

Baker, James A., III 7, 69, 72, 73, 74, 81–82, 85, 87, 89, 111, 137

Basra, Iraq 107, 108, 112, 114

Ba'th Political Party (of Iraq) 107

BBC (British Broadcasting Corporation) 100, 102, 112

Begin, Menachem 138

Bennett, James Gordon 26

Berkman, Ronald 16

Berlin Wall 79

Berri, Nabih 139, 140

Bonafede, Dom 84

Bosnia, and the ability of global television to influence foreign policy 81, 133, 134

Boston News-Letter 21

Boucher, Richard 80–81

Boutros-Ghali, Boutros 7, 134, 151

broadside 17, 21

Brzezinski, Zbigniew 68

Buchanan, James 27

Budapest, Hungary 29–30

Burns, Nicholas 70

Burundi 118, 128

Bush, George 70, 77, 79, 90; and CNN as an information source 73, 76; and CNN as an instrument for international public relations 75; and the 1991 Kurdish rebellion inside of Iraq 94, 99; and the 1991 Shiite Muslim rebellion inside of Iraq 109–110; policy toward 1990 Iraqi invasion of Kuwait 140–143; policy toward 1991 attempted coup in the Soviet Union 136–137; policy toward 1991 Kurdish refugees 97, 103–104, 112–113, 133, 152–153; policy toward 1992 Somali humanitarian relief 134, 135; public approval ratings re: policy toward 1991 Kurdish refugees 101; public opinion and policy toward 1991 Kurdish refugees 143

Bush Administration: and the 1991 Persian Gulf War 66; policy toward 1991 Kurdish rebellion inside of Iraq 94, 99–100, 109, 111; policy toward 1991 Kurdish refugee crisis 104–105, 147–148, 152–153; policy toward 1991 Shiite Muslim rebellion inside of Iraq 109–111, 114; policy toward the use of force to expel Iraq from Kuwait 142

Cambon, Jules 49
Campbell, John 21
CARE, and the Rwandan refugee crisis 121
Castlereagh, Lord Robert Stewart 2d viscount 50–51, 53
Cato (pen name for William Gordon and John Trenchard) 18–19
CBS (Columbia Broadcasting System) 34, 70
CBS news 59, 138–139
Ceausescu, Nicolae 36
Censer, Jack R. 37
censorship, government, and early printing 18–21, 25
Cheney, Dick 72
China, and the origins of printing 16; *see also* Tiananmen Square demonstrations
CIA (Central Intelligence Agency), and the 1991 Kurdish rebellion inside of Iraq 99
Citizens for a Free Kuwait 141
Clark, Eric 78
Clinton Administration: 1993–94 policy toward Somalia 123; policy toward the 1994 Rwandan genocide 120, 123, 124–125, 128; policy toward the 1994 Rwandan refugee crisis 121, 123, 125
Clinton, Bill, policy toward 1993 U.S. military involvement in Somalia 136
CNN (Cable News Network) 7, 30, 36; and international crisis management 76–78; and international relations 69–71; and public opinion 69–70, 85; and the acceleration of diplomacy's pace 81; and the beginning of the 1991 Persian Gulf War 69–70, 73; and the 1989 revolutions in Eastern Europe 36; and the 1991 attempted coup in the Soviet Union 136–137; and the 1991

Persian Gulf War 69–83; as a channel for diplomatic communication 65, 71, 73, 75, 77, 82–84, 137–138; as a diplomatic actor 69–70, 82–85; as an information source 72–73, 96, 131, 137–138; as the 6th permanent member of the United Nations Security Council 151; as the 16th member of the United Nations Security Council 7; the nature of its influence 70–71
CNN effect 74, 94
CNN International, coverage of international news compared with ABC, CBS, and NBC 70–71; foreign policy significance of 74
CNN wars (and non–CNN wars) 106, 108
Cohen, Bernard C. 131
Cohen, Herman 118
Cohen, Noel 60
Cold War, end of 86, 93
collapse of time and space 10; and communications 10, 78; and radio 32; and telediplomacy 68; and television 34, 84; and the telegraph 26, 51–52; and the telephone 29; and the transatlantic cable 28; and wireless telegraphy 31; communication, definition of 8; the four paradigms of 13–16; communication, Western, the three paradigms of 15–16; communications, definition of 8; and diplomacy's methods of practice 1, 5–8, 10–11, 48–53, 57–58, 67, 71–87, 151–154; and diplomatic outcomes 1, 5–8, 60–61, 82, 87, 88–91, 96–106, 138, 147–148, 152–154; *see also* newspapers, early effects on diplomacy; telegraphy, effects on diplomacy; television, early effects on diplomacy; television, global, and diplomatic outcomes; and the limits to its ability to influence diplomatic outcomes 117–129; and the mechanisms for its influence on diplomatic outcomes 130–148
complex humanitarian emergency (CHE) 91–92
Concert of Europe 42
Congress of Vienna, and old diplomacy 38, 47, 50–51
Cronkite, Walter, and his role in the advent of the Middle East peace

process 138–139; and the influence of his Vietnam coverage on LBJ 59
Cronkite diplomacy, and the Middle East peace process 138–139
Cuba 55–56, 80
Cuban missile crisis 72, 80
Cutler, Lloyd N. 69, 88, 130

Declaration of Independence, American, and the public's right to know 19
democracy see printing press, and democracy
democratic diplomacy 45
Der Derian, James 46
diplomacy, and advances in communications technology 6–8, 10–11, 47, 68, 71, 78, 82, 153–154
diplomacy, definition of 8–9; functions of 8–9; future of, and communications 1, 67, 151, 153–154; golden era of 41, 43; relationship to foreign policy and world politics 8
diplomatic outcomes, as a synonym for foreign policy (the product of foreign policy decision-making) 5–8, 60–61, 147–148, 152–154
diplomatic paradigms, changes in, and communications 7, 10–11, 48–49, 57–58, 60–61, 68, 78, 152
Diwaniyya, Iraq 107
Dulles, John Foster 58–59

Eagle Adrift: American Foreign Policy at the End of the Century (Lieber) 93
Eagleburger, Lawrence 69–70, 81, 130, 135
Eastern Europe 1989 revolutions and global television 36–37, 79
Eban, Abba 44, 53, 55, 60, 76
Ebo, Bosah 68
Egypt 138
electronic communication, growth of 25–26; political news 32–33; and pre-paradigm era 26; rise of 13; significance of 15
elite communication paradigm definition of 15; and the writing era 16–17, 22
England, and freedom of the press 18–21
European Community (EC), and the 1991 Kurdish refugee crisis 103

Feinstein, Diane 134

Field, Cyrus 27
First Amendment to the U.S. Constitution, and freedom of the press 20
Fitzwater, Marlin 77, 80–81, 89, 135; and the 1991 Kurdish rebellion inside of Iraq 99
Foa, Sylvana 88
Foreign Affairs 89
foreign policy: and world politics 8; as a synonym for diplomatic outcomes 5–8, 60–61, 147–148, 152–154; relationship to diplomacy and world politics 8
Fourteen Points (Woodrow Wilson), as the biblical text for open diplomacy 43–44, 86–87
France 41–42, 54; and the 1991 Kurdish refugee crisis 102–103, 115; and the professionalization of modern diplomacy 38–39; policy toward the 1994 Rwandan genocide 120–121
Francis I (emperor of Austria) 41
Franz Joseph (emperor of Austria, subsequently emperor of the Austro-Hungarian Empire) 51
free marketplace of ideas 18; legal protection of 19–20
Freedman, Lawrence 65
freedom of the press, origins of 19–20, 22
French Revolution 23
Friedland, Lewis 71
Fuller, Craig 142

Ganly, Gladys 35
Gergen, David 85, 87
Gilboa, Etyan 68
global communications, advent of 32; and the free marketplace of ideas 20; precursor of 27–28
global political crisis 91–92
global television 8; and East European revolutions (1989) 36–37, 79; and diplomatic outcomes 1, 7, 60–61, 88–91, 96–106, 116–117, 152; see also television, global, and its ability to influence foreign policy; and diplomatic representation 73–74, 83; and diplomatic signaling and receiving 74; and its ability to influence foreign policy 7, 88–89, 101– 105, 108, 111–112, 130–138, 147–148; and information

gathering 72–73, 136–137; and international crisis management 76–78, 89; and international public relations 75–76; and public opinion 69–70, 85, 97, 134, 144, 147–148, 154; and Somali famine relief efforts (1992–93) *see* Somalia 1992–93 humanitarian relief efforts and global television's ability to influence foreign policy; and the collapse of political space 36–37; and the collapse of time and space 6, 34, 36–37, 84; and the erosion of the monopoly of knowledge 37, 84; and the Kurdish refugee crisis (post–1991 Persian Gulf War) *see* Kurdish refugee crisis, and global television's ability to influence foreign policy; and the limits to its ability to influence foreign policy 117–129, 153; and the mechanisms for its influence on foreign policy 130–148 153; and the 1991 Persian Gulf War *see* Persian Gulf War, 1991, and global television's ability to influence foreign policy; and the rise of telediplomacy 6, 38; and the Rwandan genocide (1994) *see* Rwandan genocide 1994, and the limits to global television's ability to influence foreign policy; and the shaping of world politics *see* television, global, and its ability to influence foreign policy; and the Shiite Muslim refugee crisis (post–1991 Persian Gulf War) *see* Shiite Muslim refugee crisis, 1991, and the absence of global television and its ability to influence foreign policy; and the source of its influence 68–69, 133–134; and the Soviet Union (1991 coup attempt) *see* Soviet Union 1991 attempted coup, and global television's ability to influence foreign policy; and the Tiananmen Square demonstrations (1989) *see* Tiananmen Square demonstrations 1989, and global television's ability to influence foreign policy; as a diplomatic actor 81–82, 130–131; as a diplomatic broker 138–143; as a foreign policy agenda-setter 130–133, 147; as a synonym for real-time television 8; as a unique information source 133–138
Goma, Zaire 119–120

Gordon, William *see* Cato
Gowing, Nik 66, 76, 101, 105–106, 112, 132, 134
Graham, Thomas W. 144
Greece, war for independence 50–51, 53
Grossman, Lawrence 75
Gutenberg, Johann 12, 18, 20, 25, 33
Gutman, Roy 88

Haass, Richard 66, 80, 103, 111–112, 118, 136
Habermas, Jurgen 23,
Habyaramina, Juvenal 119
Halabja, Iraq 98
Hamilton, Keith 7, 39, 53, 55
Hamilton, Lee 134
Harris, Benjamin 21
Harriss, John 124
Headrick, Daniel R. 27
Hearst, William Randolph 24, 55–57
Hess, Stephen 70
high diplomacy 41
Hill and Knowlton 141–142
Hoge, James F. Jr. 89
Hohenberg, John 7, 33, 57
House Committee on International Relations, U.S. 84, 134
Human Rights Watch 121
Hurd, Douglas 108
Hussein ibn Talal, King (of Jordan) 83
Hussein, Saddam 70–72, 74–75, 77–78, 80–81, 89–90, 97, 141; and the 1991 Kurdish refugee crisis 94, 102; and the 1991 Shiite Muslim refugee crisis 105–108, 109; and the use of nerve gas against the Kurds 98, 104–105
Hutus: and 1993 war with the Tutsis in Burundi 128; and the 1994 Rwandan genocide 119–120

Innis, Harold Adams 9–10, 15, 20, 32–33
instantaneity, age of 30–32
instantaneous communication paradigm 15, 37, 67; advent of 15, 25; and telediplomacy 71
instantaneous communication paradigm, pre-paradigm era 25–26, 30–31
InterAction 97, 122
Iran: and the 1991 Kurdish refugee crisis 98, 114; and the 1991 Shiite Muslim rebellion inside of Iraq 109, 113–114
Iranian Revolution of 1979 35

Iraq 61, 66, 73–75, 78, 80, 140
Iraq, civil war, following the 1991 Persian
    Gulf War 97–98
Israel 138–140
Italian Renaissance and the rise of mod-
    ern diplomacy 6, 39
Italian city-states, and the rise of mod-
    ern diplomacy 39
Iyengar, Shanto 147

Jamieson, Kathleen Hall 83
Jefferson, Thomas 42–43
Jesser, Peter 54, 151, 154
Johnson, Lyndon Baines 59, 146

Karbala, Iraq 107
Karl, Patricia 7
Karsh, Efraim 65
KDKA, first commercial radio station 32
Keen, David 104, 127
Kennan, George F. 135
Kennedy, John F. 79–80
Kennedy Administration 80
Kern, Stephen 9, 55
Khomenei, Ayatollah Ruhollah 35
Kigali, Rwanda 118, 125
Kipper, Judith 73
Kissinger, Henry Alfred 1, 6, 41, 89
Koppel, Ted 36, 84, 93, 138
Kouchner, Bernard 105
Kuhn, Thomas S. 12, 14, 16–17, 37
Kurdish rebellion, inside of Iraq (post–
    1991 Persian Gulf War) 97–100, 127
Kurdish refugee crisis (post–1991 Persian
    Gulf War) 1, 7, 60–61, 87, 90, 94,
    113–117
Kurdish refugee crisis (1991): and global
    television's ability to influence
    foreign policy 95–105, 133, 147, 152;
    and public opinion 143, 147; as a com-
    plex humanitarian emergency 97–98;
    as a global political crisis 97–98; begin-
    nings of 97–98
Kurdistan, region of Iraq 98–100, 103,
    106, 111–112
Kurds, and Saddam Hussein's 1988 use of
    nerve gas against 98, 104–105
Kuwait: government of, and its 1990–
    1991 public relations campaign to
    encourage U.S. military action to evict
    Iraq from Kuwaiti territory 140–143;
    1990 Iraqi invasion of 74, 80, 107,

140–143; 1991 liberation from Iraqi
    occupation, 66, 97, 140–141; Saddam
    Hussein's proposals to withdraw from
    75–78
Kuwait City, Kuwait 66

Lake, Anthony 96, 136
Langhorne, Richard 7, 39, 53, 55
Lieber, Robert J. 93
Lister, Charles 49
literacy rates: England in the 1600s 18
Livingston, Robert 42–43, 47, 51, 53
Locke, John 19
Los Angeles Times 84
Louis XIII (king of France) 17, 38
Louisiana Territory 42, 47, 51
low diplomacy 41

MacArthur, John R. 141, 142
Madison, James 20, 23
Maine 56
Major, John 102–103; and the 1991 Kur-
    dish rebellion inside of Iraq 100
Marconi, Guglielmo 31–32
Marcos, Ferdinand 35
Marsh Arabs 105–106, 108; see also Shi-
    ite Muslim
Marvin, Carolyn 15
mass communication paradigm 15; advent
    of 22; pre-paradigm era 17
mass printing, and the end of the writ-
    ing era 16–17, 22; effects on diplomacy
    53–54, 152
McDougall, Barbara 130
McKinley, William 56–57
McNamara, Robert 72
McNulty, Timothy J. 7, 76
The Media and the Military: From the
    Crimea to Desert Strike (Young and
    Jesser) 151
media control see Persian Gulf War (1991)
    and control of news coverage
Metternich, Prince (of Austria) Klemens
    Wenzel Nepomuk Lothar von 41–42,
    46–47, 51, 55
Middle East peace process, beginnings of
    and television 138–139
Middle East Watch 141
Millroy, Laurie 110
ministry of foreign affairs, first 38–39
Mitterand, Danielle, and support for the
    Kurds 102

Mitterand, François, policy toward the 1991 Kurdish refugee crisis 102
modern diplomacy 39; professionalization of 38; rise of 38–40
Mogadishu, Somalia 135, 136
monopoly of knowledge 10; and communications 10; newspapers and the erosion of 23–24; radio and the erosion of 32; telephones and the erosion of 29; television and the erosion of 37, 58–61, 84, 143–144
Monroe, James 42–43, 47, 51, 53
Montaigne, Michel Esyquem de 18
Morgenthau, Hans 6, 9, 55, 78
Morse, Samuel F.B. 25–26
Motley, Langhorn 73
Muir, Jim 100
Mutla Gap, Battle of 66

Najaf, Iraq 107
Napoleon I (Bonaparte) 41, 53
Napoleonic Wars, old diplomacy and the conclusion of 41
Nasiriyah, Iraq 107
National Public Radio (NPR) 97
National Security Council 80, 103, 111, 116, 118, 136
NATO (North Atlantic Treaty Organization) 113–114, 127
Natsios, Andrew 115, 124, 133
Navarino, Battle of 50–51
Nayirah 141
NBC (National Broadcasting Company) 34, 70, 75
Neuman, Johanna 65, 93
Newbury, Catherine 120
new diplomacy 5–6, 37–38, 45; advent of 43, 152; and openness 6, 44, 53, 69; and public opinion 44–45; characteristics of 44–46; pre-paradigm era 38
Newsom, David 74, 76, 83
newspaper circulation, growth in 23
newspapers: and the erosion of the monopoly of knowledge 23–24; development of 21; early circulation in the U.S. 21–22, 24; early, cost of in the U.S. 21–24; early, effects on diplomacy 53–54, 152; mass printing of and the rise of new diplomacy 6, 152; origins of 17–18
Newsweek 101
New York Journal 55–56

New York Press 24
New York Sun 23
New York Sunday Journal 24
New York Sunday World 24
New York Times 25, 59, 100
New York World 56–57
Nicolson, Sir Harold 8, 39, 44, 46, 49, 54–55, 83
Nightline (ABC News) 36,138
N.S.C. *see* National Security Council

Ochs, Adolph 25
old diplomacy 5–6, 37–40; and privacy 5, 42, 53, 69; and public opinion 42, 55; and the monopoly over knowledge 42–43; as a function of time and space 42–43; characteristics of 40–41; original purpose 49–50
O'Neill, Michael F. 67, 137, 143
Ong, Walter J. 15
Operation *Southern Watch*, Iraq 1992, 115
Operation *Turquoise*, Rwanda 1994, 120–121
Ozal, Turgut 74, 114

Page, Benjamin I. 144
Paletz, David L. 105
"parachute journalism" 128
paradigm 12
paradigm shift 13
PBS (Public Broadcasting System) 75
Peace of Versailles, as the beginning of new diplomacy 43–44, 86–87
Pearce, David 104
penny press 23
Persian Gulf War (1991) 1, 7, 61, 68–69, 136–137; and CNN 69–83; and control of news coverage 66–67, 95, 101, 142–143; and global television's ability to influence foreign policy 1, 7, 61, 69–83, 136–137, 142–143; and telediplomacy 65; as America's first "television war" 68; as a watershed in diplomacy's methods of practice 71–72; beginning and ending times as a media-age consideration 65–67
personal media, and political space 35
Planck, Max 14
Plato 15–17, 22
Pool, Ithiel de Sola 14–15, 23
Popkin, Jeremy D. 37

Powell, Colin 72
Prendergast, John 123
pre-paradigm era 13
The Press and Foreign Policy (Cohen, Bernard C.) 131
printing: and the public's right to know 19; development of 16–17
printing press: and democracy 20, 23–24; earliest 17; machine (steam/power) 22–23
public opinion: foreign policy 86–87, 102–105, 113, 130; and foreign policy, during the era of old diplomacy 55; and government 20, 23; and the mechanics of its influence on foreign policy 143–148; as a diplomatic actor 84–87; public opinion, and foreign policy, U.S. State Department's change in attitude toward 85– 86; rise of as a diplomatic actor 54, 57, 60
Publick Occurrences Both Forreign and Domestick 21
The Public's Impact on Foreign Policy (Cohen, Bernard C.) 131
public's right to know 19; legal protection of 20
Pulitzer, Joseph 56–57

Quayle, Dan, and U.S. policy toward the 1991 Kurdish refugee crisis 100
Queen Victoria (of Great Britain) 27

radio: and the collapse of political space 32; and the collapse of time and space 32; and the decline of newspapers 33; first commercial broadcast 32–33
Reagan, Ronald Wilson 139
Reagan Administration, policy toward 1985 hijacking of TWA Flight 847, 139–140
Real-time global television 8
Refugees International 104
Remington, Frederic, and the Spanish-American War 55–56
Republican Guard, Iraq 98, 106, 108, 113
Richelieu, Cardinal (of France) Armand Jen du Plessis, duc de: and the first French newspaper 17–18; and the professionalization of modern diplomacy 38, 40
Ridgway, Rozanne 134
Roberts, Walter R. 68

Roederer, Pierre-Louise 23
Romania 36
Rosenblatt, Lionel 104
Rosenstiel, Tom 84
Rotberg, Robert I. 129
Rourke, John T. 9
RPF *see* Rwandan Patriotic Front
Russett, Bruce 9
Rwandan genocide (1994): and the limits to communications' ability to influence foreign policy 1, 8, 95–97, 117, 126–129, 153; origins of 117–118; as complex humanitarian emergency and global political crisis 118–122; news coverage of 125–126
Rwandan Patriotic Front (RPF) 119, 128
Rwandan refugee crisis (1994) 118–122; news coverage of 125–126

al-Sabah, Sheikh Ahmad (Emir of Kuwait) 140
Sadat, Anwar 138
Sarnoff, David 31
Saudi Arabia 141
Saunders, Harold 67
Save the Children 98, 104
Schlesinger, James 130
Schorr, Daniel 97, 148
Schwarzkopf, Norman 66, 107
Scowcroft, Brent 100, 135
Second Front (MacArthur) 142
Seib, Philip 57, 93
Senate Foreign Relations Committee, U.S. 69, 136
Serbia 52, 78
Sforza, Francesco, Duke of Milan 39
Shapiro, Robert Y. 144
Shattuck, John 134, 147
Shaw, Martin 97, 101, 112
Shiah Muslim (used synonymously with Shiite Muslim) 96, 106–117; *see also* Shiite Muslim
Shiite Muslim rebellion, inside of Iraq (post–1991 Persian Gulf War) 105–117
Shiite Muslim refugee crisis (post–1991 Persian Gulf War) 1, 61, 90, 106, 111–112, 116
Shiite Muslim refugee crisis (1991): and its failure to achieve the status of a global political crisis 106–108; and the absence of global television and its ability to influence foreign policy

95–96, 108, 112–113, 133, 153; as a complex humanitarian emergency 105–108; beginnings of 97–98
Shiite Muslims, and Operation Southern Watch (1992) 114–115
Shiras, Peter 97
shortwave, development of 31–32
Sigismund, Holy Roman Emperor and King of Hungary 39
Simpson, John 112
Smullen, Bill 76
Socrates 15–16
solidarity 35
Solomon, Richard H. 5, 48
Somalia 123, 125–126, 133–136
Somalia Syndrome, and U.S. policy toward the 1994 Rwandan genocide 123–124
Somalia Syndrome, in foreign policy decision-making 122–124
Soviet Union: and the use of CNN as an information source during the 1991 Persian Gulf War 72; demise of, and the loss of consensus in U.S. foreign policy 86; 1991 attempted coup, and global television's ability to influence foreign policy 137–138
Spanish-American War: and the emerging relationship between communications, public opinion, and diplomacy 55–58; and early indications of communications' ability to influence foreign policy 55–58, 60–61, 152
Starr, Harvey 9
State Department, U.S.: and international crisis management in the era of global television 69, 71, 76–81; and its change in attitude toward public opinion's role in foreign policy decision-making 85–86
strategic public diplomacy 142–143
Strobel, Warren 75, 93–94, 124
Sullivan, William H. 48
Sunni Muslims 106–107

Taft, William Howard 31
Tanzania 96
Tarnoff, Peter 75
Taylor, Philip M. 81
telediplomacy 6–7, 68–69, 72; and the acceleration of diplomacy's pace 78–81; and CNN 69–70, 73–74; distinctives of

6–7, 68–69, 89, 131, 152; emergence of 6–7, 58–61, 71, 152; and international crisis management 76–78; and the 1991 Persian Gulf War see Persian Gulf War (1991) pre-paradigm era 38; rise of and the collapse of time and space 68; and telediplomacy
Telefon Hirmondó, Hungary 29–30
telegraph: and political space 32; and the collapse of time and space 26, 28, 51–52; effects on diplomacy 52–53; first appearance of 13, 25–26; significance of 26–27; wireless see wireless telegraphy
telephone: and the collapse of time and space 29; and the erosion of the monopoly of knowledge 29; first exchange 34; invention of 28
telephone journalism 28–30, 33; significance of 30
television: advent of 33; and the erosion of the monopoly of knowledge 58–61; and the source of its influence 33; as a news source 34; early effects on diplomacy 59–60
"television war," 1991 Persian Gulf War as America's 1st 68
Tet Offensive 59
Tiananmen Square demonstrations (1989) and global television's ability to influence foreign policy 79–80, 89–90, 136–137; as the beginning of a dramatic increase in live television coverage of international crises 89–90
Titanic 31
Tokes, Laszlo 36
Tran Van Dinh 9, 60
transatlantic cable: and the collapse of time and space 28; early attempts at 27
Treaty of Versailles see Peace of Versailles
Trenchard, John see Cato
Truman, Harry S 34
Turkey 74; and the 1991 Kurdish refugee crisis 98, 100–101, 104, 113–115, 127
Turkish Empire 50–51
Turner, Ed 70
Turner, Ted 70, 82
Tutsis: and the 1993 war with the Hutus in Burundi 128; and the 1994 Rwandan genocide 119–120
TWA Flight 847 hijacking, 1985, and

early influence of television on foreign policy 138–140

U.N. see United Nations
"uncensored war," Vietnam War as the first 58
United Nations (U.N.) 68, 151; and Rwanda 120
United Nations Security Council 7, 68, 151; and Rwanda 120
United Nations Security Council Resolution 688 113, 115–116
U.S. Agency for International Development (USAID) 115
U.S. Army Rangers, and Somalia 1993, 123, 135, 136
USA Today 93
U.S. Bill of Rights, and freedom of the press 20, 22
U.S. Telephone Herald 20

VCR, and 1986 Philippines Revolution 35
Verne, Jules 28–29
Versailles, Treaty of see Peace of Versailles
Victoria, Queen (of Great Britain) 48
Vietnam War: and public opinion in foreign policy decision-making 59–61, 86, 146; and television as a diplomatic actor 152; and television's first effects on foreign policy 58–61, 68–69; as America's 1st "living room war" 68; as the "uncensored war" 68
video tapes, and 1989 Romanian Revolution 36
Visconti, Filippo Maria, Duke of Milan 39
Voice of America 99
Voice of Free Iraq 99

Walesa, Lech 35
Wardman, Ervin 24
Washington Post 59
Watson, Adam 46
Weiss, Thomas G. 129
Wentworth, Peter 18
Western civilization, origins of 15
Western communication, the three paradigms of 15–16

Western diplomacy, three paradigms of 5–6, 37–38
Wilson, Woodrow 43, 86–87
wireless telegraphy: and the collapse of political space 32; and the collapse of time and space 31; as a news source 31; development of 30–31; first transatlantic transmission 31
Wirthlin Group 141
Wolfowitz, Paul D. 66, 103
Wooten, Jim 119
World Peace Foundation 129
world politics, and communications 1, 153; see also diplomacy, and advances in communications technology; communications, and diplomacy's methods of practice; communications, and diplomatic outcomes; communications, and the limits to its ability to influence diplomatic outcomes; communications, and the mechanisms for its influence on diplomatic outcomes
world politics 8; future of, and communications 153, 154; see also diplomacy, future of, and communications; global television and the shaping of see global television and its ability to influence foreign policy; relationship to diplomacy and foreign policy 8
A World Restored (Kissinger) 41
World War I: and the divide between old and new diplomacy 6, 37, 43–44, 51–53, 86–87; communications and the causes of 52
Wriston, Walter B. 12, 77, 102
writing era (elite communication paradigm) 16–17

"Yellow Kid" comic strip 24
yellow journalism 24
"yellow press" 24; and the Spanish-American War 56
Yeltsin, Boris 137
Young, Peter 54, 151, 154
Yugoslavia 105, 134, 151

Zaire 96, 119, 122
Zenger, Peter 19–20